EVEREST
BASE CAMP

STEVE CARON
EVEREST BASE CAMP

How I trained for and trekked to the bottom of the highest mountain in the world.

DEDICATION

To Jane. It has been an absolute pleasure to spend over half my life with someone as special as you, and I cannot wait for the next part of our adventure to come.

First published 2023 by DB Publishing, an imprint of JMD Media Ltd,

Nottingham, United Kingdom.

Copyright © Steve Caron

All Rights Reserved. No part of this publication may be reproduced, stored in a retrieval system, or transmitted in any form, or by any means, electronic, mechanical, photocopying, recording or otherwise without the prior permission in writing of the copyright holders, nor be otherwise circulated in any form or binding or cover other than in which it is published and without a similar condition being imposed on the subsequent publisher.

ISBN 9781780916453

Printed in the Latvia

CONTENTS

Teenage Cancer Trust UK	7
Author's Note	8
Introduction	9
Introduction	11
Why Was I Doing this?	13
Itinerary	19

THE TRAINING — 25
WEEK-BY-WEEK DIARY — 25
WEEK 1 — 25
    Week 01 - A mainly flat walk around the Nottinghamshire/Derbyshire border — 28
WEEK 2 — 33
    INSURANCE — 35
    Week 02 - The Edale Skyline Walk, Peak District, Derbyshire — 37
WEEK 3 — 45
    VACCINATIONS — 47
    Week 03 - The Brecon Beacons Four Peaks, South Wales — 48
WEEK 4 — 57
    Week 04 - The Tissington Trail, Peak District, Derbyshire — 60
WEEK 5 — 65
    Week 05 - Dovedale, Peak District, Derbyshire — 67
WEEK 6 — 76
    Week 06 - The Yorkshire Three Peaks Challenge, North York Moors National Park — 78
WEEK 7 — 89
    Week 07 - Parkhouse Hill and Chrome Hill Loop, Longnor, Peak District — 90

WEEK 8	98
Week 08 – Snowdon, from Pen y Pass, Wales	99
WEEK 9&10	109
Week 09 – Scafell Pike, Lake District, north-west of England	112
Week 10 – Ben Lomond, Loch Lomond, Lowlands, Scotland	122
WEEK 11	131
Week 11 – A 30-mile local walk	133
WEEK 12	134
WEEK 13	137
Book Reviews:	139
THE TRIP	**153**
DAY 1 AND 2: MANCHESTER TO DOHA, THEN TO KATHMANDU.	153
DAY 3: KATHMANDU TO PHAKDING VIA LUKLA	158
DAY 4: PHAKDING TO NAMCHE BAZAAR	169
DAY 5: ACCLIMATISATION HIKE FROM NAMCHE TO THE EVEREST VIEW HOTEL	184
DAY 6: NAMCHE BAZAAR TO TENGBOCHE.	194
DAY 7: TENGBOCHE TO DINGBOCHE	206
DAY 8: DINGBOCHE ACCLIMATISATION HIKE	220
DAY 9: DINGBOCHE TO LOBUCHE	229
DAY 10: LOBUCHE TO GORAKSHEP TO EBC TO GORAKSHEP	241
DAY 11: KALA PATTHAR, THEN GORAKSHEP TO PANGBOCHE	255
DAY 12: PANGBOCHE TO NAMCHE BAZAAR	273
DAY 13: NAMCHE BAZAAR TO LUKLA	283
DAY 14: LUKLA TO KATHMANDU	294
Reflections on the trip to Base Camp	304
Reflections on Kathmandu and Patan	321
Things to do in Kathmandu and Patan	332
Day 20: The flight home	346
Acknowledgements	350

TEENAGE CANCER TRUST UK

This book is also dedicated to the Teenage Cancer Trust, especially the guardians, staff and fundraisers of the Trust.

From their website, https://www.teenagecancertrust.org/, 'Every day, seven young people aged 13-24 hear the words "you have cancer" … We're the only UK charity dedicated to meeting this vital need – so no young person faces cancer alone.

'Teenage Cancer Trust offers unique care and support, designed for and with young people. We fund specialised nurses, youth workers and hospital units in the NHS, so young people have dedicated staff and facilities to support them throughout treatment.

'We run events for young people with cancer to help them regain independence and meet other young people going through something similar.

'And we provide easy-to-understand information about every aspect of living with cancer as a young person.'

Everyone who has benefited from them, either now or in the past, will recognise what a great job they do. Please give generously to the cause.

If you are in the terrible position of currently having to use them – you can beat this and then go and enjoy life again.

All author royalties from this book will be donated to this brilliant organisation.

AUTHOR'S NOTE

This is a book written by a 52-year-old Englishman. As a result, some of the terminology and references are very much a product of my background, e.g. 1980s and '90s cultural references. TV and music feature from that era too. I also write in a chatty style, so some of the colloquial expressions may need translations for any overseas reader (and possibly even some parts of the UK).

The book is mainly written in diary format apart from reflections at the end. It details my thoughts at the end of every week while training, and every day while trekking.

Due to being brought up in a system that is part imperial and part metric, distances and heights may be in feet or metres depending on the technology used. I have generally used weight in kilograms, so no good for the Brits or the American readers, but it is a metric I now use in my day-to-day life.

I am a big football fan, supporting Derby County. Based in the East Midlands, halfway between my home town of Burton upon Trent and my current home in Nottingham, they have been a huge part of my life, and I still go regularly. Throughout the book there are references to my team, nicknamed the Rams, or you may catch a logo of them on a flag somewhere.

I do not apologise for my love of the British countryside and the first part is about my training walks across the UK. You have bought this book to read mainly about Nepal, but please do not skip some of the other parts.

I have referred to several websites in the book, so in the ebook version there are live links but for those reading the physical book, the full URL is listed.

Nearly all the photos in the book were taken using my mobile phone. The quality of camera technology in mobiles these days is phenomenal and I hope that they do the landscapes justice. There are a few in there from fellow trekkers, especially from Anton, including the cover image. Thanks for giving me permission to use them.

Thanks for reading.

INTRODUCTION

2019. I called my wife excitedly. 'I've only gone and done it, Jane.' She couldn't believe it.

After months of talking about it, I'd actually done it – I'd booked my trip.

I know you were expecting the call to be about reaching Base Camp, but trust me, after a lot of time spent prevaricating and procrastinating, this was a big step. The point of no return. If I didn't go, I would lose my flight money. A big chunk of cash. I had to go now. I was nervous. Would I be able to do it? Would I get altitude sickness? Would I be fit enough? Would I crash and burn and come home with my proverbial tail between my legs – embarrassed and disappointed? Now I'd booked it, we'd soon know.

Mount Pumori.

INTRODUCTION

2022. I called my wife excitedly. 'I've only gone and done it, Jane.' She couldn't believe it. I had to go now. I was nervous. Would I be able to do it? Would I get altitude sickness? Would I be fit enough? Would I crash and burn and come home with my proverbial tail between my legs – embarrassed and disappointed? Now I'd booked it, we'd soon know.

> Did you think this was a publishing error?
> Look at the dates on the introduction again.
> Are you getting that sense of déjà vu?

I did. Two years after originally booking the trip, getting insurance, training, mentally preparing, I had to go through the whole lot again. Like the rest of the world, Covid hit, and our lives were put on hold for so much longer than was necessary. I still tried to go in September 2020, my original date, but the world was shut. I got a full flight refund. Then in September 2021 and incredibly it still was and another refund. Now I was going to be able to finally fulfil my ambition and get to Nepal for a trip to Everest Base Camp. I flew to Nepal on 20 September 2022; I was on my way.

This book is going to take you on a journey. Not just the physical one that I took among some of the most majestic mountains in the world, but also my time preparing for the trip.

There are a lot of books about walking to Base Camp. I know, I have read a lot of them, but this is hopefully more than that. It is not just a book about kit lists, culture, or routes, although there is an element of that in there. It is also about the personal side of the trip – the training walks I undertook in the UK, a 13-week diary of my preparation which detailed the things I did (including insurance, visas, kit etc) and also the highs and lows of my attempts to be fit enough for the 11 straight days of walking to come.

It is a book packed full of photos which should not just encourage you to go to Nepal, but to visit some of the highlights of the UK scenery. It also has Strava maps and stats of the training walks and the days in Nepal. Included is an account of how I was physically and mentally feeling throughout the trek (along with my travelling companions) which may encourage you (or discourage you) from taking the plunge yourself.

There are even reviews of the books I read in preparation for the trip. Some good, some less so, but all adding a bit of extra knowledge to my overflowing brain.

Most of all though, it is a heartfelt and honest account of a 52-year-old Englishman's attempt to train for and visit one of the most incredible spots on earth. There are no holds barred. It talks about the people I met and the highs and lows of spending life 24/7 with complete strangers. There are magnificent sights, great characters and memorable experiences. If you are planning on going, then you may get some tips and a good flavour of what to expect. If you've been on the trip you'll certainly remember most of the places mentioned and empathise with my thoughts and feelings.

I hope you enjoy the story as much as I enjoyed the trip. But did I make it to Base Camp? You'll have to read to the end to find out.

WHY WAS I DOING THIS?

In 1996, just after we got married, Jane and I packed in well-paid jobs in London and went travelling around the world. The 17 months we were away really fuelled my love of travel, visiting South East Asia, China, Oz and NZ, USA and Central America. But the three weeks we spent in Nepal as part of that adventure always kept me yearning for a return. It was such a brilliant, friendly place. We visited Kathmandu, Pokhara and the Chitwan National Park, rafted on the Trisuli river, and went on a four-day trek to Poon Hill in the Annapurnas, seeing some of the most amazing views in the world.

https://en.wikipedia.org/wiki/Poon_Hill

But we had not been able to go to the Khumbu region, home of the highest point on earth – Mount Everest. I think we'd spotted it out of the aeroplane window on the way out of Kathmandu, but that was it.

Nepal had been a hazardous place for us.

We had capsized while rafting (Jane was under the water for a lot longer than she'd have liked – thank you for the life jacket and safety kayaker who rescued her.

We hadn't prepared for our trek and climbed Poon Hill (3,210m) at dawn in just shorts, a T-shirt and a thin rain coat.

On leaving Nepal, our Thai Airlines jet hit some vultures on the runway in Kathmandu which took one of the engines out, forcing an emergency landing (we even made the front page of the *Kathmandu Post*).

Over the years, I have thought about returning to Nepal, but I have never done anything about it.

In 1998, soon after getting back from our travels, we had Jim, the first of our three children, closely followed by Matt (2000) and Dan (2002). We also bought a book publishing business in 2003, so as you can imagine, time was very much dominated by bringing up three small children and keeping the business going. 'Exotic' travel definitely didn't register on our radar; we were spending great family

Jane heading for Poon Hill viewing stand after a trek to the summit for dawn. We were completely unprepared for the walk.

holidays in France instead. It wasn't until the kids were a bit older that we starting exploring some new places again such as Morocco, Montenegro, the Baltics and Croatia. Our travel bug was returning.

We did at least satisfy the mountain yearning regularly, taking the kids (from 2007) on our annual skiing trip to the French Alps. We all love waking up to that crisp air on a cloudless day and look at the mighty snowcapped peaks thrusting out of the ground into the blue sky.

WHY WAS I DOING THIS?

The Kathmandu Post
Nepal's National Newspaper

Vol. IV No. 234   Kathmandu, Thursday, October 10, 1996 (Aswin 24, 2053)

Thai jet survives major mishap

By a Post Reporter

KATHMANDU, Oct 9- A Thai Airways jet carrying 228 passengers and crew narrowly escaped a major mishap when it slammed into a group of vultures while preparing to take off from Tribhuvan International Airport (TIA) on Wednesday.

Flight TG-312 bound for Bangkok was already speeding on the runway for takeoff when a group of vultures struck the Airbus A-300-600 jet, eyewitnesses said.

No injuries were reported in the accident though five dead vultures were recovered from the site of impact, airport authorities said.

The Thai jet was lightly damaged by the force of the impact. Officials said the jet's engine fan blades were damaged and the area just above the pilot's cockpit window was stained with blood.

After impact, the Thai pilot acted swiftly and continued with the take-off procedure. Seven minutes after becoming airborne, he turned the jet around and made a perfect landing back at TIA. The Thai later cancelled the flight.

Though none of the passengers and crew were hurt in the mishap, the incident illustrates the serious bird hazard at TIA, the nation's only international airport.

TIA general manager Hari Bhakta Shrestha told *The Kathmandu Post* that bird hazards are a constant threat at this time of the year because the vultures flock to the airport grounds to feed on TIA's abundant supply of earthworms.

"The worms come out of the ground and die on the runway. This attracts the birds," he said. "We do try to keep the birds away but it is practically impossible to shoo all of them away from the airport area. Besides, the proximity of garbage dumping sites also attract the birds to the runway."

Wednesday's bird-hit could have been avoided if the TIA control tower had heeded the advice of an Indian Airlines pilot who was next in line for take-off.

Twenty minutes after the Thai jet returned to land, Indian Airlines flight IC 814 took off.

The following communication exchange between the IA pilot and tower could be heard over FM radio as it cleared the valley airspace:

IA pilot: You should do something to improve flight safety here.

Tower: Thank you, your suggestion has been noted.

IA pilot: But you shouldn't have allowed the (Thai) aircraft to take off. I had warned you there were birds there. You shouldn't have allowed the plane to take off.

Tower: It will be better if you notify the Department of Civil Aviation. Anyway your complaint has been noted.

IA pilot: Don't you have cartridges (blank gun cartridges to scare the birds away) here? I will send some from India if you don't have it.

Passengers being disembarked from a Thai airliner which made an emergency landing immediately after take off from Tribhuvan International Airport. A group of vultures had struck the Airbus on Wednesday.   *Post Photo/CSK*

We made the front and back pages of the Kathmandu Post.

Jane and I in Durbar Square, Kathmandu 1996, So young!

In 2014, I was on a year-long fitness campaign. I stopped drinking and did some triathlons and two half marathons. It was then that I discovered hiking. I was looking for an adventure and a challenge and signed up for the National Three Peaks Challenge. For those not familiar with this, you have to climb the highest mountains in England (Scafell Pike), Scotland (Ben Nevis) and Wales (Snowdon)

– all within 24 hours. The route either started in Scotland or Wales, with Scafell Pike the middle mountain, usually climbed at night. The 24-hour time limit also included the hundreds of miles of travel between them. I was on an organised group with strangers, and although we managed to complete the challenge, it was outside the 24 hours due to some of the group failing to train. They took nearly six hours to climb Ben Nevis, with the rest of the group waiting at the bottom for two hours for them to get down. We missed the 24 hours by 45 minutes! I wasn't going to be beaten and over the next four years, this time with friends, I attempted it a further five times. On my fifth attempt, I successfully made it in 24 hours. I had done it.

The attempts had failed for several reasons, including bad weather and poor planning.

Attempt 1, north to south: Slow-moving members as described.

Attempt 2, north to south: Terrible weather on Snowdon. We were within two hours of completing it, well within 24 hours. 40mph wind and sideways torrential rain stopped everyone from going up that day. We abandoned it halfway up the steep part of the Miners' Track.

Attempt 3, north to south: Terrible weather (rain and fog – visibility one metre) on Scafell Pike. Most groups didn't even try it. We did but lost GPS and abandoned the walk an hour from the top as we went the wrong way and could only retrace our steps.

Attempt 4, north to south: Thick fog at the top of Scafell Pike again; we made it to the top, but lost our bearings and ended up going down the wrong side and having to wait for daybreak to see the way back. We did the Three Peaks, but had to do Scafell Pike twice. Mountain Rescue were a few minutes from coming to find us when we arrived back to the car nine hours after setting off. It should have taken three!

Attempt 5, south to north: Completed at last, within the 24 hours. Great weather on all three mountains.

Attempt 6, south to north: Completed Snowdon and Scafell Pike. Slightly injured and too tired to go up Ben Nevis due to no sleep in the rocking minibus. I am sure I would have attempted it if Attempt 5 had been unsuccessful.

In fact, I reckon I would have still been having more attempts now if I'd not completed it. The challenges made me understand the importance of preparation. Reading the diary of my training, you will see I left little to chance.

As part of the training for these walks, I discovered the British countryside and I wanted more. You will read about some of the British countryside in the first part of the book.

As I got further into my mid-40s I had a small career switch and although we still ran our business, I started lecturing freelance at Nottingham Trent University and shortly after at Loughborough University. Loughborough is the top sporting university in the country and it was great being around such an atmosphere of competitiveness and physical prowess. My kids were also getting to the point where they were not really wanting to come on holiday with us any more. I was looking for more adventure and more new experiences.

In 2017 I auditioned for a TV game show, and when they said, 'What would you spend the money on if you win?' I replied, 'Trek to Everest Base Camp.' Not totally sure where it came from, but I wanted to say something different to get them to put me on the show (they didn't). But the seed had been planted. Was I just saying it, or was it something that had been in there all the while? The thought wouldn't go away. The more I considered it, the more I wanted to go. As Jane will tell you, once I get a bee in my bonnet about something, I get a little bit of tunnel vision. I looked at pictures of Kathmandu and Nepal and it reminded me of what a great time I'd had nearly 25 years earlier. I also read some books about the trip to see if it was possible for me. After all, I wasn't 26 any more.

Later that year, we had the news that every parent dreads. I am not going into it in too much detail (there are bits and pieces throughout the book), but I cannot thank Sophie and the staff at the Queens Medical Centre in Nottingham, and their Teenage Cancer Trust Unit enough. When you see that life can turn upside down in an instant, it makes you realise that it is for living while you can.

As my 50th birthday approached, and my 40s were hanging by a thread, I had decided. I was going to look at whether I could go. With time limited by my teaching schedule, I researched the trip – companies and timings, the logistics, the costs and the impacts on the family for such a long time away. As you saw from the introduction, it took me a while to finally take the plunge. But I did. I researched companies to go with and after reading the reviews on Tripadvisor, I picked out a local Nepalese supplier, Outfitters Nepal, rather than one based in the UK.

WHY WAS I DOING THIS?

https://www.tripadvisor.co.uk/AttractionProductReview-g293890-d12928544-Everest_Base_Camp_Trek-Kathmandu_Kathmandu_Valley_Bagmati_Zone_Central_Region.html

I selected the dates, paid the deposit, waited for Covid to be over, bought the flights, stared training and got my kit together. On 20 September 2022, it was time. Nepal – I was coming. You'd better be ready for me, because I was going to be ready for you.

ITINERARY
(from my tour operator - Outfitters Nepal)

The itinerary below was taken straight from the Outfitters Nepal website (including the grammar and spelling mistakes). It follows the traditional route, including acclimatisation days. It really fired my imagination and all my research was using this route in mind. The diary about my planning, the practice walks, all the literature I read prior to my trip was with this at the forefront of my thoughts.

The actual trip didn't quite follow this itinerary due to number of factors but the basics are there. For the detail see the later section on 'the trip'.

Detail itinerary of the Everest Base Camp Trek:

Day 01. Arrival at Kathmandu Airport and transfer to hotel.

Arrive at Kathmandu airport (1345meters) and you will be met by our airport representative and transferred to hotel, Evening free and your first overnight at hotel in Kathmandu.

Day 02. Pre Trip Meeting and Full day of sightseeing of Kathmandu valley, overnight at Hotel.

After having Breakfast – we will take you to our office and introduce with the guide and make balance payment then we take you for the sightseeing tour in Kathmandu Valley including Kathmandu Durbar Square, Monkey Temple, Pashupatinath Temple and Baudhanath Stupa.

Day 03. Fly from Kathmandu to Lukla (2886m) and Trek to Phakding (2610m) – 3.5 hours-:

Early morning drive to Airport for the 35 minutes scenic flight to the small mountain airport Lukla, after reaching at lukla our guide will introduce with the porters, then start today's trekking following mountainside on the left bank of

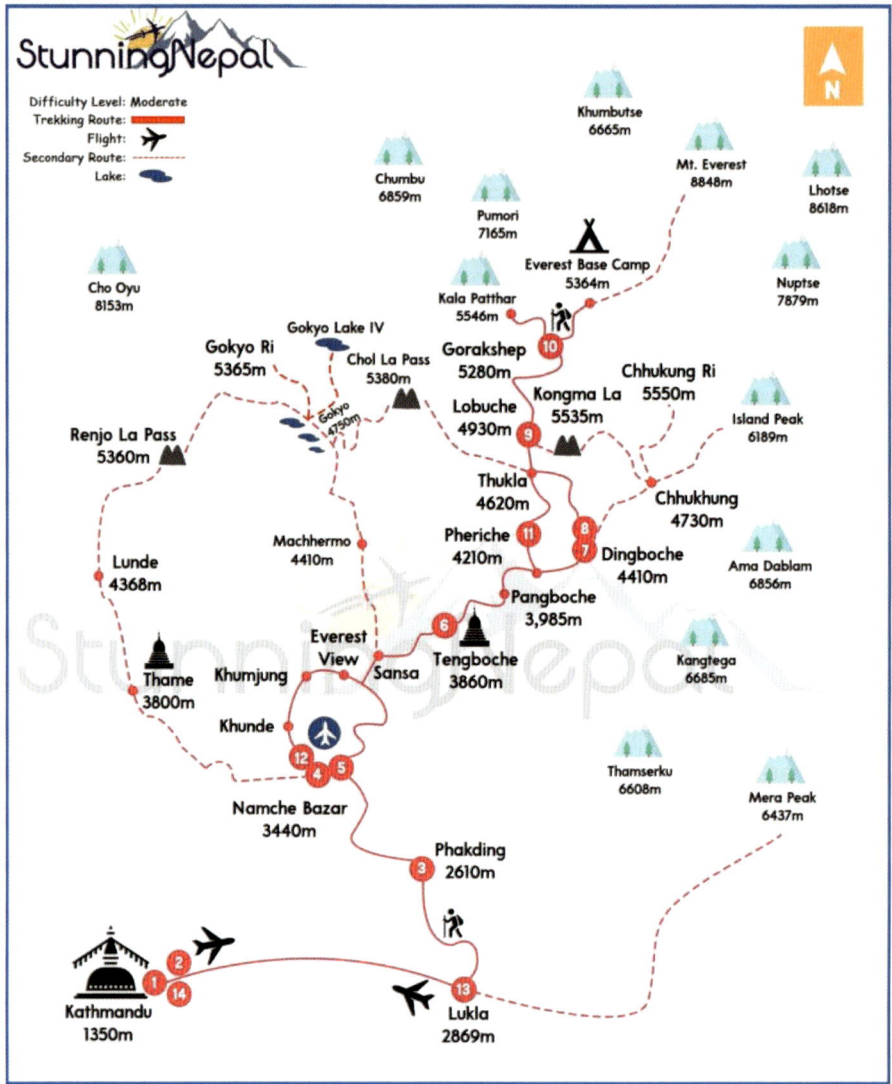

Itinerary map.

the Dudh Koshi, it is easy trekking and takes about 3 and half hour to reach at Phakding , Overnight at lodge.

Day 04. Trek from Phakding to Namche Bazaar (3440 m.) – 6 Hours:

We continue our trekking following the Dudh Koshi River and crossing it many times and we enter to the park in Jorsale and we will stop there for lunch and again we continue the trekking, after few hours walking Namche Bazar will appears ahead as you travel along the path surrounded by pines. Pass the plateau where the Saturday bazaar is held and enter the village. Namche Bazar (3440m) is surrounded on three sides by mountain ranges and opens out only where it faces the Duch koshi Koshi. The village is a central hub of the area and food, sundrie and even mountain climbing equipment may be purchased here, overnight at Lodge.

Day 05. Rest day at Namche Bazaar (3440 m) for acclimatization:

Namche is tucked away between two ridges amidst the giant peaks of the Khumbu and has an abundance of lodges, tea shops and souvenir shops as well as a magnificent outlook. It is an ideal place to spend a rest day for acclimatization to the high altitude before heading off towards Tyangboche. For the acclimatization we walk up to Khhumjung village through Everest view Hotel in Syangbuche and you will see the beautiful view of the Himalayas including Mt.Everest . Khhumjung is densely populated by Sherpa community and there is an old monastery as well so, we will visit that as well, and then Return to Namche, Overnight at Lodge.

Day 06. Trek from Namche Bazaar to Tyangboche (3867 m.) – 5 Hours:

We start our trekking with the ridge and level mountain path that offers an excellent panorama of Thamserku, Kantega, and Kusum Kangrib, after walking few hours on flat Zigzag we descend to the river and arrive at Phunki Tenga. Then we climb through Rhododendron forest to the Tengbuche, Overnight at lodge.

Day 07. Trek from Tyangboche to Dingboche (4260 m.)- 5 Hours:

We start our trekking with descending through Rhododendron forest to the Imja Khola and cross exciting suspension bridge on the Imja Khola and walk passing by a long Mani stone wall to enter the village of Pangboche. Our route continues through summer pastures to Dingboche .Overnight at Lodge.

Day 08. Rest day at Dingboche (4260 m.) for acclimatization:

Today is the remarkable acclimatization day. There are some breathtaking views of the North face of Ama Dablam and the Lhotse-Nuptse ridge as you explore this beautiful valley that leads up to Island Peak. The walk is short with a good chance to relax in the afternoon. You have another option as you can hike up to Chhukum. From where, you can enjoy the panoramic view of Island peak, Ama Dablaml, Makalu, Tawoche peak and others. Overnight at lodge.

Day 09. Trek from Dingboche to Lobuche (4930 m.)- 5 Hours:

The onward Himalayan journey leads us north for up to 50-minutes until we come to a mani-prayer Stupa then The trail is gentle looking down to Pheriche village below. Today's walk offers views of the Mt.Tawache, Ama Dablam and to the north-Pokalde (5741m) Kongma-tse (5820m) and the great wall of Nuptse. After two hours of walking, the trail from Pheriche joins near Dugla (4595m) before a small wooden bridge over the river of Khumbu glacier. Then continue for an hour up a steep hill to the top, where there are views of Mt. Pumori and other peaks west of Everest. After a short break, continue trekking up to Lobuche, Overnight at Lodge.

Day 10. Trek from Lobuche to Everest Base Camp via Gorakshep (m.) 6-7 Hours:

We start our trekking following the rocky moraine path, view icy glacial pond and icebergs down below of Khumbu glacier. After the last rocky moraine dunes, a short downhill walk brings you to Gorakshep, where we will stop for lunch and we leave all our stuff there at lodge as this is the last place where there are lodge available – then we start our Himalayan journey to the Everest Base camp- WOW !!! Congratulation!!! Your Dream come true now, after visiting sometime in the Base Camp then we return to Gorekshep, Overnight at Lodge.

Day 11. Trek from Gorakshep to Kala Patthar (5545m.) and trek to Pheriche (4243m.)- 7 Hours:

Quite Early morning, we climb to Kala Patthar (5545m.) and enjoy the view of sunrise. From Kala Patthar we can have a panoramic view of Mt. Everest and many other mountain peaks like Mt. Pumori, Mt. Lingtren, Mt. Khumbetse, Mt. Nuptse, Mt. Lhotse, Mt. Ama Dablam, Mt. Thamserku and many more, after seeing the sunrise, we trek down to Gorekshep and have lunch and start trekking down to Pheriche, Overnight at lodge.

Day 12- Trek from Pheriche to Namche Bazaar (3441 meters) 6 hours.

Now, we are trekking back to Namche, an easier descent passing through rhododendron forest. Tengbuche is a small village with a famous monastery offering you the splendid view of Ama Dablam, green hills and river views where we stopped for lunch then we will retrace to Namche , Overnight at Lodge.

Day 13. Trek from Namche Bazaar to Lukla (2886 m.)- 6 Hours:

Today is the last day of your trekking, The trekking is pleasant, except for few short uphill climbs and then down to the Bhote-Koshi River crossing it three times. The last uphill climb of 45 minutes will bring you to Lukla, Overnight at Lodge.

WHY WAS I DOING THIS?

Day 14. Fly from Lukla to Kathmandu. we will take an early morning flight back to Kathmandu, – Overnight at hotel.

Day 15- Leisure day in Kathmandu.

It's also spare day in case of bad weather in Lukla, farewell dinner in Kathmandu, overnight at hotel.

Day 16. Transfer to international airport for your final flight departure.

Attenborough Nature Reserve's natural beauty.

THE TRAINING

WEEK-BY-WEEK DIARY
Written in real time every Monday morning.

In only 13 weeks' time, or to make it less daunting, in a quarter of a year's time, I will be getting on to the plane to Kathmandu. There is a lot of preparation still needed – insurance, jabs, visa, kit, getting fit, losing weight and, well, just stuff.

This diary is not intended as a blow-by-blow account of what I did day-to-day, just a general insight into the preparation I did and some of the things I discovered. It also details when my training went off the rails and my willpower failed (beer and chocolate mainly).

As a lecturer, my busy time was nearly over until after the trip, so I could concentrate on getting ready for Base Camp while also balancing the family commitments.

NB: After each week, there is a separate account for each long training walk.

WEEK 1
Monday 20 June – Sunday 26 June – 13 weeks to go
Weight at start of week: 114.5kg
Weight at end of week: 111.9kg
Cumulative weight lost: 2.6kg
Steps completed in week: 127,588

I was into the last stretch of marking. With 250 papers to mark on my two law modules I had made a good start and was nearly through 180 of them. Monday to Wednesday saw me finish them off. It was a shame to miss one of the greatest days in England cricket's recent history when I turned down the chance to see day five of the New Zealand Test at Trent Bridge in Nottingham, and Jonny Bairstow's match-winning 136. I had been to day two, but couldn't take the risk of missing my marking deadline. It was in the middle of a heatwave, so I was able to mark in the sunshine, rather than in my office upstairs. It made up for it a little, but I am probably kidding myself.

Not too much preparation for Everest this week though, just the start of trying to get fit and losing some of the bulk I had put on over the last two months when I had taken advantage of the world opening up with trips to France and the Netherlands on a university trip, skiing with the family in the Alps, and then a fortnight on the Dalmatian coast in Croatia with Jane. Starting at just over 18st (115kg) I was aiming for 100kg by the time I boarded the flight to Nepal. Fifteen kilograms in 13 weeks. Doable, but discipline was needed.

It is always good to get the week off to a good start, when intentions are good and energy high. Three trips to the gym, a four-mile leisure walk, a 16.5-mile training walk, two over-40s hockey matches and dad dancing for seven hours at a Green Day concert (plus support) in Huddersfield was a decent start on the exercise front. Although I am overweight, I am still relatively fit, it is just difficult to keep the pounds off. Food wise, again I started well with home-cooked food and portion control. By the end of the week though I'd had three consecutive days of drinking – only in moderation mind – a 'Spoons burger and chips, and a home BBQ. A few choccies and sweets had also broken down my mind's defences and infiltrated my body.

By the end of the week, I felt a lot better, but disappointingly only 2.6kg down. Usually, it falls off for a few days after a period of weight gain, but although it was nearly half a stone, I'd hoped to be under 110kg by the end of the week. Only four days to go to do it before the end of the month.

Nothing much on the preparation side, apart from buying three books on walking to Everest Base Camp. Being halfway through a classic Wilbur Smith, I couldn't start them straight away, but by Sunday, Wilbur was complete and the research could begin in earnest.

Miles walked: 20.

* * * * *

TRAINING WALKS

With 13 weeks to go, I knew that I needed to get some miles into my legs. I planned 13 long walks across the length of Britain, some hilly, some just long.

TRAINING

These are logged and discussed over the training pages, including maps, stats and pictures. Some I was joined by friends, some I was on my own, but each one had the effect of getting me used to being on my feet and fighting through any pain and doubt that I knew I would encounter on the slopes of the Himalayas.

They are also a really good way of testing kit: do the new boots hurt, what blisters did I get, what chaffing, what food and fluids worked to give me an energy boost along the way.

The final benefit was getting out into the open air. Living in Nottingham and working as a lecturer and business owner, my job is very indoors and although I do try and get outside as much as possible, the training walks really helped me to see parts of Britain that in most cases I haven't seen before. And what a fabulous country it is for walking and nature.

The walks in order:

Walk 1 – 24/06/2022:	A mainly flat walk around the Nottinghamshire/Derbyshire border
Walk 2 – 28/06/2022:	The Edale Skyline Walk, Peak District, Derbyshire
Walk 3 – 08/07/2022:	The Brecon Beacons Four Peaks, South Wales
Walk 4 – 12/07/2022:	The Tissington Trail, Peak District, Derbyshire
Walk 5 – 20/07/2022:	Dovedale, Peak District, Derbyshire
Walk 6 – 28/07/2022:	The Yorkshire Three Peaks Challenge, North York Moors National Park
Walk 7 – 02/08/2022:	Parkhouse Hill and Chrome Hill Loop, Longnor, Peak District
Walk 8 – 10/08/2022:	Snowdon, from Pen y Pass, Wales
Walk 9 – 17/08/2022:	Scafell Pike, Lake District, north-west of England
Walk 10 – 21/08/2022:	Ben Lomond, Loch Lomond, Lowlands, Scotland
Walk 11 – 01/09/2022:	A 30-mile local walk

Training Walk 1
24/06/2022: The Nottinghamshire/Derbyshire Border, 16.2 miles.

To kick off my training in earnest, I stayed local. I am incredibly lucky to live in Attenborough, six miles from Nottingham city centre towards Derby in the west. Within a mile of my house, we have the benefit of Attenborough Nature Reserve. Built on the site of old gravel pits, it is now somewhere for locals and visitors alike.

https://www.nottinghamshirewildlife.org/attenborough

From their website, 'Attenborough Nature Reserve was established in 1966 and was opened by Sir David Attenborough. This much loved, nationally important site is best known for its birds with over 250 species recorded, but also provides a home for hundreds of species of plant and insects. It is cited as one of the best places in the UK to see kingfisher and is also home to rare wildlife including bitterns and otters. The reserve attracts around 500,000 visitors each year and holds a special place in the hearts of many.'

A promotional piece for sure, but not far from the truth.

It has been the home of bike rides, runs and walks at least once a week for the 24 years that I have lived near there. Despite its many divergent paths and hidden cut-throughs, I have come to know it very well, but it never disappoints. Turn left

Attenborough Nature Centre in the heart of Attenborough Nature Reserve.

at the river and you can go all the way into Nottingham (via the River Trent or the Beeston Canal); turn right and you can go to Sawley, across the Nottinghamshire/Derbyshire border. It is also a big protection for the residents of Attenborough and Chilwell against the high waters of the Trent in the wet months of autumn and winter as it offers a good overflow when the banks of the river cannot take the strain of the British weather.

Whether it is the height of the summer sun, the snow and ice of winter or the changing colours of spring and autumn, each day offers different sounds and sights. My particular favourite is a weir from one of the overflow lakes that goes under one of the bridges. Always busy with birdlife, including swans, Canadian geese and ducks, you can often find a noble heron, standing on the edge, scouring the water for something to eat. If you're in luck he finds something to snack on or he spreads his wings and flies off into the distance. Magnificent.

* * * * *

So the reserve was an obvious place to start my training walks.

I was planning to do a 20-miler, but it was cut short for reasons to come. Heading out through the Nature Reserve towards Trent Lock near Sawley, I would join the Erewash Canal and head through Long Eaton, Sandiacre and Stapleford, before going back into Nottinghamshire and climbing the Hemlock Stone Hill (the steepest hill near me), through Bramcote Park and then back into Chilwell and the nature reserve to finish off. I missed the last part. It is a route I know well, but mainly as a cyclist, thanks to my good friend Dave Jones who showed me the

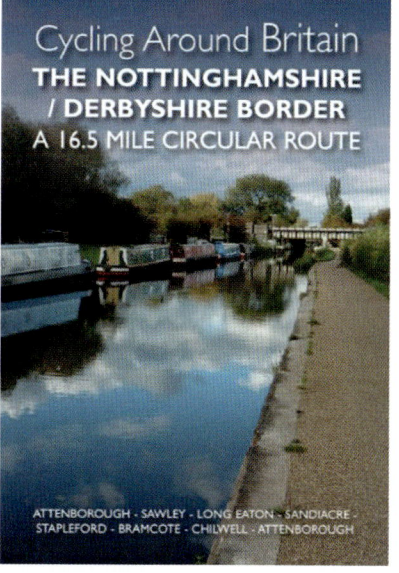

route about 15 years prior. In fact, in the early days of ebooks, I did a guide to the route and it is still available on Amazon.

https://www.amazon.co.uk/Britain-circular-Nottinghamshire-Derbyshire-Attenborough-ebook/dp/B006FXVJF6/ref=sr_1_1?crid=2UY46FCMA8W6K&keywords=steve+caron&qid=1656144685&sprefix=steve+caron%2Caps%2C135&sr=8-1

Starting at 9am, I thought I would aim for a three-miles-per-hour pace, including breaks. I have a tendency to just push through without really stopping, but I knew that on the walk to Base Camp we would be stopping for meal breaks and for slower moving walkers. The point of the training walks is to be prepared, so I needed to be used to stopping and starting – getting those muscles moving again after a break. Easier said than done – I walked at my usual pace of 16.5-minute miles, nearly a third faster than I intended. Would I suffer from it later?

I have recently bought some new boots from Decathlon, and although I have worn them for shorter walks, I haven't been anywhere over six miles in them. They are really comfy though, especially as I followed some advice from years ago by a running shoe salesman that I should put gel inserts into them. I have done this in every pair of trainers, running shoes and walking boots ever since and have no painful feet after this tactic.

The day was great for walking, about 20 degrees celsius, dry with a nice breeze. The previous few days had been a heatwave, over 27 degrees. Not much for some of you reading this, but remember we are British. Anything over 22 degrees and we start moaning like mad. Mind you, anything under 17 degrees and we moan like mad too. You'd have thought that we'd have got used to the British weather by now.

There were a few other walkers and cyclists on the paths as I headed for Sawley, but not too many. Once you're out of the nature reserve itself, it stops being a circular route, and is a destination track, so having to come back the same way puts a lot of walkers off making the outward trip. However, a four-and-a-half-mile stretch of the River Trent was not a bad start for me.

One of the features of the walk was the skyline, with the looming cooling towers of Ratcliffe Power Station switching position from my left to my right depending on the meandering of the river. What was obvious was the sheer size as they came closer. My first job was at Drakelow Power Station in Burton upon Trent and although the generator buildings and chimneys were ugly, I was always in awe of the towers, with their beautifully contoured bodies that were perfectly designed to condense the steam back into water. On an open day in the 1990s, they closed one off and visitors could go inside and release a helium balloon, watching it float away through the perfectly round caldera. Only from the inside can you truly appreciate their magnificence, so before they are all knocked down in the rush for green energy, see if you can experience this before it is too late.

Trent Lock itself is at the junction of the Trent and the Erewash Canal and it is a little hive of activity for visitors as there are a few pubs and cafes but it is also home to long-term canal folk. Repair yards, paint shops and holiday lettings make it a busy hub for canal users, but calm and tranquil for those who just want to enjoy a coffee and scone or a pint.

The canal itself runs for nearly 12 miles between the River Trent and Langley Mill, and for the most part it follows the River Erewash, which forms the boundary between Nottinghamshire and Derbyshire. It was built largely to bring coal out of the Erewash Valley pits and down to the river Trent for onward trade to Nottingham and Leicester.

A right turn on to the canal, and I started on a six-mile stretch through the old industrial heartland of south Derbyshire. This is one of my favourite walks in the locality. Taking you off the roads, you can see some real examples of how the past would have looked at its height, when factories had extra tall chimneys to make sure the smoke from the furnaces cleared the Erewash Valley basin.

The final stretch would take me back into Nottinghamshire. Cutting through Stapleford, I had some proper hill training at last. Only 331ft high, Stapleford Hill (or as it is known by me, the Hemlock Stone Hill) is a very steep climb which

Along the Erewash Canal through Long Eaton – the old bakehouse chimneys.

The Hemlock Stone. No one knows how it got there.

gives you good views over the local area. Now a designated area for mountain bikers, you need to keep your wits about you as you're climbing, but both sides are generally respectful of each other. The trig point was my first real break, so I had lunch and enjoyed the view. I was about 12 miles into my walk and no sign of stiffness. Good news.

The Hemlock Stone itself is believed to be over 200 million years old and is worth a look. There are many theories as to where it came from, either man-made or just as part of the general geology of the region.

After lunch, it was another couple of hills through Bramcote Park and over the A52 and then back towards home along the tram track and the nature reserve.

After only three miles, I realised that I had made a big mistake in my preparation. My Fitbit had already run out of battery, my phone had already gone on to the backup charger in my bag and was now in low battery mode, and my earpods started to tell me that they were running out of juice. So much for digital tech!

I made the decision to cut short the walk by three miles or so and head straight home through Chilwell instead of the extra loop of the nature reserve. It was actually three and a half miles short, but not to worry. I had got through the trip in a good time, only four hours 38 minutes of walking time, at an average moving pace of 17.08-minute miles.

Nothing hurt, I'd tackled a couple of hills and the day was pleasant. A most enjoyable trip.

Stats for the day:
Steps: 49,735 (taken as a combination of Fitbit and the phone app when Fitbit ran out of battery)

WEEK 2
Monday 27 June – Sunday 3 July – 12 weeks to go
Weight at start of week: 111.9kg
Weight at the end of week: 110.5kg
Cumulative weight lost: 4kg
Steps completed in week: 129,609
Cumulative: 257,207

It was a really strange week this week. I did a lot of walking, over 40 miles, and a couple of visits to the gym but I was really struggling to get my weight down. The mark of any true yo-yo dieter is the phrase 'the diet starts tomorrow', usually on a Sunday afternoon as the third or fourth roast potato is polished off or the late-evening bowl of cereal comes out of the cupboard. I am no different. Monday and Tuesday was great, a double 12-mile round trip walk to Nottingham and back for uni and a 21-mile walk around the Edale Skyline in Derbyshire with an old friend and her son. It had me feeling fit and nearly a kilogram down from Monday morning. By Saturday it had virtually gone back on again. A couple of days of relative inaction, snacking (I eat when I'm not doing much), then a BBQ with our really good friends Pete and Ali (and lots of booze) on the Friday meant I was way behind schedule. I have learned though that the booze stays on me for a couple of days and then goes again, so a good day Saturday and a really good day Sunday and I went below the 111kg mark to 110.5kg for the first time since the beginning of May. Next week, I am aiming to be below 109, not seen since April. I have been trying to reduce my drinking anyway. I was never a regular drinker, just a binge one, so I am aiming to only have a beer once a week maximum from now on. Let's see if that helps. Pete and Ali are on holiday now for a fortnight, and as they are my usual partners in crime, I may even have a fortnight off. If I can ramp up the training, eat well and not drink much, I should be in a much better position.

The walk on Monday was another old favourite. Through the Attenborough Nature Reserve and on to the canal, it is a five-mile walk into Nottingham, past Boots HQ and into the heart of the city. One of my jobs is lecturing at Nottingham Trent University, so whenever I can, I walk there. It is just over six miles in total, and takes between 90 and 100 minutes depending on how quickly I go. Whenever I mention it to students or fellow lecturers, they always look at me amazed, but it is something I have done for years. Mind you, a good podcast or three certainly helps. My go-to podcasts, in order are *Fighting Talk* on BBC Radio 5 Live, *The Frank Skinner Show* (on Absolute Radio), *Planet Normal* from the Daily Telegraph, *Triggernometry* (a really interesting discussion show that is not afraid of tackling the issues of the day) and *What Most People Think* by Geoff Norcott, a very funny British comedian with a political slant. With over five hours of content a week, it certainly keeps me occupied. I also have a 'Longlist' on my Spotify with nearly 54 hours of my favourite songs – just in case I run out.

Tuesday was my big training walk of the week to Edale in the Peak District, which you can find at the end of this entry.

The rest of the week was spent working on my business and catching up on some university admin, and fitting in a couple of visits to the gym (just walking up the highest incline on the treadmill or the stepper). Sunday I did manage another training walk. There are not many hills near us – the canal walk as you can guess is completely flat. However, in Bramcote Village, there is a park called Town Street which is a half-mile circuit, with a steep incline either side. For some good quick cardio, and some good downhill training (which you cannot get in the gym) I did eight laps, in just over an hour. It is only a 30m incline, but it does burn when you go for it. It is almost a classic HIIT session – with boots on. Before the National Three Peaks attempts, we used this regularly. I had almost forgotten about it, but now it will become a regular training route. Maybe I need a dog to take with me.

Planning for week three's walk is complete. A trip round to the Brecon Beacons in Wales on Friday 8 July, with another of my oldest friends, Steve 'Boggie' Booth. As it is three hours away, we will be stopping over, so with the accommodation booked, the route chosen, the map downloaded and the weather forecast favourable, I am ready.

One major thing I did manage to sort out this week was my insurance for the trip. Obviously being airlifted off the mountain due to injury or altitude sickness can be a big expense, so the insurance companies who supply this are specialist, and I suggest you shop around. Following this entry, there is detail of my insurance search.

The final task of the week was to sort out my clothes cupboards. I have shirts that don't fit, walking gear all over the place and my sock drawer would test a

INSURANCE

I normally leave holiday insurance to Jane. Before 2019 we generally got annual insurance which includes skiing, and it doesn't seem too expensive, but as I was going to 5,500m, I thought I'd better check out the specific insurance needed for something so out of the ordinary and I'm glad I did. With helicopter rescue from the mountain being the biggest cost, the specialist companies make a big deal of it. Last time, my insurance was with a company called PJ Hayman, and when Covid hit, it was rolled over, but when I couldn't go in 2021, we just cancelled it as they couldn't roll it over twice (not sure why). This time, I wanted to go through the process again, so selected three companies to choose from: PJ Hayman again, True Traveler and World Nomads.

I started with World Nomads and I wasn't impressed with them. The agent wanted me to go online and process the quote there. I wanted to chat it through. He just went through the website himself and came back with a figure of £719.28 for standard and £867.51 for the premium. I was shocked. I was sure it was only about £300 last time. I checked with Jane, and she thought it was only about £260. Can it really have gone up that much?

After a chat with True Traveler, I was relieved to find they were back in the ball park at £250.84. I talked through the issues with a knowledgeable and friendly agent called Chris. He even showed me how I can add things easily on their website (once I had chosen my options from the conversation).

When I got a reply from PJ Hayman (Adventures Specialist Travel Insurance), I went through the quote with another good agent, Ethan, and they came back with a figure of £343.50. The documentation for the quote was emailed and I set about deciding which of the two to choose.

Apparently, there is a scam in Nepal which I had been warned about last time, whereby the travel operators are in cahoots with the local helicopter companies. For a fee, the travel operators will call up their mates and get you helicoptered off the mountain at the first sign of altitude sickness – obviously a hazard at that height. According to one of the insurance reps I'd spoken to, the easiest way to overcome altitude sickness is to just descend a couple of hundred metres and drink lots of water. I had no intention of finishing early, but it was something to consider. As a result, the premiums are high to mitigate some of the risk. True Traveler were very clear that unless they had authorised helicopter evacuation, it wouldn't be covered.

After comparing the two quotes and details, I decided to go with the higher quote. I am not sure why I chose it to be honest, just some higher cover in areas, less generic in others, and just a sense that this was very specific to the task I wanted to undertake.

It was a relief to get the insurance. Although I had only paid a $150 deposit towards the actual trek, I had paid for the flights. If they were cancelled for Covid as before I'd get my money back, but if I had to cancel for any reason, I'd be the thick end of a grand out of pocket.

Job done, now I needed to just print off the documents and make a note of the emergency helpline.

INSURANCE COMPARISON CHART:

Summary of Cover – Section & Cover Limit per Event Excess* person (up to) Premium	PJHayman – Adventures Travel		True Traveller	
	info@pjhayman.com		sales@truetraveller.com	
	https://quote.adventurescover.co.uk/trip-details		www.truetraveller.com	
	02392 419 070		0333 999 3140	
	Benefit	Excess	Benefit	Excess
	£343.50		£263.77	
PART A				
1. Medical & Emergency Expenses	£10,000,000	£100	£5,000,000	£75
Emergency dental treatment (for relief of pain only)	£300		£350	£75
Physio	£ -		£350	£75
Burial Costs / Body Repatriation	£3,500			
Hospital Inconvenience Benefit	£400	£ -		
Search & Rescue costs	£50,000	£500	£15,000	£750
2. Personal Accident	£5,000	£ -	£15,000	£75
3. Personal Liability	£2,000,000	£ -	£2,000,000	£75
4. Activity Equipment	£1,000	£75		
Delayed Activity Equipment (over 12 hours)	£200	£ -		
Activity Equipment Hire	£300	£ -		
5. Legal Expenses	£25,000	£ -	£15,000	£75
6. Curtailment	£2,000	£100	£3,000	£75
PART B				
7. Possessions, Personal Effects, Money & Documents				
Personal Possessions	£2,000	£75	£2,000	£75
- Single items, pair or set limit	£300	£75	£250	£75
- Valuables limit	£300	£75	£350	£75
Delayed Possessions (over 12 hours)	£200	£ -	£105	£75
Loss of Personal Money	£300	£75	£250	£75
Loss of Travel Documents (including Passport)	£1,000	£75	£250	£75
8. Cancellation, Loss of Deposit or Curtailment	£5,000	£100	£3,000	£75
9. Unexpected Events				
Travel Disruption (costs to reach destination)	£1,000	£ -		
Travel Delay	£120	£ -		
or Abandonment (after 12 hours delay)	£5,000	£100		
PART C				
10. Optional Independent Traveller				
Extended Cancellation or Curtailment	£5,000	£100		
Extended Travel Delay	£120	£ -		
Extended Travel Disruption (costs to reach destination)	£1,000	£ -		
Accommodation	£5,000	£100		

Mensa student. So after the walk on Sunday, while listening to Wimbledon, I had a clear-out. THREE bin bags of clothes got sent to the recycling centre or the local Marie Curie charity shop. Feeling a real sense of achievement, I can now see exactly what I have when deciding what I still need for the trip to Nepal.

The final thing to mention is that I started one of my Everest Base Camp books, *One Step at a Time* by Paul Tallett. It is a sobering read and reminds me that I have some way to go to be fit enough. Paul was only 40, was a regular walker in the hills of Scotland and had a major weight advantage on me. And he still struggled on some of the days. With 11 weeks to go I need to up my training – starting on Monday!

A full review of Paul's book is found elsewhere in this volume.

Training Walk 2
28/06/2022: The Edale Skyline Walk

After the relative ease of the walk around the local area in week one, I decided to go for one of my favourite walks – the Edale Skyline. Set in the heart of the Peak District, only 75 minutes from Attenborough, it is an eight-hour, 22-mile walk around the top of the Hope Valley. Reaching a height of over 500m at Mam Tor, it is a long and varied walk around the ridge surrounding the valley – but what views. Hopefully the photos in this section will do it justice, but I suspect not. The only way to experience it is to do it, whether it is just sections or the whole distance. I chose the 28th as the weather forecast was the most benign in the week. In other words, it wasn't going to rain.

The Peak District is the UK's oldest National Park, yet it was only established in 1951. Covering over 500 square miles, it has 20 million people living within an hour of it, including the cities of Manchester, Sheffield, Stoke, Derby and Nottingham. Split between the Dark Peak (largely uninhabited moorland and gritstone) and the White Peak (farmland and limestone gorges) it attracts millions of visitors each year. I go regularly to visit, but also travel through it on my way to Manchester where my son lives. The A57, between Sheffield and Manchester, is one of the great scenic routes in the UK, with winding roads, hills and valleys, bleak moorland and lakes.

https://www.peakdistrict.gov.uk/
https://www.peakdistrict.org/
https://en.wikipedia.org/wiki/Peak_District

Although I tackled the first training walk solo, I'd asked friends if they wanted to come on any of my trips, and for this one I was joined for the first four hours by one of my oldest friends, Helen. I met her at Preston Poly in 1989 and we have kept in touch ever since. How she managed to drag along her 20-year-old son, Ed, as well is a mystery, but I was pleased as it meant I didn't have to worry about her getting back to Edale when we parted company at Jacob's Ladder (more to follow). He added a really different dynamic as he listened to our stories from the 'Poly' days without getting bored. He was probably trying to get some gossip – and therefore, some leverage.

* * * * *

There are several places you can start the walk, but as it was the Hope Valley, the obvious place was Hope. I had done the walk twice before, both in 2021, so I was familiar with the route, but both times it was anti-clockwise. As Helen and Ed were only going to do part of the journey, we decided to go the reverse route so that they could see Mam Tor, one of the highlights of the trip. It also meant an easily navigable but long trip back to Edale where they were being picked up by Helen's husband, Nick. A cyclist, not a walker, he spent the time on the cycling friendly roads around Castleton.

The start of the walk, looking up the path from Hope to Lose Hill.

TRAINING

Hope is a village near Castleton, probably the most well-known town in that part of the Peaks, but there are a few good pubs and facilities, as well as a railway station. To get to the skyline, you have to go up, and having experienced it twice, I knew it was going to be a leg and lung-burner whichever direction we took. Lose Hill, the first destination, stands at 476m and to get there was relentless.

It was as I expected, and I wondered if I would put Helen and Ed off, but they tackled it without complaint – in fact with humour and enthusiasm. I knew that the effort would be worth it, but they didn't and could have been a bit grumpy. It is always a worry that you overstretch those who haven't been used to training for long walks, but those worries were allayed immediately and I knew it would be a good trip.

From Lose Hill, you can see the whole valley and the sheer size of the task. The first part was an obvious path of two or three miles to Mam Tor. For anyone familiar with the Channel 4 'metal logo man', used to introduce some of their TV shows, you will recognise this stretch of path. For those reading this in an ebook, you can see the advert.

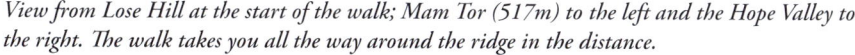
https://www.creativereview.co.uk/channel-4-logo-c4-giant/

Mam Tor is the highest obvious point on the walk at 517m and getting to the top is the most popular walk among visitors. Easily accessible from Castleton and Edale (you can even park nearby) it is a reasonably challenging climb, but not too difficult for the 'fitness challenged' if you take your time, as there is a very defined paved route to the top. I had been up there three times recently and the weather is very changeable, from hail (even though it was sunny at the bottom) to blazing

View from Lose Hill at the start of the walk; Mam Tor (517m) to the left and the Hope Valley to the right. The walk takes you all the way around the ridge in the distance.

My travel companions for part of the journey, Helen and her son Ed, at the top of Mam Tor.

sunshine. On this occasion it was very blustery – but dry. It is a great place for taking in the views though as you can see down to Edale and across the Hope Valley or turn the other way and you get Castleton and Winnats Pass – a limestone gorge that has a steep winding road through it. There were plenty of other visitors hanging around on top so we joined them for the photo opportunities and the views.

We'd been walking about two hours, so we were all starting to feel peckish – it was lunchtime. I normally try and leave early on these walks, around 8am, but Nick is a dairy farmer, so had the morning jobs to do before they set off from Staffordshire. We met at 10.30am in the end, but as it was only a week after the longest day, there was no danger of finishing in the dark, even starting nearer midday. We didn't leave Hope until 11am, so 1pm seemed about right for some food. Settling in at a quiet spot overlooking the valley and Edale, we watched the activity around us. Some model plane enthusiasts were flying their gliders across the landscape and there were many schoolkids all on their Duke of Edinburgh Award expedition. Even after two hours of walking the challenge ahead was plain to see. The final climb would be Win Hill, and I could see it in the background, behind Lose Hill. Not only did I have to walk around the other three sides of the valley, the final ascent was going to be long.

TRAINING

The view back towards Lose Hill with the opposite side of the valley clearly seen on the left. At the back, on the right, is Win Hill (463m), the final climb of the walk.

I had always known that Helen and Ed would leave me after the first part of the walk so we chose a route for them to go back down into Edale. The beauty of the Hope Valley is that there is always an 'out'. Even if you intended to go round the full skyline, there are so many paths back into the centre, you can plan your route depending on time available. Unfortunately for them, the next 90 minutes were probably the most boring part of the walk. Round the back of the valley up to Brown Knoll, there was a paved route on the peat landscape. It was paved to stop people sinking into the peat when it was wet, and was a great piece of engineering. The views weren't great until the exit to Jacob's Ladder where if you looked away from the Hope Valley you could see the city scape of Manchester in the distance. It was not the clearest day, but you could still make out some of the recognisable buildings.

* * * * *

Edale is the start of the 268-mile long Pennine Way. According to the National Trails website,

'The route follows England's rocky spine from the hills of the Derbyshire Peak District and the Yorkshire Dales, through the stunning Swaledale Valley, across the North Pennines and over Hadrian's Wall in Northumberland to the Cheviot Hills, ending in the Scottish Borders in Kirk Yetholm.'

https://www.nationaltrail.co.uk/en_GB/trails/pennine-way/

Many have said that they are going to walk it – sometime. Including me. Many have not even started it. Including me. But it is a good ambition to have.

Some of the landscape up close. A really good example of how the rocks and formations have been there for thousands of years. Note the peat nature of the ground and the many paths round the rocks.

The start of the Pennine Way takes you up a steep winding path called Jacob's Ladder. At the junction with my path, we parted company, and Helen and Ed descended into the valley down the ladder, while I continued up towards Kinder Scout, the highest point in the Peak District at 636m. My route wouldn't quite get me there, but I was tantalisingly close and I was really tempted. Maybe if I'd still been with Helen and Ed, we'd have gone.

Across the back of the Hope Valley, the path shifted from something very defined to something more haphazard. There was still a general direction that was obvious, so no worries about getting lost, but you had to pick your way through rocks, and different paths that fellow walkers had made over the years. Sometimes, you'd find yourself a few metres away from where you had expected to be. It was a

Looking back towards the back of the valley. The distinctive path going down towards Edale is the start of Jacob's Ladder, a popular route from Edale.

A view of Win Hill from Crookstone Out Moor. The route takes you along a path by the trees in the centre of the image.

fascinating place though with overhanging rocks, rock stacks and boulders strewn all over.

With the skyline taking in many outcrops into the valley, I found myself going the long way round on several occasions. Instead of cutting across the top of the outcrop, I would walk to the end, and then have to double back on myself. I needed to consult my map more often but I had a problem.

My phone is nearly two years old and the battery is not as reliable as before. Despite it being charged before I set off, it had already run out and I was charging it on a powerbank, but it was painfully slow. To preserve the battery in case I needed the phone later I switched it off. This meant I lost my online map. I did have the classic paper version of the Ordnance Survey map with my route on, but I had lent it to Nick for his bike ride as I had a downloadable version – which of course was on my phone. Going the reverse way round compared to my previous two visits, I kept missing the cut-throughs. It probably added about a mile to my route. The other downside of the battery outage was that I couldn't track the stats on the walk accurately. I knew I'd have the 'steps' and 'floors' on Fitbit, but the Strava tracker would be inaccurate. As a result, the map from Strava at the end of this section is for the identical walk I did last year.

It was approaching 5pm and I could see Win Hill in the distance around the valley. It didn't look too daunting so I pushed on. Down from Win Hill, was a long stretch of trees which I remembered from my last walk there. Not obvious from the photos at a distance but they formed the boundary of Ladybower Reservoir. Even if I didn't fancy the walk, I definitely wanted to see the reservoir.

Approach to Win Hill (463m), then back down into Hope.

Ladybower Reservoir was built over eight years from 1935. It is next to the Derwent Reservoir and it was here that the Dambusters practiced their raids before deploying Barnes Wallace's 'bouncing bombs' in enemy territory. Now it is a scenic place for tourists and locals alike.

The final leg of the trip would take me to Win Hill. At 463m, it was the smallest of the three that I had climbed that day, but it was a long way to the top as the skyline dropped from Crookstone Out Moor, meaning I had to climb again. At one point I came to a fork in the path. Hope (and the car) was only 30 minutes away downhill, or up to Win Hill and another 90 minutes. My resolve nearly cracked and I considered going right to Hope, but then I remembered why I was here. If I took the easy option at the end of a seven-hour day in the relatively low hills of Derbyshire, how would I cope at the end of the eighth day in Nepal while walking at the top of the world. So despite some aching limbs, I chose left. It was actually not as bad as I thought it would be. It also helped that I wasn't alone. Obviously work had finished for the day and the path was buzzing with mountain bikers. Despite sticking my thumb out, no one would give me a lift, but their energy inspired me to get to the top.

It was literally all downhill from here. The climb up to Lose Hill at the start of the walk was tough, but looking down towards Hope from Win Hill, it made me wonder whether I had made the right choice after all. It was steep and long and passed through a few fields with cows in. I didn't think I'd even be able to outrun a tortoise after 20 miles never mind a charging cow protecting her calf, but I passed through without incident. I could have done with a couple of walking poles to take the strain from my aching knees, but after 30 minutes or so, I crossed under

TRAINING

Strava map of the walk from 2021. The route was the same, just the direction was different.

the railway bridge on to the first bit of tarmac for eight hours, half a mile from my car. I had made it. It was 6.50pm, just short of eight hours from start to finish.

I had a really good sense of achievement and it was a great day. A chance to catch up and have a laugh with a good friend, stunning scenery and another 22 miles in the legs.

Next week, the Brecon Beacons.

Strava Stats from 2021:
Distance: 21.7 miles
Elevation Gain: 3,474ft (approx. 1,050m)
Fitbit stats for the day:
Steps: 49,735
Floors: 473
Calories: 7,894

WEEK 3
Monday 4 July – Sunday 10 July – 11 weeks to go
Weight at start of week: 110.5kg
Weight at the end of week: 110kg
Cumulative weight lost: 4.5kg
Steps completed in week: 137,002
Cumulative: 394,209

So much for not boozing. From promising to having a fortnight off, I actually had a drink on three separate days. Granted none of them were binge drinking (one pint on Thursday, five on Friday, and three on Saturday) and in mind all very justifiable, but it did contribute to me only losing half a kilogram in the week. A lot below my target of 1.5kg on the week. I'll keep that again as next week's target as I have a lot of walking planned.

I started the week slower than usual. Normally I walk into Nottingham for my weekly student meetings but they all wanted to have them online, so I missed out on my 12-mile Monday. To compensate I went to the gym for an hour on the treadmill, with full kit, including boots and rucksack – only a few strange looks. This was after a trip to the private travel medical practice to discuss vaccinations. There is a separate section on this with a lot more detail, but I was pleased to hear that my vaccinations were still up to date from my aborted trip in 2020. No more cost there. It was also the last week for the hockey masters, the over-40s summer tournament that I play in for Boots Hockey Club. Three matches in 20+ degrees celsius was too much for me after the gym. Was I trying to do too much?

On Tuesday, we had the news we had been waiting for when my youngest, Dan, got signed off at the hospital after five years of check-ups. The words 'go and enjoy your life' from the consultant, seemingly so simple, had a profound effect on us as a family. It was surprisingly emotional. We had been expecting it so it wasn't a surprise, but the invisible pressure valve released. To celebrate, I took Dan and Jim golfing as Jane was at work, and then had fish and chips for tea. So very British.

I did a longer local walk on Wednesday, about eight miles up and down some local hills including Bramcote Park and the Hemlock Stone again. It was a good workout actually as I did push it. I also bought a new high-capacity powerbank and solar charger. I am currently testing them, so when I get the results I will let you know whether they do the job that is promised.

I had a cultural experience on Thursday where Jane had a concert with her orchestra group, Music For Everyone. It is a great organisation, 12 weeks of rehearsals, then a concert. I don't get a chance to watch her that often due to work, but the music was uplifting, the conductor very energetic and Jane's clarinet playing (to my ears) mistake-free. They are not professionals, it isn't perfect, but they have a great enjoyment of music and it shows. Great fun. Boris also resigned as the Prime Minister. Quiz night in the local with some friends Paul and Sharon

VACCINATIONS

Please note – I am NOT a doctor. The details below are my experiences only. Please see your own doctor before you travel and take their advice about what you need before travelling.

It is very difficult to see a doctor in the UK these days. I made a telephone appointment to talk about altitude sickness and it would be a MONTH before they could even call me. There was no chance of having a chat about vaccinations with them.

Prior to my first aborted trip, I did have a lot of jabs privately, so I booked another appointment with Traveldoc, a franchise I think, but they certainly had an office in Nottingham. So I went along to see what else I needed and whether my current jabs from 2020 were still valid.

What I needed?
- Tetanus / Polio / Diptheria – administered at school, so most UK citizens will have it
- Typhoid - £50
- Cholera - £75
- Rabies - £195 (3 doses of £65 each)
- Hepatitis A - £45
- Hepatitis B - £135 (3 doses of £45)
- And Covid of course.

Luckily for me, I am still covered for all of these from my aborted trip. I asked about malaria and Japanese encephalitis, but these are both mosquito-borne diseases and there wouldn't be many of them in the Himalayas. Any further travel in Asia and you may need to consider them.

I did ask the prices, which I have put alongside the individual vaccinations, so if you were going privately, it would cost you the thick end of £500, and you need 28 days for the jabs that require three doses. Make sure you plan it into your schedule. None of them should have any side effects, so will not interfere with your training or make you ill before you go though (according to the doctor). I asked if any were available on the NHS, and apparently typhoid and cholera are, but to get an appointment is very difficult, and apparently there is a shortage due to Covid. No surprises there. Funny how private healthcare providers always manage to get access.

in the evening was meant to be booze-free, but Paul has been holed up in hospital for a fortnight, so when he had his 'one' pint for the night, I felt that I should join him. It was only one, and a good job as I had a late-evening rescue mission to get Matt, my middle son, from the middle of the Derbyshire Peaks, as his cross-country train from Manchester had stopped in the middle of nowhere. Not great prep for an early start, a four-hour drive to Wales, then a seven-hour walk.

Friday was my big walk, this time 14 miles in the Brecon Beacons. You can read about it in more detail as usual, but it was my first time there and in the beautiful sunshine and steep terrain, it was another good chance to get some miles in the legs.

I thought I would ache in the morning after the walk, but my fitness must be improving. It was no issue driving back for three hours, not even a hint of cramp. All I need to make sure I do is get a lot more of these in, so that I don't ache after 11 straight days. I am not holding out much hope, but delaying it as long as I can in Nepal is going to make my experience so much more enjoyable. On getting home, Jane and Matt suggested lunch at a local pub with a beer garden, then a couple of beers at home in the sun rounded off the day. I don't get to see Matt much as he lives in Manchester, so it was nice to catch up.

With the weather still staying gorgeous, and with training in mind, it was not a tricky decision on Sunday to walk the six miles to Trent Bridge to watch England v India in the final T20 of the series. It is not often you get world-class sport in Nottingham, and the venue is one of the best in the country for cricket, so it is hard not to go on the big occasions. With a crowd that was about 50/50 in terms of supporters, the atmosphere was great, and the crowd was in really good humour. I do love the attitude of cricket fans. You have a beer, sit next to a rival supporter and chat, clap even when the opposition do well (half century for a batsmen, 200 runs for the team etc) and chill. I do like football as a sport more, but it is a very different viewing experience.

With a few big walks, I upped my step count again for the week, and I have started to see the benefit in my legs. I am not losing weight as fast as I would like, but I am more confident about my fitness. With ten weeks to go, I need to keep it up.

Training Walk 3
08/07/2022: The Brecon Beacon Four Peaks

I was a bit nervous about this one. I had never been to this part of Wales before and I had seen people get sponsored just for climbing Pen y Fan, and, more worryingly, news reports of how the British Army used it for training (sometimes fatally). It sounded tough. If ever there was a time for getting a good-weather day, this was it. Navigating without distance vision is always trickier, and of course you do miss the views. At 16 miles and with lots of incline, it would be a really good test for me. Was I able to manage it more easily than expected, or did it give me more doubt about my ability to tackle the Himalayas?

The marketing slogan for the Beacons is, 'Always changing, forever beautiful.'

After the walk, it was very difficult to disagree with that sentiment. For more details on what else you can find there, see:

https://www.beacons-npa.gov.uk/
https://www.breconbeacons.org/

I had another companion on the trip, this time for the full journey. Steve 'Boggie' Booth is my best mate from uni and someone I still see a few times a year. We met on day one at Lancashire Poly in Preston 1988 as we were both doing the same accounting degree and he was in the same seminar group due to our surnames being 'B' and 'C'. Three years of going to all the same classes, flat-sharing while playing pool, darts and cards, beer and a bit of study thrown in and we would be the classic friends for life (a bit like Helen last week – without the pool, darts and cards).

It was Boggie who came on my first attempt at the Edale Skyline last year, and we vowed then to do a walk every year. In fact we planned the Brecon Beacons a while ago, and it fit perfectly into my training schedule. Unlike Edale where I came home straight after the walk, we agreed to stay over in Wales and have a few beers afterwards. A good job as it was a three-to-four-hour car journey. After checking the weather, we could see that there would be no issues so we agreed to meet in Stoke at 7am and share a car down to Merthyr Tydfil on the edge of the Brecon Beacons.

I have now read a few books on trekking to Base Camp (see book reviews) and one thing that comes across is fatigue. Lack of sleep, five hours a day walking, the Khumbu cough and freezing conditions means that you must have stamina and determination to keep yourself going even when you are tired. Inadvertently, I practised this.

The night before the walk, I set my alarm for 5.15am, so I could get ready and drive the hour to Stoke to meet Boggie. Jane and I were at a local pub quiz on Thursday night, but I wasn't drinking and we were planning on being home at

10pm. That was the plan anyway. At 9.45pm we got a call from Matt, our middle son, who lives in Manchester, and was due home on the train that night. His train had broken down in the Peak District as it crossed the Pennines and he was faced with a very expensive taxi ride to 'civilisation' (i.e. Sheffield). Could we pick him up? Of course we could, that's what parents do. So an hour each way and I arrived back after midnight, only five hours to the alarm. With a four-hour drive and a seven-hour walk – all on four hours' sleep – if I could manage this, even for a day, I knew I would have a chance in Nepal. Throw in the sticky weather which further hampered sleep and I was up before the alarm even sounded.

Boggie was on time. I know that sounds obvious, but it is a first. He left his car at the fantastic Trentham Gardens just off J15 of the M6 and we headed to Wales. Four hours later after a pit stop and some strangely signposted roadworks, we pulled into the Blaen-y-glyn car park and set off on the route I had picked out from my Ordnance Survey map (OL12) which originally appeared in *Trail Magazine* in December 2019, the Pen y Fan circuit; 24.42km, six hours and rated 'Difficult'.

Only we had to go back as Boggie had left his food in the car. Off we went again, only we realised we were going in the wrong direction. So glad we had GPS that tracked our movement on the downloaded map – but the path had looked obvious. Luckily we passed the car again, as I realised I was still in my driving shoes, not my walking boots, so another pit stop. We'd walked about half a mile, had three false starts and were back to square one. What a way to kick off the day. It was funny though.

Almost immediately we were going uphill. After half a mile and a 750ft elevation climb (229m) we reached the top of the first hill, Fan Big. The views of Brecon started to become spectacular. Grand open valleys, hills, forests and water was all we could see. Very few roads or cars, and because it was a Friday, very few people. It was like being on our own private grounds. One thing we did notice was the lack of sheep. Not sure why we thought of it but I do know it's not what you think, even though I am a Derby County fan (nicknamed the Rams) with the inevitable chants of 'Sheepsha**er' from the opposition supporters.

The path stretched out in front of us, and for the next two or three miles, we hugged the ridge. No sign of the four peaks yet, but they were looming on the map. It was as simple as turning a corner which we duly did. There they were in the distance – Fan y Big first, then Cribyn, Pen y Fan (the highest) and eventually

TRAINING

A look back down the route where we'd already walked – back towards Fan Big.

Corn Du. We'd only done about four miles, and they didn't seem that far away – mind you they looked challenging. Looking back down the path, it was a surprise to see how steep the slopes into the valley were next to the path we'd come down. I never really noticed it before, despite my fear of heights. Was I overcoming this, or had I just not noticed as I was chatting to Boggie. I noticed it later!

The walk up to the top of Fan y Big (literally translated as 'point of the peak') was very gentle. After all the play-on-words schoolboy jokes (go on work it out, it is not difficult), we'd obviously come at it from the easy side as a group of students were at the top relaxing. They had come from Cribyn and were shattered due to the climb. We'd be going down that of course. After taking in the views, and having our lunch, we set off to Cribyn ('little ridge').

It was steep descending to the bottom, but hill walking is not just about the ups, it is the downs as well, and often the more elderly walker (okay, over-40s)

The Four Peaks (l-r) Corn Du (873m), Pen y Fan (886m), Cribyn (795m) and Fan y Big (719m).

51

start to have knees that have seen better days. Boggie especially found it easier going uphill rather than downhill, something a lot of my friends also echo. Not something that especially bothers me though, I prefer the downhill walks because I find them easier, but I prefer the uphill because of the views, and again we weren't disappointed. The walk downhill from Fan y Big was 100m of elevation, followed by a 170m of elevation to the top of Cribyn (795m). It was a real workout for the heart and lungs. I have a tendency to breathe heavily as I climb, even though I feel fine. Boggie kept asking me if I was okay; I think he was worried about me – or more likely how he'd be able to explain it to Jane if I keeled over.

As we approached the top of Cribyn, a group of younger walkers (aged 20 to 40) congratulated us on our climb. They must have seen a couple of old, grey-haired blokes panting their way to the top and thought we'd done well. We got chatting and when Boggie mentioned that I was going to Everest Base Camp, they changed from being congratulatory to a little awestruck. As I mentioned my past walking exploits, National Three Peaks, Yorkshire Three Peaks, Edale etc, they all said that I should post about my adventures in Instagram. As a 52-year-old, I have never been on it, but it is food for thought. They were especially keen because they have formed a group called #offthebeatentraxuk to encourage people of all ages to enjoy the wonder of the British countryside and they are trying to spread their message via social media. One of them took my LinkedIn profile and later connected. Who knows, we may even meet again as I may ask them if they fancy any of my future training walks.

Boggie (third from the left) and I at the top of Cribyn with the guys from #offthebeatentraxuk. Fan y Big in the background.

Pen y Fan from halfway down Cribyn. It looks a lot steeper from this angle than it did at the top of Cribyn.

They were going in the opposite direction to us on the walk they had christened the Harper Route, so we fist-pumped our goodbyes and set off for the highest point of the day, Pen y Fan.

At 886m, Pen y Fan (Top Spot), was 90m higher than Cribyn. With another descent (which we'd not seen from the top) of 130m, it meant the climb to the top spot was a massive 220m. Over about 800m in distance. It was a steep climb, but as it was the last major obstacle of the day we climbed with only a couple of stops to get a breather.

It was worth it. The views were spectacular, especially on such a beautiful day. There was a stag do at the top, all dressed as *Lord of the Rings* characters, complete with hunting horn for the groom to neck a can of Corona after a shot of Scotch malt whisky. Only a few mixed cultural messages there, but they were good fun and greeted us warmly.

It was at this point that I had a lightbulb moment, which of course I should have realised hours, days, weeks, or even months ago. At all the high points there was a distinctive flat area, with a cairn in the middle. I just thought it was for the walkers.

From Wiki, 'Historically, beacons were fires lit at well-known locations on hills or high places, used either as lighthouses for navigation at sea, or for signalling over land that enemy troops were approaching, in order to alert defenses. As signals, beacons are an ancient form of optical telegraph and were part of a relay league'

I had only just spotted this and it dawned on why they were called the Brecon Beacons. Each flat area was where the bonfires were lit for this communication. Boggie was amused. I was meant to be the one who knew my history. Just not language apparently.

Boggie and I at the top of Pen y Fan with Cribyn and Fan y Big in the background.

After another snack and drink we headed to our last peak, Corn Du ('Black Horn') and at 873m it was only at a slightly lower elevation than Pen y Fan. No big up and down here though, just a gentle gradient both ways, and we had completed our four peak challenge.

It turned out to be the best part of the walk too. We were just over seven miles into the 16-mile total. For the next four miles or so we started back along the opposite ridge to the four peaks. The views were still pretty good and our legs were still holding out.

Then the leg wobble started. I have hinted that heights are not great for me. Not true, it is the fear of being near an edge. It could be 20m or 200m and I would feel the same. The path

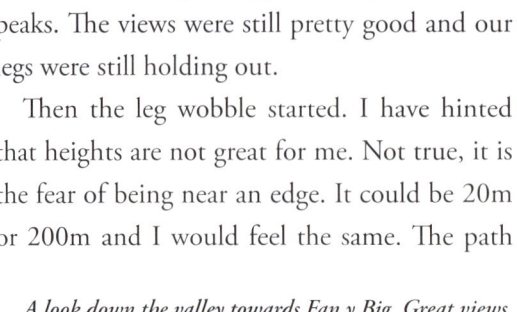

A look down the valley towards Fan y Big. Great views.

TRAINING

The path going very close to the edge down towards Cefn Cull. Not good if you don't like heights.

home went very close to the edge of the valley walls. Ludicrously close (for me). Boggie doesn't have the same fear, so he walked closer to the edge than I dared, which somehow made it worse. I couldn't enjoy the views as much as I was picking my path very carefully. I was so pleased it wasn't blowing a gale. It was a pity really, and I felt such a wuss, but after half an hour or so, we were past the worst part and it was heading for home.

The final four miles were a drag. The views had gone and we walked alongside a fence. The path wasn't defined and we ended up in a marsh. Both of us had water-in-the-boots moments, in fact I nearly faceplanted as I tried to jump between two seemingly firmer footholds. Boggie sensibly went around this.

We were pleased to find the road and headed back to the car park, forgetting that it was predominantly uphill all the way, the last thing we needed after a long walk. But the sense of achievement on reaching the end was there for both of us.

Home for the night. And another 500 steps maximum!

A much-deserved beer at the end.

Distance: 16.3 mi
Elev Gain: 3,313 ft
Time: 6h 4m

We were really pleased we'd not decided to drive straight back home, so after a 30-minute drive to Rhymney we checked in to the Prince of Wales pub. It looked like it had seen better days from the outside, but the welcome was warm, the beer tasted great and cheap, the locals were friendly and the twin room was clean with everything you needed. We didn't need much. A walk back inside for pie and chips, more beer, chat and people watching and at 10pm we were both knackered and crawled to bed. Apparently, it was only two minutes before I was catching zzzzzzzzzzzzzzzs.

It was a truly great day. It is always special to catch up with Boggie with lots of family news, reminiscences, the inevitable lists – favourite book, film, band, TV – and of course the best part, the scenery and the activity. Please don't ignore this part of the UK, make sure you add it to your list of walks, whether you are training or just doing it for fun.

Strava stats:

Distance: 16.3m

Elevation gain: 3,313ft (approx. 1,010m)

I couldn't use my Fitbit as it stopped working. I wondered if I had put my hand in the marsh when I nearly faceplanted. It kicked back into life the following evening. The steps count is from my phone counter, so not as accurate.

Daily steps: 39,502

WEEK 4

Monday 11 July – Sunday 17 July – ten weeks to go

Weight at start of week: 110kg

Weight at the end of week: 109.3kg

Cumulative weight lost: 5.2kg

Steps completed in week: 171,781

Cumulative: 565,990

A week of really piling up the step count. After the Brecon Beacons and cricket, I didn't want to lose momentum. With three days at Nottingham Trent this week, I was able to walk there and back on two of them, a 12-mile return trip on each day. On the other day my rucksack strap broke which was very frustrating so I walked there but had to get the tram back. Not only did I miss the training, I also missed the scenery. It is such a lovely way to get to Nottingham, along the canal.

The canal path at Beeston Rylands.

I have put a few pics in to show how idyllic it is. What a lovely slow pace of life canal folk have. And a pleasure to train on there.

Sandwiched between these days was my longest walk ever, 27 miles up and down the Tissington Trail on the edge of the Peak District near Ashbourne. There is a separate report of the walk which was pretty uneventful and relatively flat, but 27 miles was long. Like Brecon Beacons, I was really surprised that I didn't ache the next day. I am definitely getting fitter.

The final walk was back to Mam Tor and part of the Edale Skyline, this time with Jane. We're planning a trek up Ben Nevis at the end of August as part of our trip to Scotland to see Coldplay at Glasgow's Hampden Park, so Jane needed to start training

The canal path near Nottingham.

TRAINING

Jane climbing up Lose Hill.

for that (and try her new boots out). The Hope Valley is such a lovely part of the world that I don't mind going again and again, and for Jane, this was her third visit to Castleton, but only her second time up Mam Tor, and her first walk to Lose Hill.

In total we walked six miles, up and down from Mam Tor to Lose Hill, so some hill practice for us both. I found it really easy, whereas I remember my first time really huffing and puffing to get up there. More evidence that the training is working. So from the previous Friday to this Friday, I had walked a total of 92 miles in eight days. And no pain either. I am trying to have as many consecutive long walks as I can, to replicate Nepal, where you don't have rest days – you have to just keep going.

Jane and I at the top of Mam Tor.

The long walk streak was ended on Saturday and Sunday, but I felt satisfied that I had achieved another goal in my training.

I read another Nepal book this week, a 1983 copy of Lonely Planet's Kathmandu and Everest which I'd picked up for a couple of quid in the local Oxfam charity shop. It was a lovely nostalgic reminder of how I had used these books religiously while backpacking in the mid-1990s before the internet. One thing did scare me though and that was the description of how much uphill and downhill there is on the EBC trek. I naively assumed that it would be a reasonably steady uphill journey over the eight days of actual climbing to Base Camp, but the author talked about the overall ascent on the walk being the equivalent to climbing Everest twice. Not just base camp, but 18,000m of incline. I think he was basing it on the walk from Kathmandu to Lukla too, but still, this was a scary thought; 27 miles down the relatively flat Tissington Trail was good for endurance but not so good for the type of walking I would be facing. Next week, I will try and get out to Dovedale and just walk up and down Thorpe Cloud a few times.

This is where there appears to be a real gap in the literature about the trek. There is a lot of info about the relative incline between the end-of-day stops, and the time it takes to walk it, but there is not much on the up and downs within the days. Hopefully, I will be able to add this detail to this book and give the reader a real sense of which days are harder than others.

The final part of this week's diary is the weight. After a great start, I was down below 108kg at one point in the week, but after a very hefty BBQ at my sister's on Sunday (with far too much to drink) it crept back above 109kg. It will soon drop off again, but it is frustrating that it set me back. It is more frustrating as it is blatantly self-inflicted – once again.

* * * * *

Training Walk 4
12/07/2022: The Tissington Trail - Derbyshire

After last week's trip to the Brecon Beacons, I was more confident of the big hilly walks. I had planned the Lake District Ten Peaks Challenge, from Ambleside to Scafell Pike (the highest mountain in England) and back. I'd bought the map, planned the route, packed my bags and set my alarm for 5.15am to get there for a 9am start.

At 10.30pm, I completely lost my bottle. I was travelling alone this week, and I started thinking about the two times I had been lost on Scafell during my National Three Peaks attempts (once we were up there for nine hours). I didn't want to go solo in such a difficult terrain, and a long way from any town. Despite GPS, I didn't fancy getting lost again. So I changed my alarm to 6.15am and thought I'd go local again – another trip to the Peaks, and a walk up and down the Tissington Trail. It wouldn't be hilly, only 300m of elevation, but at 13.5 miles in length, it would be a 27-mile return trip, more than I'd ever walked in a single day before. Not challenging from an up and down perspective, but a challenge for sheer length.

From the Peak District website: 'The London and North Western Railway (LNWR) between Buxton and Ashbourne first opened in 1899. Following the closure of the line around seventy years later, the Peak District National Park bought the route in 1971 and turned it into a traffic free trail for walkers and cyclists.

'The Tissington Trail runs for 13 miles from Parsley Hay (53.1706°N 1.7828°W) in the north to Ashbourne (53.0196°N 1.7397°W) in the south.'

https://www.peakdistrict.gov.uk/visiting/places-to-visit/trails/tissington-trail

It is a very popular route for cyclists and walkers, and I remember cycling it with the kids when we were camping near there about 15 years ago. For a test of stamina and distance it would be perfect.

An example of the quality of the path on the Tissington Trail.

The walk starts in Ashbourne, a small town on the edge of the Peaks. It is a lovely place and attracts many tourists every year, either day-trippers, or people staying at the many camping spots. It is very close to Dovedale, one of the most-visited places in the Peaks due to its shallow river, the famous stepping stones across the river, and the chance to climb Thorpe Cloud, the highest peak in the local area. We used to take the kids there a lot when they were little.

The actual walk will not take too much time to describe. The path is excellent all the way – flat and wide and a gentle incline north to Parsley Hay, and the reverse on the way back to Ashbourne.

It was another good British summer's day, about 20 degrees and dry, and I was able to abandon a lot of my usual kit list – map, compass, whistle, light sticks, emergency blanket! There was no way I was going to get lost. Hot and tired, yes, but not stuck on top of Scafell Pike in fog.

It really was just that, straight up and down again. What was so nice about it was the proximity to the local farming community. Rather than seeing barren but beautiful, hilly landscapes, there were distinctive fields, some harvested, some about to be. There was a dairy farm with the cows undertaking their morning milking. There were cuttings where the rock had been carved away to allow the old train line to pass. And in the background you could see Thorpe Cloud and the surrounding hills. A lovely way to spend the day.

There were a smattering of people using the trail. Mainly cyclists, but a few walkers with their dogs only doing part of the walk. It took about four hours to go the 13.5 miles south to north – slightly uphill and I did get a good sweat on, mainly

The old station house at Hartington.

TRAINING

Halfway at Parsley Hay, now back to Ashbourne.

because I was trying to keep my pace up. If I couldn't get the cardio from the hills, I would get it from the speed.

As I approached Parsley Hay, I came across an old railway station at Hartington that had serviced the old railway line. It was a lovely reminder of how Britain used to be, before the Beeching cuts in the 1960s ripped out some of the less-popular lines. An act of wanton vandalism that led to more cars on the roads than are necessary.

At the end of the trail was a cafe and car park. I had already walked a half-marathon in just under four hours, so I definitely deserved a 30-minute break. There were plenty of cyclists having the same thought. The legs were feeling good, my body was well refreshed, my bladder was emptied, and I returned back towards Ashbourne.

Jane often asks me if I get bored while walking. I spend many hours walking alone, whether it is to Nottingham for work or around the local area as part of my training. In all honesty, I don't. I enjoy the solitude sometimes, whether it is listening to music or podcasts, or just alone with my thoughts. I am pretty comfortable in my own brain – maybe it was the 36-hour train journeys while backpacking, or just sat pondering next steps for my business or lecturing life.

On the way up the trail, I listened to podcasts, but as the reception started to disintegrate near Parsley Hay, I relied on the tried and trusted downloaded music in Spotify. Four hours and five albums later, the time flew by. *Bat Out of Hell* (Meat Loaf), *American Idiot* (Green Day), *St. Jude* (Courteeners), *Sam's Town* (The Killers) and *Waiting for Bonaparte* (The Men They Couldn't Hang) are five of my go-to albums, and as the path was quiet, I took the opportunity to belt them

Great scenery – rocks, plants and bridges – what more could you want?

out at the top of my voice – after all, I wasn't on the bus or tram. Nice weather, a downhill walk, the English countryside and a mini, one-man karaoke and I was like a pig in muck.

Even the scenery changed, despite going on exactly the same route but in reverse. I suppose you're always looking forward, so don't see the scene behind you. Now I did and although it looked sort of the same – it was different.

I ignored the legs that had started to ache, and the shoulder that had to be relieved of the bag every so often, and just sauntered home in exactly the same time as the northward journey, three hours 49minutes. Not bad for a 13.5-mile trip. Just over 17-minutes-per-mile pace, way faster than I would need in Nepal.

From start to finish, it had taken me less than eight and a half hours, with a nice stop in the middle. No stops in the actual walk though. Without the big lung-busting hills I just push through. It must have been hot though as I drunk four litres of water on the trip in total. No altitude sickness for me!

My legs certainly ached, and after driving the 40 minutes home, I did tenderly get out of the car, but as the muscles warmed up, and a bath, they were fine. Nothing in the morning either. These practice endurance walks are certainly giving me confidence in my physical capabilities.

WEEK 5
Monday 18 July – Sunday 24 July – nine weeks to go
Weight at start of week: 109.3kg
Weight at the end of week: 107.1kg
Cumulative weight lost: 7.4kg
Steps completed in week: 137,440
Cumulative: 703,430

A much less intense week on the walking front (only 51 miles) but a great week on the waistline – over 2kg lost, putting me below 17st at 16st 12lb. Only another stone (6.5kg) to go with eight weeks of training left. I would love to be in the 15s when I get on that plane on 20 September. So what caused it – well, firstly no alcohol, despite a couple of opportunities including another BBQ at my sister's on Saturday. I was a model of sobriety and I felt better for it. A few lapses in food (pizza and chips on Thursday before watching *Elvis* at the cinema) pushed me back above 110kg on Friday morning, but three good days and it dropped off.

The big news of the week for the country was the heatwave. In Britain it hit over 40 degrees celsius for the first time ever on Monday and Tuesday, and the whole country went into meltdown – and I am not talking about the temperature. Panic set in. Advice was even given on the news about how not to die in the heat. I think the mainstream media had forgotten that Brits love travelling to hot countries, and they go for a fortnight. Two days of heat was not going to stop us and the beaches were packed and shirts were off. Remember Noël Coward saying that only mad dogs and Englishmen go out in the midday sun, well he was proved right this week. I was working at NTU unfortunately, but two lovely walks back and forth along the canal to Nottingham (yes I know, even in that heat, surely I was going to die) on Monday and Tuesday added a further 24 miles to the tally.

On Wednesday, it was my day's training walk and I returned to the Derbyshire Peaks, this time Dovedale, and spent six hours and 14 miles going up and down Thorpe Cloud, Bunster Hill and enjoying the views along the river Dove. A great day, in the now 'freezing' 21 degrees.

The rest of the week was steady. Walks around the nature reserve and to Beeston with Jane (seven miles), back and forth from the car to Pride Park to see the Rams (three miles) and an hour's uphill walking in the gym (three miles) was all I did, but it kept my feet in motion.

From a preparation perspective, I have still not decided on the solar charger for my powerbank. It does charge, but not especially quick and it is reasonably heavy. As I don't want to lose battery on the trip, I will probably take it; after all, even a bit of juice is better than running out. I also tested out my electrolytes on the training walk. Cola-flavoured – just about passable (see training walk section). Now I just need to test them with the water purification tabs to see if they hide the taste. That's for next week.

I also bought a blood oxygen monitor for my finger. Apparently, if you go under 70 per cent blood oxygen, you are on the verge of serious altitude sickness, so I will be keeping an eye on that on the trip. I am 95 per cent at sea level in Nottingham. Another couple of Base Camp books read (see book reviews) and I am starting to flip-flop between excitement and trepidation as the days get closer. Only eight weeks to go now. I am fitter, lighter, more prepared and better trained for hills. So why am I worried? Because it is 5,500m and very cold, that's why!

One more piece of good news is that I have had confirmation of my booking for a round of golf at the Gokarna Golf Resort in Kathmandu on 23 September.

TRAINING

https://gokarna.com/ I cannot wait to see what it is like at such an altitude. Hopefully my drives will go so much further.

I also had it confirmed from my tour company that they will be providing a down sleeping bag, down jacket and a duffle bag. This will save me some cost and free up the luggage space for other essentials. Good news.

* * * * *

Training Walk 5
20/07/2022 - Dovedale - Derbyshire

Still without a 'volunteer' to come to the Lakes, I was solo again. After reading a guide which said the actual uphill parts of the EBC trek was twice the height of Everest, I needed to find somewhere that could give me this. I mentioned Thorpe Cloud in last week's walk, so I decided to spend a boring day walking up and down it. At about 250m in elevation, I thought I'd go up and down all day. Tedious for sure, but great training.

As it was near Ashbourne, about an hour away, I didn't need to get up as early as usual for this day trip. Good job really as we were on the back of the two hottest days 'ever' in the UK and barely anyone in the country could sleep. We don't bother with A/C here as it never gets that hot so we all spent the night trying to keep cool – and failing badly. Mind you, it gets difficult to sleep when it's only about 15 degrees centigrade at night here and we still don't learn. The shops immediately sell out of electric fans and we spend a day or two moaning about the heat. An anathema to residents of hot countries, but not to the Brits where weather really is a national obsession.

I tried another bit of EBC preparation as well on the trip. I had read about water purification tablets and electrolyte tablets being added to the water bottles. The first to make sure you weren't ill, the other to re-energise AND to hide the taste of the purification tablets. The electrolytes also had added caffeine and B vitamins. I don't know what all that means for the body but it sounded good and couldn't hurt. I started with the electrolytes only for this trip. I had bought some 'cola'-flavoured ones from Science in Sport (they were the cheapest flavour) and added four to my three-litre bladder. The instructions said add one per 500ml of water, but to take no more than four a day. Slightly contradictory but I erred on the side of caution with the four and I was pleased I had. It tasted okay (six would

Looking towards Thorpe Cloud (at the back of the pic) from Bunster Hill.

have been a really strong taste), but I would have preferred the orange flavour. Too cheapskate to spend that extra £5 you see. It didn't have any side effects so the practice worked and I will persevere with them for the rest of my training.

Arriving at the Dovedale car park at 9.30am, they were just setting up the ice-cream shop and the pay desk, so I waited for them. I'm really pleased I did as I got chatting with one of the park wardens and she gave me some really good tips on how to spend the day. She also pointed out that a lot of the area was open access, meaning that you could wander anywhere. I tend to stick to the paths to save the hills from erosion, but there weren't really defined paths on a lot of the park.

I had been to Dovedale over 20 times over the years (the kids used to love it) but it seemed I had only seen a fraction of it. From a really boring day ahead, I was going to experience so much more than expected (without skimping on the point of the day – the uphill bits).

A view of Thorpe Cloud from the top of Bunster Hill.

Opposite Thorpe Cloud, there is a large cliff (the edge of Bunster Hill) which I have often looked at but never thought about climbing. Well, I did today. The path rose sharply and the landscape was extremely dry due to the mini-heatwave. The peak was way off up the hill to my right, so I started climbing. With just a few sheep for company, it took a while to climb the 180m of incline to the ridge. I could then take a right turn to the cliff edge, or left to the 'spine' of the hill and the highest point. I chose right. There were lots of small peaks along the way and I climbed them all.

At the edge I looked out across the valley to Thorpe Cloud. I had never seen it from this angle and it made me realise what an interesting peak it really was. Not quite as high as Bunster Hill actually but a really unique formation. Just shows what perspective does for your opinion of things.

After admiring the view for a short time, I set off in the opposite direction and headed for the peak of Bunster Hill and a look out towards Ilam and the Walton Hotel. I met a couple from the south coast who had spent their honeymoon there 44 years ago, and had come back to see it again which was lovely. The ridge to the bottom looked inviting (and steep) so I walked all the way to the bottom and back up again. Going down was much harder. Without a defined path, it was almost baby steps to keep my balance and I could feel my feet slamming into the front of my boots.

Going up was not as lung-busting as I thought, once again showing that I am getting a lot fitter. I employed an old technique Jane and I used in our original Nepal trek 25 years ago and which I have used on various walks since. Take it in stages – 100 steps and then a 20-second breather. It makes a massive difference

The famous stepping stones, without any queues.

Image from the Derby Evening Telegraph showing the stepping stones on a busy day. Copyright Gareth Butterfield.

without taking much rest time. Six reps of 100 steps and I was back at the top. Another tricky and painful descent back towards the car park and I was ready for Thorpe Cloud.

It is a short walk to the stepping stones at the bottom of Thorpe Cloud, and it brought back fantastic memories for me of bringing the kids here when they were little. Jumping in and out of the river (Matt fell in when he was in nappies once), scrambling up and down the scree, searching for sticks (all small boys love carrying sticks), hiding between the trees, and of course crossing the stones. There was a furore a few years ago when the Peak District National Park decided to make them safer by cementing flatter and higher surfaces to the existing stones. Of course I was a traditionalist and didn't want them changing but they were sympathetic to the original look and feel, and now they look like they've been there forever. At the weekend, it gets busy here, and as there is no passing on the stones, you have to wait for the other side to finish crossing before you can go from your side. Sometimes large queues form as people keep crossing from the other side even if they've not been waiting as long. Imagine you're at temporary road work traffic lights, only yours stays red until the other way is clear. I have seen 'crossing rage'

TRAINING

Bunster Hill from half way up Thorpe Cloud.

many times as someone starts from the other side when the last person is only a couple of stones from the end. Very funny, unless you're on the end of it. No such worries today as it is not school holidays yet so relatively quiet.

There are three ways up Thorpe Cloud; one is very steep, the other two more meandering tracks. The park are trying to encourage people to go just one of the ways to protect the hill from erosion, which for me is a mistake as the only 'suggested' path turned out to be dry, slippery and quite tricky to navigate, especially downhill. I took the steep route up, the one I have been up on 95 per cent of times

At the top of Thorpe Cloud - the first time.

My Strava route and stats for the morning walk – lots of back and forth. Bunster Hill on the left, Thorpe Cloud on the right.

to Dovedale. There is a lovely halfway point where you get to see down the valley back towards Bunster Hill, or in the other direction towards Milldale. With no one else on this side of the hill, it was nice to reflect and reminisce and although it sounds really cheesy, I did feel a real glow inside. And it wasn't just the heart beat going like the clappers.

Another few reps of 100 steps and I had made it, and reasonably in breath too. The wind was up as I walked across the ridge and after two days of stifling heat, it felt good to be cool. After the now-customary selfie (for proof) I started my descent.

I had planned to climb Thorpe Cloud another couple of times using the different routes, but with the paths having signs asking you not to use them, I only did it one more time. But only after I'd descended all the way to the bottom into

TRAINING

A look down the river towards the stepping stones from the bottom of Thorpe Cloud.

the valley. It wasn't just steep hills I needed to walk up, but the longer more steady climbs. The end result was the same, just the means of getting there different.

Before going up again, I was going to climb another adjoining hill. As I walked up the valley towards the start of this ascent, I saw a flag on the top of the hill. Of course I didn't know what it was, until I saw many signs at the base of the hill. After going out of my way to read one, it was clear – this hill was used as a shooting range and if there was a flag, then it was live ammo. Not a tricky decision then, so a quick change of direction and it was back up and down Thorpe Cloud again.

By now I had walked 7.3 miles, and gained approximately 700m in elevation. Not a bad morning's work. It was slow at three hours five minutes, but speed wasn't the challenge today.

Back to the stepping stones for lunch, I realised I had forgotten my fork, not handy for my lunch of tuna pasta mayonnaise. As I was already feeling tired due

Some caves on the way to Milldale – great for exploring.

Looking back to Thorpe Cloud with Bunster Hill to the left.

to lack of sleep and couldn't replenish myself as well as I'd like (midget gems and crisps only), I considered going home. I'd also developed my first blister in these boots, from the downhill pressure on my little toe.

But I couldn't just 'go home' in the Himalayas, I would need to push on past the setbacks and energy deficits and reach the days destination. So I applied a 'magic plaster' (Compeed to you and me) to my blister, put my day pack back on and set off on a five-mile round trip to Milldale along the Dove Valley. It was going to be easy, just straight down the valley alongside the river and back, so a compromise on the hill training but it was another couple of hours on my feet. There was even going to be a shop at the end. Nothing is ever as it seems though if you're prepared to change your plans.

The walk to Milldale was lovely, and I was shocked by the realisation that I had never done it with the kids. We'd always been happy to hang around Thorpe Cloud and the stepping stones and although we'd walked about half a mile towards Milldale, we'd never gone all the way. I will change that when the grandkids come along (no pressure lads) as there was loads that would interest them.

A gently burbling river, rocks, trees and caves made the trip not only beautiful but really interesting and it was a shame to get to Milldale in the end. But I could always look at it again on the reverse journey. Or could I?

After a chat with the man in the shop, and with a second wind in my heels after this gentle stroll, I decided to look for an alternative route back. He suggested going around the back of the hills on the opposite side of the valley where it would eventually lead me back to Bunster Hill, where I had been in the morning. If I'd not been that way earlier, I would have been more reluctant but now I was armed

TRAINING

My Strava route and stats for the afternoon walk.

(with information and experience), I was ready to go. It would also have some more up and downs, the purpose of the day.

After a false start (fork in the path, and I took the wrong one), it was a steep climb to the top of the valley side, but then the countryside opened up and it was a lovely rolling walk back to the car park. Coming around Bunster Hill, I thought I'd be walking across the bottom of it as I passed through on the semi-path that was there, but I actually crossed it halfway up, a few hundred feet in elevation from the road. This was the hairiest part of the whole day for me. The path was more an accumulation of footmarks rather than anything defined, and I slightly strayed off it on to a rocky part which was slippery. With 300ft of steepish rocky terrain below, one false move could have been hazardous. One slip later and I was six feet further down the hillside than I intended with much more to slip into, but I managed to dig my boots into the hillside, get my balance and scramble to safer ground. It was like digging my ski edges into the piste in the French Alps on a tricky black run, so it was nice to see my transferrable skills in action!

Keen to get back to the car park and wrap up for the day, I slammed the metaphorical accelerator on and two minutes later, I had completed the walk. Another six and a half miles and 300m of elevation, made it a day of nearly 14 miles covered, 1,000m of climbing and as importantly another six hours of walking.

Rather than go back to Nottingham, I had a prearranged curry night in Burton upon Trent (my home town) with some old friends later, so it was back to my parents for a cold bath and a catch-up before the evening's food. A great end to a much more interesting day than I was expecting.

WEEK 6
Monday 25 July – Sunday 31 July – Eight weeks to go
Weight at start of week: 107.1kg
Weight at the end of week: 108.3kg
Cumulative weight lost: 6.2kg
Steps completed in week: 150,444
Cumulative: 853,874

A funny week all round for me. A great test of fitness on Thursday on my long walk around the Yorkshire Three Peaks, followed straight away with an eight-miler in Dovedale with Jane. This showed how far I have come and how my muscles can recover quickly. However, I only did one other reasonable day of walking (12 miles on Monday) and then bits and bobs all week. On three of the seven days, I did not even get to 10,000 steps and no trips to the gym. I suppose I still covered over 50 miles (including a round of golf and walking to watch Derby from the car), and 150,000 steps, including some large inclines in Yorkshire but I feel disappointed and a bit deflated.

I am wondering if I have hit mid-training mental fatigue as my body is fine. I really look forward to the days away, especially when I am with someone as I was on two occasions this week, but the nitty gritty walks around the local area are not as appealing as they were. I really need to get my mojo back to make sure I am even fitter for the trip which is now just seven weeks away.

I even managed to put weight on. On Friday morning I was down to 106.5kg, by Monday morning it was 108.3kg, so more self-inflicted setbacks. I am now behind schedule against all my monthly targets and most importantly, the 20 September one.

The weekend gain was in a good cause though as we hosted a BBQ (three beers for me) with some friends and Matt's friends to watch the England women's football team – the Lionesses – beat Germany 2-1 in the final of the Euros. It was great to watch. I have really bought into the women's game, especially at international level. Great skill, and, unlike the current men's game, they look to pass the ball forwards all the time. Very refreshing and certainly a lot less boring.

I also had a quick drink on Saturday to celebrate Derby winning their first match in League One for over 30 years. With a massive crowd, and Matt coming from Manchester to watch with me, it was good to see our promotion challenge on track from day one.

Some of the training things I did this week:

I read that to mitigate against upset stomach while away, take some probiotic yoghurts for a period beforehand. This was an easy one for me as I try and do this anyway, but after reading this, I make sure I do it every day, not 'when I remember'. I also take daily Vitamin D, Magnesium, Vitamin C and Cod Liver Oil tablets. The D was to ward off Covid (I still haven't had it) and the others are to make me feel better. I am rarely ill so whether this helps, I am not sure, but they cannot hurt. I will be taking my quota to Nepal, apart from the probiotics.

On my Monday walk round Bramcote and the local area, I added a water purification tablet to my water supply to see what the impacts were, especially taste. With the cola-flavoured electrolyte tabs, I couldn't taste anything horrible which was a good sign. What wasn't good was having to dash into a local pub halfway round to use their facilities. I don't know whether this was related, or whether my 'latchkey incontinence' kicked in when I knew the pub was coming close, but I will have to test it again, and make sure I have some loo roll in my bag if I am going more rural.

My boots got drenched on Thursday in Yorkshire. I do have my old ones as a spare which I used in Dovedale on Friday, but I won't be taking them to Everest. I am wondering whether to get a good pair of trekking trainers to take with me in case this happens in Nepal. I don't want to travel on the plane in my boots if I can help it so I would need alternative footwear and these could serve two purposes. I need to see what the weight load is when I start packing and maybe get some, while still giving me time to break them in.

I am having a flag made with some logos and a message which hopefully I will be able to unfurl at Base Camp. My good friends at Mad Dog Sports in West Bridgford, Nottingham, have  kindly done this for me, so I will give them the plug they deserve. Even if you don't live in Nottingham, they do mail order, so get online and give them a go. Independent sports shops are a dying breed, so look past the big chains and put your money into expertise from the staff and great customer service.

https://maddogsports.co.uk/

Finally, I read my best book so far – *A Trekker's Guide to Everest* by Radek Kucharski. It has everything I need to know including great information about preparation as well as a detailed description of each day's walk, including the height elevation and descent each day – just what I have been after. A full review can be found later in the book.

* * * * *

Training Walk 6
28/07/2022: The Yorkshire Three Peaks Challenge

I had been looking forward to this. I think it was to see exactly how far my fitness had come. While training for my National Three Peaks attempts, I had completed this walk four times previously and I knew that it was a really tough walk. With 1,500m of elevation and 24 miles of walking in total, it was the classic challenge.

Set in the Yorkshire Dales, in the north of England (for our overseas readers), it is a challenge that attracts all level of walker, from experienced hikers to one-off charity novices.

According to the website https://theyorkshire3peaks.com/, 'In our humble opinion the Yorkshire Three Peaks Challenge offers some of the best scenery in the country. Set in the beautiful Yorkshire Dales National Park, the 3 Peaks lie at the heart of an area of outstanding natural beauty and scientific interest. Even on a wet and windy winters day the Yorkshire Three Peaks offer a spectacular challenge, one that will rest in your memory for many years to come.'

TRAINING

Strava map of the walk.

I do not deny that on the wet and windy day it is a challenge (I have been drenched more than once on here) and I cannot argue that it rests in the memory. As a training walk it is perfect – beautiful countryside, a nice, defined path so you cannot get lost, some fellow walkers to chat to, even on quiet days like mine, and best of all, a really physical challenge, both of hills and stamina. It has everything you need for mountain training as the hills are all different. Whernside has a long uphill at a nice steady gradient, followed by a steep step-heavy path downwards, whereas Ingleborough and Pen-y-ghent have steep climbs and long descents. It tests all your walking muscles in one way or another.

The challenge is to complete it in 12 hours – all in, including breaks. I had always come inside that comfortably and I didn't want to be outside it this time.

After a couple of weeks of training alone, I was joined once more by one of my oldest friends from university. I am so glad that as a collective we have all kept in touch. Denise and her partner Rich live in Yorkshire, so were local. However, they only wanted to do part of the walk, so we agreed to meet at the Ribblesdale Viaduct near the bottom of Whernside where they could leave their car and we could drive to the traditional start of Horton-in-Ribblesdale, for them to pick up after walking from Pen-y-ghent.

It was going to be another test of stamina in other ways too as I was going to drive there and back either side of the walk. Having not had too much sleep for two nights, my alarm was set for 4.15am, ready for a three-hour drive to Yorkshire from Nottingham, to meet at 8.15am. I was early, Denise and Rich rocked up at 8.40am. Looking at the map, we decided to skip the trip to Horton and start at Whernside as there was an easy way for them back to the car. I had not even considered it, but on hindsight, it worked well, and I may consider it again for future attempts. We set off around 9am, not the 8.30am I was hoping for, but it was fine, what is half an hour between friends. As it happens it cost me my dryness later.

The Ribblehead viaduct is very impressive, and always a good meeting point for organised Yorkshire three peakers on their charity runs.

Beginning the walk at the Ribblesdale Viaduct with Denise and Rich.

TRAINING

All three peaks in one view, Whernside (736m) on the right at the end of the path, Ingleborough (723m) in the middle and Pen-y-ghent (694m) on the left.

According to the website http://www.yorkshiredales.org.uk/places/ribblehead viaduct/, 'Ribblehead viaduct is just over the border from Cumbria into North Yorkshire and is undoubtedly the most impressive structure on the Settle-Carlisle Railway.

'Hundreds of railway builders ("navvies") lost their lives building the line, from a combination of accidents, fights, and smallpox outbreaks. In particular, building the Ribblehead (then Batty Moss) viaduct, with its 24 massive stone arches 104 feet (32 metres) above the moor, caused such loss of life that the railway paid for an expansion of the local graveyard.'

And Wiki says (https://en.wikipedia.org/wiki/Ribblehead_Viaduct), 'The viaduct was designed by John Sydney Crossley, chief engineer of the Midland Railway, who was responsible for the design and construction of all major structures along the line. The viaduct was necessitated by the challenging terrain of the route. Construction began in late 1869. It necessitated a large workforce, up to 2,300 men, most of whom lived in shanty towns set up near its base. Over 100 men lost their lives during its construction. The Settle to Carlisle line was the last main railway in Britain to be constructed primarily with manual labour. By the end of 1874, the last stone of the structure had been laid; on 1 May 1876, the Settle–Carlisle line was opened for passenger services.'

To the outside world, it is very reminiscent of the Harry Potter films and the Hogwarts Express journey to school from King's Cross, and it does have that feel to it, but to the Brits it is just another fantastic piece of Victorian engineering that you can see all over the UK.

The walk up Whernside is long. At 736m, it is actually the tallest of the three peaks. Starting at a base of just above 300m, it has over 400m of elevation, but over a distance of about five miles. It is not a tough climb for most of the way, but it just seems to go on and on. The route takes you up alongside the viaduct through the valley before taking a left turn up and over. If you imagine a Brontosaurus, you start on the end of the tail which curls round before you start climbing its back. If you're in the Y3P race which is held every year, you actually race up the proverbial side of the dinosaur, a lot steeper and tougher. I unknowingly attempted the Y3P walk on race day once, and saw paramedics attending to athletes at the top of Whernside who had not been able to cope with that terrain.

As you approach the top, you can see all three peaks at once, one of the few places on the walk you can do this. And I have said this tongue in cheek, as this is the only time I have ever managed to do this. The Yorkshire Dales are gorgeous but they do have a reputation for changeable weather and on previous trips it has either been raining or cloudy at the top of here. We were lucky; the temperature was mid-teens Celsius and although it was overcast, visibility was great. This remained for most of the walk – almost perfect walking weather.

As we approached the top, Denise commented that as well as being struck by the scenery, she felt safe. I had not thought of it like this before, and tried to put myself in the position of the chief of a people who were under threat of being attacked by marauding armies. With steep hills either side, and visibility for miles, I too would have felt safe. That's why it is always great to go with other people on trips like this. It gives you different perspectives.

The downhill was tough, lots of steep steps and some loose rocks. My knees were being battered with the impact but they were holding up well. I am trying not to walk with a pole. Not sure why. Maybe I am worried I will lose my balance

The landscape between Whernside and Ingleborough. One of the shake holes to avoid.

by overstretching with the pole or out of sheer middle-age bloody-mindedness (surely I don't need one yet). I think it is the latter, so logically, I may need one in Nepal, and I should train with one. Maybe next week.

We met a few groups coming up the other way and I could tell that they thought we had the easiest direction. Looking back up the hill where we had come, I think they were probably right.

Just behind the trees ahead (which took nearly an hour to reach) was a good rest stop, with a cafe, toilets and shelter. I had taken advantage of it many times in the past so was an obvious lunch spot. It had taken us over three hours to walk the eight miles, a lot slower than I was hoping for, but not unexpected. The company more than made up for it. By the time we'd finished lunch, four hours had nearly passed and I was itching to get going again. Only eight hours left.

After only another 200m or so, Denise and Rich would be looping back towards their car, so we said our farewells, and promised to meet in a pub next time. I then put the afterburners on.

In the cafe there had been a couple of blokes that we had chatted to, and I had joked that I would catch them up when they left 15 minutes before me. They were now my target. I could see them in the distance, so I set off at a quick speed across the relatively flat fields towards the bottom of Ingleborough, normally the nemesis of many a walker as it had a very steep part to get to the ridge (imagine going up the side of the dinosaur this time). The terrain was very varied. Some of it was very soggy peat fields (I think) with some stone paths and bridges which were traversed, as well as some unusual rock formations and large 'shake holes' that needed to be avoided.

The moon-like surface at the top of Ingleborough.

After overtaking a couple of other groups, I could see my targets ahead of me, halfway up the steep hill approaching the ridge. I remember it being really tough, so I steeled myself for the latest lung buster. Employing the 100-step technique described last time, I got to the top in six reps. When you think you're at the top though there is another 400m or so (in distance) to the actual trig point, and then you come back on yourself to descend. On previous trips, I have seen many a charity walker miss that out as it is too much after 19 miles to even go that extra distance. It is a shame because it is one of my favourite parts of the whole Y3P challenge. It is relatively flat and the surface is very rocky, but not big rocks that you have to pick through, just a flat moonscape feel to it. When it is really cloudy, it is eerie, but not today. I could see the trig point in the distance as well as the rest of the local area, stunning.

As I started this part of the walk, I passed my two fellow walkers coming back the other way having reached the top, and said I'd try and catch them up. They said they'd be happy for me to join them which gave me an added incentive as I do like to chat to people en route. After the selfie at the top of the hill (to send to Denise), I started heading down the five-mile path to Horton. In the past this has been a real slog as you are wanting to just finish, but with only two hills done, I was still full of energy. I also had another 14 miles or so to complete so was ready to go at pace.

At the start it is not easy to pick your way through the rocks and peat and I could see my new 'friends' marching away a few hundred metres ahead. I felt that I was almost running in places as the path became more predictable and I think that this made a huge difference in my final time. With two miles to go to Horton, I

Horton-in-Ribblesdale station. A real picture postcard depiction of rural Britain.

TRAINING

Pen-y-ghent from below.

managed to catch them up. I had been constantly edging closer and I'd finally made it. They were very welcoming and a similar age, so we spent the rest of their trip (but not mine) chatting about Everest, the National Three Peaks (which they wanted to do) and the Knaresborough Bed Race (look it up).

One of the unexpected pleasures of walking is the chance to talk to complete strangers and have something in common. You are both doing what you are doing for different reasons, but there is this common purpose. The camaraderie among walkers is always great, and this is one of the things I am looking forward to most in Nepal. As I am travelling alone, I hope to be able to meet lots of new people on the way and hear their stories.

At the top of Pen-y-ghent. All downhill from here.

I walked with them to their destination, the brilliant Red Lion pub on the edge of Horton in Ribblesdale after crossing over the railway line at the station. It is one of the loveliest stations in the UK for me, so small, quaint, well-kept and quintessentially British.

They had completed their challenge in nine hours 15minutes, well within their target of ten hours. If they had gone so quickly and I had caught them up, I must have really made good time. According to Strava, it had only taken me two and a half hours to get up and down Ingleborough. I was chuffed. Would I be able to get to the viaduct in ten and a half hours? Four hours and about ten miles to go. Should be possible.

Pen-y-ghent ('Hill on the border' or 'Hill on the Heathen'; the meaning of Ghent is a little disputed) is the usual starting point of the Y3P and I have never found it too difficult before. However, I did recognise that it would be like climbing Ingleborough for most – the end of the walk and therefore the most foreboding. It was two miles to the top, and as the starting point was the lowest elevation, was probably the highest climb of them all. I needed positive thoughts going through my head.

I passed some contractors laying a path at the start of the walk up the first hill. It is becoming common across Britain for these paths to be laid on popular routes, and it is brilliant that they do it. It shows the way for the novice walker, but it does protect the terrain well too, keeping it available for generations of walkers to come. It is always done using huge pieces of local stone so that it is in keeping with the region. I donated some cash to the cause in the collection box to help ensure they can continue their work.

Up ahead, there was no one to pass. Starting this hill last was rare, so most people had already completed this part of their challenge. With no one to aim for, it was a battle of willpower. It was also steep, especially nearer the top. As the legs were starting to ache it was definitely slower going for me and I wondered how I would be at the end of a long day in Nepal, at over 3,000m higher than I currently was. I certainly needed to maintain my training.

It took me an hour to cover the two miles, including some scrambling up rocks towards the top. I was overtaken by a young teenage lad in jeans and T-shirt. Not a traditional walking outfit, but it was for him as he was racing his sister to the top. She was nowhere to be seen. He passed me but we had a chat at the top and he kindly took my photo for posterity. As most young uns these days, he knew his

WALK 6: THE YORKSHIRE THREE PEAKS CHALLENGE

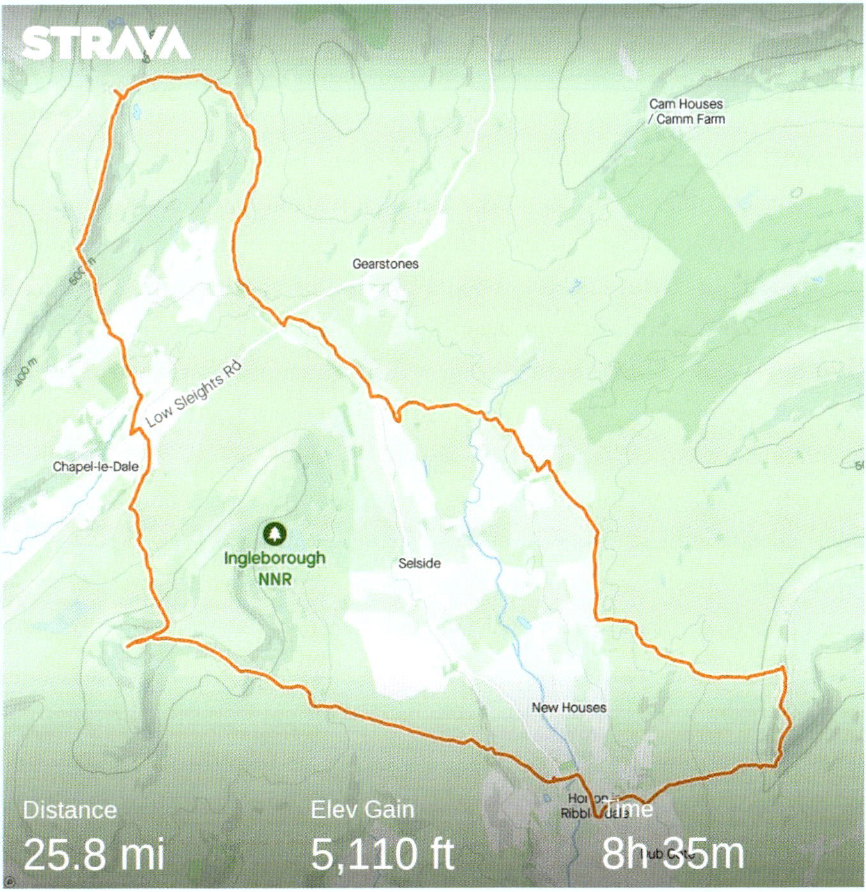

STRAVA

Distance: **25.8 mi**
Elev Gain: **5,110 ft**
Time: **8h 35m**

Elevation

Elevation Gain: 5,110 ft

Max Elevation: 2,424 ft

Pace

Avg Pace: 19:56 /mi

Moving Time: 8:35:19

Avg Elapsed Pace: 23:18 /mi

Elapsed Time: 10:02:27

Fastest Split: 16:27 /mi

way round a smartphone camera and took a few at different angles to make sure I got a decent one. I'll let you decide if he managed it.

I had a revelation at the top of Pen-y-ghent, and it is one that I should have discovered 30 years ago. Fitness is not just about being able to do stuff – run marathons, play hockey, bench press 50kg etc, it is about how quickly you get over it and can carry on. All you fitness people reading this are currently rolling your eyes at my innocence on this subject but better late than never. After only a few seconds' rest at the top, I was ready to go again. I have talked throughout this book so far about how I was able to get going again without too much trouble the day after a walk which is true, but I'd not really made the connection, assuming that it was just the training of the muscles. Maybe it is that too, but looking back at past attempts I recalled being really troubled during the Y3P and desperate to get home. Now, I was feeling good, and I was raring to walk the last eight miles to the car.

I saw some people coming up the other side and wished them well when we passed as I descended quite sharply on the path down towards the viaduct. It wasn't difficult, just long. About eight miles of fields passed quickly. I remember doing the walk in the past and this section was a slog as it was just getting to hill two (Whernside). Now it was getting to the end. It only took me about two and a half hours to walk back, so I had obviously recovered from the steep climb quickly and got back into my stride.

The last two miles were grim though. The weather finally broke from overcast to light rain to torrential rain. I had a raincoat in my bag, but with the car so close and a change of clothes in the boot, I just stuck it out. It was never cold, but the rain went into my boots, down my neck and in places you don't want to know about. If only we'd started half an hour earlier as planned.

I finished in ten hours two minutes, just before 7pm. A little frustrating that I'd not gone inside ten hours, but after the strolling nature of the walk with Denise and Rich and a long lunch it was actually a really good time. Strava says I walked for only eight hours 35 minutes, so I was really pleased with it.

A quick change under the open boot of the car providing shelter, and I was on the way home, arriving at just after 10pm. Strava said I had covered nearly 26 miles. All the literature says it is a 24-mile walk. Of course, I am going with Strava.

A long day, but a fantastic one. I am now a lot more confident about Nepal. I don't think I'll have trouble with the endurance, it is now the altitude, and there is not much I can do to replicate that.

WEEK 7

Monday 1 August – Sunday 7 August – Seven weeks to go

Weight at start of week: 108.3kg

Weight at the end of week: 107.4kg

Cumulative weight lost: 7.1kg

Steps completed in week: 121,360

Cumulative: 975,234

The target was to hit the one million steps mark this week, and I just missed it. My 'big' walk this week was an intensive, but short, 11-mile walk up lots of hills in the Peak District. Great for training, but not for the step count. I also did a nice round trip to Nottingham and back along the river and canal (13 miles) on Thursday as well as a couple of Bramcote/Town Street loops. Forty-five miles in total for the week. Another decent effort and I feel I'm back on form after last week. With six weeks to go, and three big training walks planned, I should be okay.

Another funny weight week, ruined by another boozy BBQ on Saturday. The weather in England at the minute is just too good to let it go to waste, and what better way than an evening in the sun with good friends and a few bottles of San Miguel! I was down nearly a kilogram on last week but still not caught up the gain from the previous week, so really a couple of weeks wasted and I am well down on my target. I need a really good week, with some intermittent fasting (16 hours a day) and a booze-free week (fingers crossed). Hoping to go under 105kg by Sunday. Depends on the weekend, the weather and my willpower.

A few trip things have happened this week.

Sponsorship – I have decided to get sponsored at last. I have been umming and ahhing about it for some time, and went for it on Thursday. As a family we are grateful to the Teenage Cancer Trust charity and so I set up a Just Giving appeal. As I write this (Monday 8 August), I'm up to nearly £300 towards my target of £500. I really hope that I can reach it as that would make a massive difference to the charity. I'll see if I can request that it goes to the TCT centre at the Queen's Medical Centre in Nottingham, but if not, anything to help is fine.

Altitude sickness pills – I finally had the call from the doctor, who surprise surprise, couldn't help me. It is so frustrating to use the NHS at the moment. I was advised to go to a specialist travel doctor, i.e., private. I went back to the place that I had had my vaccinations and they were happy to see me for a £95 appointment and a £25 prescription. Having read a lot of books on the trek, there is a lot of detail on how to avoid it, and Diamox (or the generic drug name – Acetazolamide) is recommended in all of them with seemingly few side effects. In one of the books I read, the author bought his online, so I did the same. After some research, I plumped for www.theindependentpharmacy.com and ordered 28 250mg tablets. The service seemed efficient. They asked lots of questions about general health, age, medications etc, and I have since received an email with a full list of faqs about altitude sickness. So far so good. They certainly look genuine. When they arrive, I will test them as not only are they are a diuretic (makes you want to wee), I need to be sure I don't get a reaction from them. Better at sea level in Nottingham than at 5,000m in the Himalayas. I also need to test them with my water purification and electrolyte tabs. I'll report back on how they have gone.

Water purification – on this subject, I bought a different brand, and tried them out on a short eight-miler on Sunday. Within four miles I was rushing into the same pub as last week to use their loos. This is a worrying trend. It probably didn't help that my stomach was gurgling already due to the previous night's beers, so I need to test them again. It may be in my head, 'the latchkey incontinence' that I mentioned last week, or it could be a genuine physical reaction. Either way, I need to get on top of it as I'll be drinking four or five litres of water each day, which is a lot of running behind the nearest rock with my emergency loo roll and cigarette lighter to burn the evidence.

Kit – every book that I read adds a little extra learning as to kit I should take. This week, another couple of tops were bought, and I am nearly at the end of that buying streak. I also picked up a good tip from the Lonely Planet I read (see book reviews) to take some car air fresheners to put in your boots at night, and some tumble dryer sheets to keep the clothes fresh in the main bag. They have now been ordered. I haven't really sorted my kit fully so hopefully it won't be too heavy.

* * * * *

Training Walk 7
02/08/2022: Parkhouse Hill and Chrome Hill Loop, Longnor, Peak District, Derbyshire

All my walks so far have been well-defined and easily researched, or certainly part of my knowledge base to date. This week, I was at a bit of a loss of where to go. At Dovedale I had been told by one of the National Trust volunteers about a place

Across the valley from near Longnor, Chrome Hill, the highest peak, on the left.

near Buxton (a small town in the Peak District, between Ashbourne and Manchester) where there were lots of hills including an iconic one called Chrome Hill. So iconic, I had never heard of it. I wrote it down and vowed to look it up. I am so glad I did. You will see later some of the photos, but it is spectacular, and it is not alone. In all, I ended up walking for four hours, ten miles and five steep inclines. Not my usual day trip, but as a trip within an hour of my home, it was lovely to see a part of the country I was not familiar with.

Researching walks around Chrome Hill, I was given a rough idea of where to go, but they were all five miles or so. I was lucky that I had an OS map of the region (OL24) which covered the White Peak area of the Peak District as opposed to the

Looking down the ridge from High Wheeldon.

Dark Peak on my other excursions into Britain's oldest National Park. From Wiki,

'The White Peak, also known as the Low Peak, is a limestone plateau that forms the central and southern part of the Peak District in England. It is mostly between 270m (900ft) and 430m (1,400ft) above sea-level and is enclosed by the higher altitude Dark Peak (also known as the High Peak) to the west, north and east.'

One route useful for research was at:

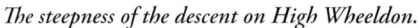

https://www.visitpeakdistrict.com/things-to-do/parkhouse-and-chrome-hill-p689991.

I could see that there were many hills near Chrome Hill, so I plotted a rough trip around them, and planned to wing it while I was there, thus making it longer than the five miles. As they were all near small towns and villages, I couldn't go too wrong – I certainly couldn't get lost. Starting in a lovely little village called Longnor, with free parking, pubs, cafes and shops, the plan was to start at the end of 'the Dragon's Back Ridge' as it is known. With a hazy day due to the threat of rain, the scene was atmospheric, and reminded me a little of my time in Yangshou in China back in the 1990s. Hills rising out of the mist with the promise of mystery.

After a steep uphill walk on the road back towards Crowdicote, the path veered left over a stile and the climb up High Wheeldon began. Unlike a lot of the walks I'd been on recently, this route was less travelled and the path was more a trail in the mud, rather than a deliberate stoned area. It turned out that I was unsure underfoot for a lot of the hills, especially downhills, and that reduced my pace significantly. I imagine the EBC trek is going to be more well-defined, but some practice on different terrain cannot harm, can it!

The steepness of the descent on High Wheeldon.

TRAINING

The steep path up Parkhouse Hill.

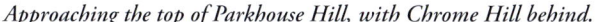

At the top of High Wheeldon (422m), you could see the route ahead. Parkhouse Hill was like a Cornish pasty, sticking out of the ground, with Chrome Hill behind it. One of the articles I read described it like walking across the back of a stegosaurus, and from this angle, I could see what they meant. Being wary of heights (see the Brecon Beacons walk) the peaks looked very narrow and although very photogenic, scary at the same time. It makes me sound like a real baby here I know, but I was on my own, it was drizzling rain by now, and very windy. Not a great set of conditions for this particular phobia.

The walk up High Wheeldon was fine, very little impact on me due to the training I had done, but the downhill was really steep and grassy, with a path that was defined but not well trodden. I much prefer steps. I gingerly placed my feet one after the other while keeping an eye out for parts of the path that could be extra treacherous. After a slip that took me five metres lower down before I could stop myself, and with flashbacks of my Dovedale experience (see walk five) I was getting really worried that the next slip would be longer and potentially more debilitating. Employing another good ski technique, I started to traverse across the slope, so the descent was longer but less steep. I almost imagined myself doing snowplough turns at the end of each run. It probably took me fifteen minutes to descend 100m, but I was down, including a

Approaching the top of Parkhouse Hill, with Chrome Hill behind.

Parkhouse Hill descent looking from Chrome Hill. I'm glad I avoided it.

small run and a hop at the end as I finally lost concentration and then balance.

I had hoped to walk all the way across 'the ridge', but as you can see from the picture, the next hill was a cliff face (Aldery Cliff), so I set off alongside the ridge looking for a path up it. After the hairy descent, it was actually a relief to spend the next part of the walk on the road, but it seemed to go on for ages. I ended up in Earl Sterndale, which a lot of the online walks started from. I am glad I'd researched the area as the pub they all mentioned had shut down, and the path up to Hister Hill (the next on the list) was through their back gate. Another relatively easy walk to the top (348m) and it was another

At the top of Chrome Hill, Parkhurst Hill in the immediate background.

TRAINING

Downhill from Chrome Hill, less scary than it looks. Hollins Hill on the left.

steep downhill. Well-practised at downhills now, I took the long route, with a more well-worn path – it must be part of the usual short walk that people go on, to make the path as defined as that.

Ahead was Parkhurst Hill (360m) which loomed up out of the ground. It was thin at the top and imposing. The path to the top was steep and although reasonably well-defined, the weather made it slippery. There were lots of paths going off the side of the hill which baffled me, but later I was to understand why.

The walk up was a lung-buster, but recovery didn't take long. What did take long though was my decision on what to do at the top. The views were superb, and Chrome Hill looked stunning from this angle, but the path down to Chrome Hill looked terrible. I had read that there was some rock scrambling needed on the walk and such was my brain fog I couldn't even remember if it was this direction or even of it was this hill. I bottled it and turned around and decided to take advantage of one of the paths I had seen before. I passed the only other walkers I saw all day and expressed my doubt about the direct route,

A look back up the valley from Hollins Hill. L-r, Chrome Hill, then Parkhouse Hill, Hitter Hill and the high point in the background, High Wheeldon.

WALK 7: PARKHOUSE HILL AND CHROME HILL LOOP, LONGNOR, PEAK DISTRICT, DERBYSHIRE

Distance 10.8 mi
Elev Gain 2,619 ft
Time 3h 51m

Elevation

Elevation Gain — 2,619 ft

Max Elevation — 1,485 ft

Pace

Avg Pace — 21:20 /mi

Moving Time — 3:51:29

Avg Elapsed Pace — 22:54 /mi

Elapsed Time — 4:08:26

Fastest Split — 12:31 /mi

but they were two lads in their 20s who were bound to be less risk-averse than me. Twenty minutes later, I noticed that they had made the same decision.

After bottling the descent of Parkhouse Hill, Chrome Hill (425m) looked a lot more intimidating. Not the walk up, but the narrow ridge and steep drop at the top. I half expected to come back on myself again. I wasn't going to die in Derbyshire. Not today. How melodramatic. I had completely over-reacted. The walk up was steep again, but this was my goal of the day and it didn't take too long to reach the summit. In the middle of the ridge, I was so pleased I had come somewhere new. The British countryside really is fantastic. One of my favourite travel writers is the American, but self-confessed Anglophile, Bill Bryson. His love of our landscapes is beautifully written, far better than I could hope for, so try him out (*Notes from a Small Island* or *Little Dribbling*) or even better, get your backpacks on, and experience it for yourself.

So what to do? Repeat my Parkhurst Hill retreat or push on. It did look intimidating, with outcrops rising into the sky and no clear route, but a relatively easy looking path caught my eye lower down. It didn't look too bad, as long as I could get there. Pressing on, it was the right decision; I joined the path quite quickly, and had a lovely descent.

The countryside was up and down towards the end of the valley, but nothing to worry about. It was time to start the return. I could have come down the road, but Hollins Hill was a much better option. It was lovely to be able to make the steep climb, and then the gentle descent back towards Longnor. The views of the Devil's Back were superb, so much better than they'd be on the road. As the path descended more steeply, it was obviously less well-travelled as fern and brambles blocked the path, but channeling my inner Indiana Jones, I pushed my way through until I hit the road.

I'd only been walking for about three and a half hours, with 30 minutes to the car along the roads, and I suppose I could have gone back on the reverse route for more training, but after five hills, with steep up and downs, I actually felt I had done enough for the day. The weather was now warming up and the steep road back was easy. I remember the walk back to the car after Brecon Beacons and how tough it was. Now it wasn't. More evidence to give me confidence for Nepal.

WEEK 8

Monday 8 August – Sunday 14 August – Six weeks to go

Weight at start of week: 107.4kg
Weight at the end of week: 107.5kg
Cumulative weight lost: 7kg
Steps completed in week: 115,855
Cumulative: 1,091,089

So this week I smashed through the one million steps mark, in just over 50 days, giving me an average of approximately 20,000 steps a day of training. I wanted to make sure I gave this trip my best and I hopefully won't look back and blame lack of training. Not as many weekly steps as I'd like, but with only three longer training walks all week (although one did include climbing Mount Snowdon) I had dropped down to 33 miles. I'm looking to push it up next week as I have two 950m mountains planned in the Lakes and Scotland as well as day to day training which I am going to ramp up.

Weight wise, I was down to 105.4kg at one point, then two BBQs on Saturday and Sunday (one boozy) put me back where I started. I'm not worried. It will drop off this week after a couple of good days. One more major blowout next week as we're on holiday in Scotland with friends, then it will be on the home stretch to Nepal, and booze-free healthy eating Monday to Sunday, and not just until Friday night.

Packing – call me obsessive if you want (I like to think I am organised and well-prepared) but on Monday, I had nearly packed – six weeks early. Using all the books so far (see review section) I have a pretty good idea of what I need and I have been gradually buying anything I have not already got in the cupboards. I haven't weighed it all yet, but I am sure that it will be under 20kg in total, some of which I will leave in Kathmandu when I am trekking. As I am staying in Kathmandu for a few days before the trek, I do need extra clothes (including my golf glove for a round at altitude – cannot wait), but I am confident I won't have to jettison anything. I will do a last check before I go.

Altitude pills – I tried half a pill before my walk on Tuesday (ten miles) and in the two and a half hours around Trent Lock and the Erewash Canal (part of training walk one), I needed a wee twice. Looks like the diuretic part works. I didn't have any other after-effects though. The pill was used in isolation, so I didn't try it with my electrolytes and water purification tabs. I will try that next week and see if the combination causes me any issues.

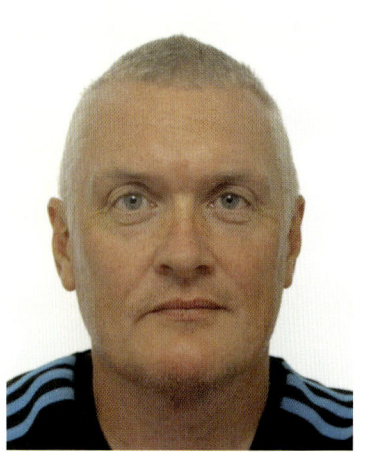
Passport photo.

Purification tabs – after the rush to the Sherwin Arms last Sunday, I wondered whether my new water purification tablets were the cause, or whether it was the beer from the night before's BBQ. Thankfully, it looks like it was the beer and not the tablets, as I tried them again this week and there were no effects. A relief, but I need to experiment more to be absolutely sure.

Passport photo – I have not needed a formal one for a while, but as I will need some for the trekking permits in Nepal, I headed for the nearest large Tesco and their photo machine. It cost £8 – when did that happen! The machines are pretty good and can tell you whether the photo is suitable for passports, and you can have up to ten goes to get it right. I took six. There were options for visas, but Nepal wasn't one of them, so I have to assume that any one will do. The classic British passport photo is very dull as you aren't allowed to smile. Mind you, when I am walking up a 200m incline at 5000m, I'm sure it will more accurately reflect my face than a beaming smile ever would.

The big walk of the week was to Snowdon with my youngest son Dan, his uni mate Andrew, and Andrew's dad. We are still in the summer heatwave so the sky was cloudless and it was fabulous. Snowdonia is such a fabulous place, if you have never been, add it to your bucket list.

Training Walk 8
10/08/2022: Mount Snowdon, from Pen y Pass, Wales

This was a walk I knew that I would enjoy, and I wasn't disappointed. Most people have heard of Mount Snowdon (1,085m), the highest peak in Wales, and part of the National Three Peak challenge. In fact so many people have heard of it, that there were huge queues on the paths last year as the country emerged from its Covid induced slumber and started to explore the British countryside again. A taxi driver I spoke to reminisced about three-hour queues at the peak to touch the trig point and get the Insta photo. I hoped it wasn't as busy today, but as it was midweek, I wasn't expecting too many problems.

As part of my National Three Peaks (N3P) exploits (see earlier sections) I had been up Snowdon three and a half times, and once each with family and uni

Miner's Path and Pyg Track Map. © APCE_SNPA 880

friends, so as a six-attempt veteran, I considered myself a relative expert. I knew what to expect in terms of scenery, but that didn't take anything away from the natural beauty and wow factor that I get every time I go. It is a cliché, but I do fall more in love with it each time and always discover something new.

'Snowdon (Yr Wyddfa in Welsh) is the highest mountain in Wales and England. It's one of our most famous and recognisable landmarks and is well worth a visit. Standing tall over the village of Llanberis, Snowdon is part of a close-knit family of jagged peaks and can offer views of Snowdonia, Anglesey, Pembrokeshire and Ireland. Choose from six different paths to conquer this 1,085 metre (3,560 feet) giant which are the Llanberis Path, Pyg Track, Miners' Track, Watkin Path, Rhyd-Ddu Path or the Snowdon Ranger Path,' according to https://www.visitsnowdonia.info/snowdon-walking-routes.

The usual paths for the N3P challenge are the Pyg Track and the Miners' Track, and I planned to follow this tried and trusted approach. My favourite path of the

At the start of the trip, left to right, Andrew, Lee and Dan.

two is the Pyg Track, quite tough at the beginning but then a lovely walk across the middle of the mountain where it joins the Miners' Track before heading to the summit. For extra training though, I considered doing both and summitting twice. Ambition was greater than reality in the end as you will see.

Last week, I flippantly asked my youngest son Dan if he wanted to come. We'd taken him up there a few years earlier when he was not really in a physical state to do it. It is a major regret of mine, completely overestimating his recovery at the time, and I thought it had put him off for life. But surprisingly and pleasingly, he said he wanted to come. His summer job, running Segway events, is not nine-to-five, so we saw when his day off was and chose Wednesday. As an added bonus, his university housemate Andrew and Andrew's dad Lee also wanted to come. I'd never met Lee, but if Andrew was anything to go by, I knew we'd get on. We did.

With a four-hour drive each way, and potentially walking up twice, we needed to start early. Andrew and Lee live on the other side of Nottingham so were to meet at ours at 6am. I set my alarm for quarter past five, with the message to Dan to let them know not to be late as it is something I cannot stand. At 5.50am, they fulfilled their side of the bargain and knocked on the door. Unfortunately, I had not been woken by the alarm, and neither had Dan. Not a great start for us,

On the Pyg Track, looking out towards Y Liwedd, Snowdon off to the right and my mea culpa.

but we were mostly packed up from the night before, so we were out the door by quarter past six. I know I will get an early morning knock on the door from the guide in Nepal, but I much prefer to be ready in plenty of time, and not just in time.

We arrived at Pen y Pass car park around 10am, only to discover that it was pre-booking only. That was new. I knew it might be busy, but pre-booking! Last year's crowds must have made them become much more regimented. Understandable, but I am a traditionalist at heart, and I don't like changes of rules that make things harder. The marshal directed us to a park and ride scheme three miles down the hill towards Llanberis. Before we even arrived at the park and ride, an enterprising farmer had opened his field for a fee of £5 a car, and minibus taxis were on standby for £10 per trip, or £2 a person if there were five or more. In the car park were a young couple from England and a solo traveller from Europe, so we all jumped

Andrew and Lee taking a break on the Pyg Track with Snowdon in the background.

TRAINING

in and travelled back up to the starting point. We saved just a couple of quid, but the others made big savings.

It was going to be hot; the forecast was 28 degrees, with barely a cloud in the sky, so we had come prepared with three litres of water each. In the rush to get out though, Dan forgot his festival bucket hat, so we hoped the shop sold them – sunstroke was a real threat today. They didn't, but they did find a cap in lost property which they lent us, as long as we returned it. Great service.

We set off on the Pyg Track, and like a lot of mountains I have been up, the start is where you gain a lot of initial elevation and it was hard work for a bit. I wondered how Dan would be this time, but he was fine. After a 20-minute upward hike, the path forked. To the right was the notorious route via Crib Goch – a narrow ridge which has proved fatal to some walkers in the past. With my memories of Chrome Hill from last week fresh in my mind, it wasn't a difficult decision to keep to the left path down the Pyg.

I don't know if it because I am getting older (52 and all that), but I was pointing at two peaks on the ridge ahead of us, and saying that the one on the left was Snowdon. The large peak further to the right of them was just an optical illusion because it was closer. Dan wasn't convinced at all; he even said he could see people on the top, but as I'd been up there six times, and Dan only once, it was obvious that I was right. In the words of Yoda, a bit too big-headed I was, and after another five minutes of walking I was eating humble pie as Dan was obviously right as I started to recognise the paths to the top of Dan's choice and saw other hikers on them. I think I'd got my lakes mixed up. At the bottom of Snowdon are some of the clearest mountain lakes I have seen, and as there are four of them on this section of the walk, I had misremembered where the Miners' Track climbed up to meet the Pyg Track. After all, Llyn Lydaw and Glaslyn were similar weren't they? I suppose that is the reason, but a terrible excuse. I teach my students about decision making, avoiding bias and collecting evidence. I had relied on my anchoring and authority biases and ignored the biggest evidence in front of me – a really big hill with people at the top. I'm sure Dan will keep reminding me about it for some time (only 20 years if I'm lucky).

Snowdonia is magnificent. Views from both sides stretch as far as you can see. I think it had even been voted Britain's best view at one point. Andrew and Lee were Snowdon virgins and were loving it. Wait until they try and climb it in 40mph winds with torrential rain as happened on my second attempt – but not today

At the top with Dan, although not at the very, very top!

so I cannot blame them for their initial opinions. Great weather has been a good feature of a lot of my walks during my training, and it really makes a difference. Bloody hot, but the benefits hugely outweigh the costs, as long as you are prepared with the right kit.

The Miners' Track and the Pyg Track meet about 40 minutes' walk from the top, and the first half is a slog, as tough as the original section. We only needed a couple of quick breaks and we were on the ridge, where the view on the other side of the mountain came into view. Lee joked that there would be a housing estate, but I knew he would be blown away and he was. Looking out to the left you can make out Anglesey across the Menai Strait, and to the right the path toward Llanberis and the railway line.

Snowdon is the only mountain I know (certainly in the UK) where there is a railway line to the top. Loads of day-trippers save themselves the exertion of the walk and come for the views. There is even a cafe at the top, and it has been frequented a few times by me in the past – sometimes to warm up and on others to get a refreshing drink and loo break. Not today. The railway line was being repaired near the top and the train didn't come all the way. I suspect that there were still many at the summit who hadn't walked all the way though. As a result, the cafe was shut until 2023, including the toilets. I am glad I had not been

Looking down to the west towards Anglesey from the top of Snowdon.

relying on it (see 'latchkey incontinence' in my diary) and I could see that some of the walkers were really disappointed. Later, we saw a family walking uphill with a reluctant child shuffling along, with the promise of the cafe at the top. Dare we tell them?

As we approached the very top, we could see that a queue had formed to get up the stone mound that marked the summit. We suspected that a lot in it were train passengers. It didn't seem to be going down very quickly and it was obvious why. People were going up in their singles, pairs or little groups and spending ages getting the perfect photos and enjoying the views. I do find the Insta culture so self-absorbed, stupid and irritating. On every other occasion I have been up Snowdon, there has been a constantly moving queue as people go to the summit, take a quick pic (shock horror – maybe even with other people in the background) and then move on and enjoy the view and take the scenery and group photos from

The Llanberis path (down to the left), with the railway line and Clogwyn Station.

ten metres lower. We saw a couple of kids go up the unsignposted 'exit' so we followed, touched the top and descended, with one of the Insta stars giving us a 'polite' mouthful about how we should have queued. It was all a bit pathetic really. Pathetic that we didn't join the queue as good British people should, pathetic that the queue had even formed in the first place and pathetic that there wasn't more chuntering in the queue about the delay. No wonder there was a three-hour queue at its busiest last year if every party wanted their three minutes at the top.

We'd prepared a packed lunch and went and sat on the platform of the station to take in the views on the other side of Snowdon. I think that this was the first time I had really done this. On four occasions I had been rushed as part of N3P, with the family we had been concentrating on getting something for the kids, and with my uni mates it had been very cloudy, with little long visibility. With plenty of time and great visibility, I could trace the other paths down the mountain, to Llanberis, the Snowdon Ranger Path and the Rhyd Ddu Path. Next time I come, I am going to be a lot more ambitious and climb it from the 'other side'. Maybe even before Everest, we'll see.

Lee fancied going back to Pen y Pass over the Crib Goch ridge – or he said he did to wind me up. I had never really seen it this clearly before, so regardless of the motive there was no chance I was attempting that. It was so narrow. In Nepal, I hope I don't have to encounter anything with sheer edges; I will be a quivering wreck.

The rest of the group didn't want to go down and up again to complete the training I had originally planned, and to be honest, I am not sure I did as it was so hot, but we did walk about 400m down the Llanberis Path, before turning back

Glaslyn Lake at the bottom of the steep section of the Miners' Track. A great place to cool off, especially in 28 degrees celsius. Snowdon is majestic in the background.

WALK 8: MOUNT SNOWDON, FROM PEN Y PASS. WALES

Distance	Elev Gain	Time
9.6 mi	2,713 ft	4h 6m

Elevation

Elevation Gain	2,713 ft
Max Elevation	3,507 ft

Pace

Avg Pace	25:37 /mi
Moving Time	4:06:51
Avg Elapsed Pace	37:30 /mi
Elapsed Time	6:01:21
Fastest Split	18:24 /mi

and started descending with the promise of the waters of Glaslyn at the forefront of our thoughts.

The walk down was a lot easier. My knees never seem to be bothered by the downhill parts of the walk, and I have never used a walking pole to aid me. I think I will now follow this tactic in Nepal. I'm not sure I want to use poles for the first time, hate them, and then end up carrying them for 11 days. The path down was narrower in places than I remember, and we did have to wait for people to pass, or to let us pass. At high season (especially weekends) this could have caused some mutterings, but not today. The steep descent down from the Pyg Track/Miners' Track junction to the lake made me glad that we'd chosen the Pyg Track to ascend. I had done the Miners' Track up Snowdon twice before and I remember how hard this section was. The beetroot faces of those coming up past us, showed me that they thought the same.

As we approached Glaslyn, we saw that there were already people in the lake. For reasons mentioned before, time or conditions on previous trips were always an issue, and I had never had the time or inclination to have a dip before. I wasn't going to miss out this time. All the rest of the group felt the same, so we stripped off most of the way and dived in. It was very cold, we were at 600m above sea level after all, but so refreshing. Dan and I stayed in the longest, probably about ten minutes. As the water was so fresh, I dived under and opened my eyes to see the sunbeams driving through the water towards the depths. With a little bit of turbulence caused by some frantic arm waving, the bubbles also caught the luminescence of the sun. It was magical.

Lying on the banks to get dry, Dan suffered some bad cramps in his legs and feet. Some of the drugs in his treatment had caused severe cramps, and even five years later, I suspect he was still susceptible to the after effects. It took some time, and some salted cashews from Lee for it to subside enough for us to continue.

The last three miles were largely flat or downhill, so there was not going to be a fitness issue ahead of us, just time on feet. Dan seemed fine now, so it was really a case of enjoying the views, looking longingly at the water again and following the path back to Pen y Pass. I would consider coming for a full day trip here (on a sunny day of course) and picnicking and swimming in the lakes, as one large family were doing. I wished Jane, Matt and Jim were here too.

While Dan took his hat back with Lee and Andrew, I jumped in a taxi with a family of four from Barcelona to get my car and then went back and picked up my fellow walkers. As I drove back up the road, I could see the hills rising up above me, saw the Pyg Track snake up to the ridge and recalled what a great day it had been.

On the way home, we stopped in Betws-y-coed for fish and chips. I had only driven through here before, but it has a really good vibe and it is another place on the list to visit when more time is available, especially the babbling stream where many tourists and locals were cooling off.

At ten miles only, the walk was not as long as some of my training days, but with 28,000 steps, 2,713ft of elevation and more endurance (eight hours of driving and six hours of walking in 28-degree heat), it was another large tick on my training chart and a massive step in the right direction.

WEEK 9 & 10

Monday 15 August – Sunday 28 August – Five and four weeks to go

Weight at start of week: 107.5kg

Weight at the end of week: 107kg

Cumulative weight lost: 7.5kg

Steps completed in weeks: 220,214 (120,402 and 99,812)

Cumulative: 1,311,303

Fundraising total to date: £422.19

A double diary entry this week, as I was on a five-day stay in Scotland from Friday the 19th to Wednesday the 24th so thought it would be best to track what has happened across the whole time. In short, the training has really dropped off, and taken a turn. I have still done two big training walks, both in week nine. After the joys of Snowdonia last week, I was in two more stunning locations – the English Lake District and the Scottish Highlands. The first was up Scafell Pike (977m) with Dan and his mates again, followed by Ben Lomond (975m) with Jane and our friends Pete and Ali. Both of these walks showed me once again that I am now very capable of distance, time and the uphill bits, but to be honest, I am flagging a bit from the training. Not the physical side, but the mental side and the daily walks around Nottingham have really dropped off.

As the departure date gets closer, (only 23 days as I write this on Monday 29 August) I am itching to go. It is like waiting for Christmas as a kid. The first of December is very exciting, as you're in the final month of the year and you open door one on the advent calendar, then as you get closer to Xmas Eve, you get more

The Devil's Pulpit, near Drymen.

and more impatient and you can never see it coming. I am on 20 December I reckon, and as the days to Nepal get closer, I just want to get that final viewing of *The Great Escape* and *The Sound of Music* under my belt and put out the whiskey glass and carrot and wait for the sweet sound of the clock chiming 6am on Xmas Day so I can open my pressies.

The other side of the wait for the 20th is that I now have to do some marking and begin prepping for my lectures which start when I get back from Nepal. With three weeks to go, I have to think that I just cannot go out walking for three hours easily now. I do need to do some work, and keep writing this book. I have started to go back to the gym, but rather than spend 90 minutes on the stepper or the treadmill walking uphill, I am running again. Only five kilometres at a time but the speeds are gradually getting quicker. I used to do quite a bit of running, but I cannot remember the last time I ran for 30 minutes without stopping. Maybe 12 months. Perhaps this is the wrong strategy, I will only know when I am away, but I think I have the walking miles in my legs. Now if I spend three weeks getting the heart rate pumping it may help me when the oxygen is thinner. No doubt the trip log will tell you if this decision was stupid.

My weight is also frustrating, but once again self-inflicted. In the last fortnight I have fluctuated from a low of 105.2kg (after my walk up Scafell) to a high of 108.9kg. The trip to Scotland and eating out and boozing every day certainly didn't help with that, but I felt like a last 'blast' before three weeks of sobriety. It wasn't like I wasn't exercising. With a trip to Loch Lomond and Glasgow, you cannot help but be out and about, and we made the most of it. Exploring Loch Lomond by car, boat, swimming and on foot, was a thrill.

Highlights:

A gem of a place called the Devil's Pulpit near Drymen, a small gorge with blood red water (from the sandstone rock) was a real unplanned bonus. The Drover's Inn at the top of Loch Lomond, supposedly the most-haunted pub in Britain. Wild swimming in the freezing cold loch at the picturesque village of Luss. The walk up Ben Lomond itself. And finally, the reason we were in Scotland in the first place – to see Coldplay at Hampden Park in Glasgow. Chris and the gang delivered and my feet hurt from dancing as much as my throat from singing.

Now I am back in Nottingham, it is a three-week fitness final streak. No rubbish food, no booze, and a real reduction in the amount of Diet Coke I drink. I need to be weaned off it before Nepal. It could be the trickiest thing of all. I tried giving up caffeine a few years ago when I worked in an office which involved a lot of tea and coffee as well as the Coke. After three days, my body almost shut down with the withdrawal symptoms. I only drink decaf coffee now and peppermint tea, so my caffeine intake is well down from then anyway but the Coke has continued apace. I also know I won't get it on the mountains easily, so I need to break the psychological hold it has on me.

I was proud of my willpower on Saturday, as it was my son Jim's 24th birthday BBQ with 25 of his mates from Nottingham and Hallam Uni all descending on our house. A really great bunch, but as the beer and rum flowed I managed to restrain myself, and tempting as it was, I didn't join in with the boozing – just the BBQ and (some of) the banter.

* * * * *

Not much bought for the trip recently, a couple more wicking T-shirts from Mountain Warehouse in Glasgow only. By the end of this week, I will be unpacking and repacking to make sure everything is there that I need. Then it is the dreaded weigh-in to see what I need to ditch.

I haven't even read a Nepal book for a fortnight – more lethargy I suspect. I have two more to go, I will start one tonight.

To end, the sad news is that my tour operator still hasn't found anyone else to go on my trip. I am really disappointed. I know I will be okay, and I will meet people in the hostels and on the trails, but they won't be in 'my gang' and I think it could be lonelier than I would have liked. Someone said recently that I would make lifelong friends on the trip, and normally I would agree, but I am not convinced now. I hate the impacts that the political over-reaction to Covid has had on the world. I am convinced that without the restrictions there would be a full complement of walkers. Either through being scared of travelling, a general nervousness about being out and about after lockdown or being wary of the costs (all we get on the news at the moment is 'cost of living crisis') – it has made the world a less-travelled place, and that can only be a bad thing for society.

Sorry to finish on a downer. I am normally a really positive person, so I promise to be back on form next week when the proverbial Christmas *Radio Times* hits the doormat and I can see that the Christmas Day *Top of the Pops* is back on the TV listings, just before The Queen's speech.

Training Walk 9
17/08/2022: Scafell Pike, Lake District, north-west of England

I have looked forward to most of my training walks so far, but this one I was more concerned about. Scafell Pike is the highest mountain in England at 977m, and is another element of the National Three Peaks challenge. I have attempted Scafell Pike seven times before and only completed it on four of those occasions – once spending nine hours on there (we went down the wrong side after losing our bearings in the terrible fog). After the fourth climb, and finally a successful attempt at the N3P, I vowed 'never again', yet here I was going for my eighth climb.

The difference this time is that there was no time limit as I wasn't dashing off to Snowdon or Ben Nevis, and it would be during the day. As it is the middle mountain on the N3P it is usually completed at dusk or even during the night, so being able to see the full majesty of the Lakes during the daylight was going to be a real bonus. I was also with Dan again. Snowdon hadn't put him off. Last week Andrew and Lee had gatecrashed my trip up Snowdon. This week I returned the 'favour' and joined them on their three day trip to Wastwater, the four-mile lake at the bottom of Scafell Pike. It wasn't just Andrew and Lee this time either; there were also Andrew's brother Matt and his girlfriend Lois, as well as Lee's brother Nick. It was a real family affair.

The Lake District is arguably Britain's finest national park. The strapline is 'Discover. Explore. Inspire.' And it hits all three of these. https://www.lakedistrict.gov.uk/. It was established in 1951 and covers an area of 2,362 square kilometres

At the start of the walk. Scafell Pike (977m) directly ahead, Scafell to the right.

(912 square miles). With hills, water and few major roads, it welcomes millions of visitors a year. One of the UK's natural wonders.

The rest of the group had planned to walk up Scafell Pike on the 17th (Wednesday) and I watched the weather closely in the week leading up to it. The heatwave was coming to an end, and despite hosepipe bans springing up all over England, heavy rain was the order of the day. Apart from the Wednesday. We agreed a meet time of 9.30am at their hostel for a walk up and down Scafell Pike.

A 9.30am meet meant a 5.30am start for me, followed by a four-hour drive. Each way. It was going to be another test of stamina, not just in walking stamina, but in concentration and physical activity. I was slightly late due to a car standoff on the narrow roads, when two cars couldn't decide who was going to move over first. One of the hazards of driving on country roads in the UK.

Wastwater is the deepest lake in England at 79m, and has always been a welcome sight as I've approached Scafell Pike in the past. It also has a chequered history as it was the site of an infamous murder.

'In 1976, The Wasdale Lady in the Lake – Margaret Hogg, was murdered by her husband and her body was disposed of in the lake. She was found after eight years, with her body preserved like wax due to the lack of oxygen in the water,' says Wikipedia.

It is long but it isn't wide, you could swim across it if you were a decent swimmer, but it is impressive.

At the edge of Wastwater, there are two car parks for the ascent of Scafell Pike, one in the village of Wasdale Head, and one a mile closer to the Lake – that is the one I have always used, so like all good traditionalists, I went back there without

Halfway up, looking back towards Wastwater – the deepest lake in England at 79m. Sellafield can just be seen at the back right of the picture.

even considering the other. It had had a facelift and it was a big improvement. There was a small shop, credit card facilities for parking and proper toilets, rather than the pongy portaloos that used to be there. Apparently it had been upgraded over three years prior – is it really that long since I last visited? Oh yes, I forgot, Covid restrictions knocked 18 months off everyone's life and our point of reference has been altered. The car park was packed; it was going to be a busy day. After paying £9 per car for the day, we unloaded the cars, picked up our packs and set off.

The weather was perfect, late teens centigrade and overcast, but great visibility. Maybe it wouldn't be so bad after all.

I remember the last time I climbed it, and the final time I said 'never again' after three other times saying 'never again'. It just dragged on and on, and just when you think you're at the end, there is another uphill section. I vaguely remembered there being a plateau for some respite, but I knew that the first hour was a slog – uphill and relentless. You could see Scafell Pike looming in the background, with its sister mountain Scafell to its right. It is a rock giant with little vegetation at the top, so it was a case of getting to it.

Approaching the top of Scafell Pike, very rocky underfoot.

Although it was tough, the views were magnificent. I know I have extolled the virtues of the British countryside throughout these training walks, but I am not employed by Visit Britain, I just love it. It has been a real summer of outdoors activity for me, and just for that alone, the trip to EBC has been worth it, and I haven't even stepped foot on a plane to Asia. If Nepal is even half as good it will be magnificent.

The walking party at the top of Scafell Pike. I'm next to Lee, then Matt, Lois and Nick standing. Dan and Andrew squatting down.

After following the mountain stream up the first section of the walk, we turned and looked back across Wastwater. I had planned to come back to the car a different way if possible, even if the others wanted to come straight back the same way, so I drunk in the view. In the rear, slightly spoiling it was Sellafield, the nuclear power station on the edge of Cumbria. I had never had good enough weather or light to see it before.

As expected, there were many people on the walk, and we played tag with several of them as we kept taking breaks at different times and overtaking each other. I got to know Nick, Matt and Lois a little better and the mood was good. Everybody seemed keen to get to the top and find an alternative route home, but there was no rush and we had plenty of rest and view breaks.

I spent a few minutes with Dan reminiscing about the only time I had attempted Scafell Pike without it being part of the N3P. In August 2014 (Dan was 12), the kids wanted to go and see Derby in the cup away at Carlisle (the most northerly football club in England). I agreed to take them, as long as they climbed Scafell Pike on the way. What a terrible parent. ● We got most of the way when the weather closed in, and at the time I was not completely familiar with the

Looking back towards Lingmell (left - 807m) and Great Gable (centre - 899m), with the choice of path in front. Part of the path down to Skyhead Tarn (lake) can just be seen on the right in the distance.

mountain, so with three kids under my charge and a kick-off to get to, we turned back. This time, there was nothing stopping us getting up.

There was the plateau as I remembered, but it was only a couple of hundred metres (if that) so the natural rest I was after didn't happen. The path underfoot became rocky and quite tricky, but there was no way to get lost in this weather as you could see the peak with lots of people snaking their way to the top.

There were never *too* many people though, with plenty of room at the top. It was an opportunity to take 'the photo' and many people were also sat around eating their lunch or just taking in the views. Compare this to the 'queue' at Snowdon and it was a real change in attitude. Maybe the walk to the top (rather than taking the train) gave a sense of camaraderie for the walkers who didn't mind taking each other's photos and manoeuvring around to clear the shot for the exclusive 'family' photo.

We followed suit and settled down for lunch. I had not really seen the other side of the mountain before. The only time I had, I was not in a good mood (our eight-hour trip involved getting lost on the other side as we had descended the wrong

The view down through Middleboot Knotts towards Great Gable.

way on the fog). I tried to trace the route of the Lake District 10 Peak Challenge from my OSL6 Ordnance Survey map, and I picked out a few. I was glad I had not attempted it on my own as I had originally planned (see training walk four). Even though it was good weather, we were sweaty, so it didn't take long for the cold to set in and coats and jumpers were donned. They weren't on for long.

The valley back to Wasdale Head with Lingmell Beck feeding Wastwater. The path back can be seen halfway up Great Gable. Kirk Fell (802m) and then Red Pike (826m) next to Great Gable.

After about 15 minutes, we had decided to head back down the same way, but instead of turning left back to the car, we were going to turn right towards a lake we could see in the distance, Skyhead Tarn. There was a distinctive path, and Lee vaguely remembered coming up that way on a previous trip ten years earlier. The whole group agreed, so we were able to stick together for the whole trip.

Ahead of us was Lingmell, one of the '10 Peaks', and there were a few hardy walkers ascending it. I was keen, but the others not so. I have done many hills now, so I wasn't going to argue too much – especially as it was only up and down, there was no alternative route back. The rest of the view was filled with hills, water, paths and sky. Andrew said that he actually preferred this view to Snowdon. Dan said it looked like a film backdrop it was so perfect. It was hard to disagree with either of them.

I was on virgin territory. I had only ever gone up and down on the same route, and on reflection, this was my favourite part of the whole walk. It descended a lot more leisurely and I can imagine that coming up that way would be a lovely route. I will mention it to Jane when we fancy a trip to the Lakes as I have definitely put her off the steep route.

There was one tricky part when you had to do a little rock climbing. No equipment needed, but you just needed to be careful of your footing. Dan was

WALK 9: SCAFELL PIKE, LAKE DISTRICT, NORTH-WEST OF ENGLAND

Distance: 9.2 mi
Elev Gain: 3,394 ft
Time: 4h 11m

Elevation

Elevation Gain — 3,394 ft
Max Elevation — 3,199 ft

Pace

Avg Pace — 27:16 /mi
Moving Time — 4:11:50
Avg Elapsed Pace — 37:27 /mi
Elapsed Time — 5:45:56
Fastest Split — 15:48 /mi

TRAINING

Dan and I at the end of the walk outside the Wasdale Head Inn.

concerned about me which was touching – role reversal after 20 years. A fork in the path had us reaching for the map again. Left looked really picturesque, and would get us home quicker, alongside Middleboot Knotts, but it was really steep once you were past the gorge. Not being in a hurry, we opted for the right path, and although not as dramatic visually, it was certainly the correct choice.

Looking across the valley, I didn't fancy the walk across the middle of Great Gable. The path seemed very narrow and with the scree cascading down the side, I visualised slipping to the bottom. Irrational, but that is what fear does for you. We eyed up the path down the river (Lingmell Beck) and headed left across country to try and reach it.

We ended up on the high path! Not sure how, I think the boggy ground meant we just looked for a way to get to a path, any path. I do admit I was nervous, then I saw a ten-year-old girl coming the other way with her dad and that gave me the kick up the backside I needed. Like any fear, the prospect was far worse than the reality and it was a gentle walk back to Wasdale Head and the promise of the pub. Dan and I walked ahead for the final part of the journey and we had a good chat about politics, the environment and woke culture. It was pleasing to hear that not all 'youngsters' think the same as the media say they do.

The end point was the Wasdale Head Inn, a mile from the car park. With a four-hour drive back to Nottingham, it was only a Diet Coke for me, but most of the others wet their whistle with a pint. With six of them, they wouldn't have all fit in one car back to the hostel, so leaving five of them there for a second round, I took Dan back to the hostel.

After last week's dip at Snowdon, we took the chance for a little more open-water swimming and jumped into Wastwater. It was, as expected, very cold, but calm and clear. My muscles immediately responded to the temperature – a natural ice bath. I am not too scared of the cold showers in Nepal now. Famous last words I know.

It was another good training walk, with great company, some good memories with Dan, and no rush. With five weeks to go, I am thinking of scaling back the mountain walking. I am in Scotland for a few days when I will certainly do at least one more, then I will see whether to rein it back. I don't want to get injured and I want to preserve energy for EBC. Let's see if my body allows me to do this, or will it be raring to go before then?

Training Walk Ten
21/08/2022: Ben Lomond, Lake Lomond, Lowlands, Scotland
I had every intention of doing an 11-day National Three Peaks challenge (okay, I know it's not the same as 24 hours, but still decent). After my two trips with Dan up Snowdon and Scafell Pike I was going to go up Ben Nevis, the highest mountain in Scotland and also Great Britain. The trip to Scotland had been planned for months. As soon as Coldplay announced that they were playing Hampden Park in Glasgow, Scotland's national football stadium, Jane and I, along with our gig buddies, holiday pals, and oft drinking partners Pete and Ali, booked tickets. We often go away to see bands or visit cities with them, and it was perfect timing. So it was a question of what else to do while in Scotland and how long to stay.

Pete has been on all but one of my N3P walks, so we know the route to Ben Nevis well, but had never really stopped along the way due to the mad dash nature of the 24 hour schedule, hence bypassing Loch Lomond completely as a way of getting from Glasgow to Fort William. Now was a chance to experience it. Jane and Ali were all for it, so we booked the first three days at a lovely small town called Drymen, ten minutes' drive from Loch Lomond, and planned a day to go up Ben Nevis. The final two days would be in Glasgow ready for Chris and the gang. With only a week to go though, Pete mentioned Ben Lomond as an option.

Some of the islands on Loch Lomond, known as the 'Narrows'.

Only half an hour from Drymen (as opposed to two and a half hours to Fort William) and after a tip from mutual friends, we switched plans and aimed to climb Ben Lomond instead. Not as high (it was 974m as opposed to the 1,345m of Ben Nevis), but it was new for me and a challenge for the others who had understandably done nowhere near as much training as me – and we did want it to be fun. It turned out to be a great decision.

Ideally we'd have gone on the Saturday, but with the weather forecast showing us that this could have been a bad choice, we went with the forecast and chose Sunday. Trips away with Pete and Ali can be boozy and Friday was no exception (for me anyway); I went too hard too early and was inspecting my eyelids in the pub at 10pm. I wasn't going to make the same mistake on Saturday night, so in anticipation for the walk the following day, it was just a couple of pints.

Earlier that day, and in preparation, we took a two hour boat trip on Loch Lomond and couldn't help but be transfixed by the natural wonder and sheer scale of the surroundings.

From Wiki at https://en.wikipedia.org/wiki/Loch_Lomond, 'Loch Lomond is 36.4 kilometres (22.6 mi) long and between 1 and 8 kilometres (0.62–4.97 mi) wide, with a surface area of 71 km2 (27.5 sq mi). It is the largest lake in Great Britain by surface area; in the United Kingdom, it is surpassed only by Lough Neagh and Lough Erne in Northern Ireland. In the British Isles as a whole there are several larger loughs in the Republic of Ireland. The loch has a maximum

Ben Lomond from the middle of the Loch.

depth of about 153 metres (502 ft) in the deeper northern portion, although the southern part of the loch rarely exceeds 30 metres (98 ft) in depth. The total volume of Loch Lomond is 2.6 km3 (0.62 cu mi), making it the second largest lake in Great Britain, after Loch Ness, by water volume.'

With islands, castles, villages, boats, wildlife and the imposing mountains surrounding it, we knew we'd made a good choice.

According to the VisitScotland website, 'Loch Lomond and The Trossachs National Park – At the heart of the park is Loch Lomond itself. You won't find a bigger loch or lake in the whole of Britain and you'll have a hard time finding a more beautiful one, too. Take a cruise on the waters and admire the mighty bulk of Ben Lomond, Scotland's most southerly Munro, as

The route map at the car park. The Ptarmigan route goes to the left, the Tourist route on the right.

TRAINING

Loch Lomond from halfway up. The moody sky really frames the sheer size of the landscape.

well as the jagged shoulders of the Arrochar Alps. You could maybe even visit one of the loch's 30 islands.' https://www.visitscotland.com/see-do/landscapes-nature/national-parks-gardens/loch-lomond-trossachs/

Ben Lomond loomed over the lake though, and it daunted Jane and Ali a bit. Pete was quiet, and I suspect it did him too. I was raring to go and was very excited about another hill to climb and another new experience. It was over 3,000ft, which meant it qualified to be a Munro, of which there are 282 across Scotland. Over 6,000 people have 'bagged' them all and if you want to break the record you have to do it in under 39 days and nine hours as Stephen Pyke did in 2010. A brilliant effort. https://www.visitscotland.com/see-do/active/walking/munro-bagging/

With the preparation done, and the relative sobriety in the pub on Saturday night, we were up early and ready to go. Arriving at the car park in Rowardennan, we chatted to the volunteers from the Scottish National Trust who said that there were two routes to the top, the tourist route or the Ptarmigan route. According to Walk Highlands, the return trip on the tourist route is seven and a half miles. The volunteers said it was 'about 2km' longer than the Ptarmigan route but much easier 'like walking up Sauchiehall Street' (a famous retail thoroughfare) in Glasgow. https://www.walkhighlands.co.uk/lochlomond/ben-lomond.shtml. The rest of the party were happy to 'go shopping' so the tourist route was taken.

The sheer rock face that tested my nerve. See the path to the right – far too close to the edge for me.

The first part of the walk took you uphill through the trees pretty quickly, and you were soon out of the trees and able to see the loch for the first time. It was unclear which the peak was at this point – so much more difficult when you are not able to judge the relative heights from a distance. The route was busy and we were overtaken by several different parties, but we did note that they were all younger than us!

As the view of the loch started to open out, we were not only stopping for a rest but to drink in the scenery. Having been on the boat, we could pick out the 'Narrows', a group of islands in the middle and home to wild wallabies (true fact). From higher up, the full magnificence of the loch's 20-mile length was evident, and we really looked forward to seeing it from 3,000ft at the summit. Only another 2,000ft to go.

It is hard to really capture the essence of the route. The path was obvious, so there was no getting lost, and in the main, it was well maintained. In parts, you could even describe it as a bit boring. If you want a really adventurous climb, then I wouldn't recommend it, but that wasn't the purpose of our trip at all. After following the incline for what seemed like ages, we hit a plateau and could see the final peak above us. As we got closer, it seemed less difficult, with a zig-zag path back and forth to take away the worst of the incline. I found it easy; Jane said her

We made it! Jane and Pete in matching hats.

legs had stopped working. I remembered back to some of my earlier walks and knew exactly how she felt.

It started to get cold, and for the first time on my training walks, it was time for hats and gloves. Jane had left her hat at home, so Pete lent her his spare – a corporate gift from his employers Vauxhall Finance. It really suited her. They became hat twins.

The last part of the ascent, after the zig-zags, was a 300m gentle stretch of path to the peak – or so I thought. As I rounded one section, the opposite side of the mountain descended sharply. My knees turned to jelly and I started to back away from the edge. Ali was just merrily taking photos of the view while standing near the edge of what I thought was a sheer rock face – I didn't dare go closer to find out. I was willing her to hurry up and move away. It's strange how your fear transfers to a perception of the dangers others face. Like Boggie in the Brecon Beacons, Ali was never in danger, but it rattled me badly and my own irrationality spoiled my enjoyment at the top.

It should have been an exhilarating last 100m to the top. As the trig point came into view, the other side of the mountain could be seen. I thought Snowdon was my favourite view in Britain, then I transferred it to Scafell, now Ben Lomond

What a view. A small snapshot of one of the finest vistas I have ever seen.

nailed it. I am constantly overwhelmed by how much nature can completely capture the human spirit. I have often wondered whether we are programmed by society to love the natural scenery of the world, or whether it is inherent within us. TV shows, parents, friends – even Microsoft Windows screensavers – constantly bombard us with images of nature and we are told that they are fantastic. Are we programmed? I don't think so. I think we are just awestruck by the beauty, purity and simplicity of the natural world and we seek out things to enable this emotion – whether it is a small stream, a baby rabbit in the hedgerow, a mighty canyon, the sky at night or the longest lake in Scotland surrounded by hills. Simple pleasures passed down through society for thousands of years. Maybe that is what is really driving my desire to go to the Himalayas.

Safely by the trig point, I took a 360-degree look at the horizon and relaxed for a moment to really enjoy it. With decent visibility, we could see for miles in every direction – just like I had been able to at Snowdon and Scafell. It was mesmerising. It had taken us over three hours, but the time and effort was worth it.

We had planned to have our packed lunches at the top, and fellow walkers at the top had had the same thought, absent-mindedly eating their sandwiches while sitting on the edge, but I was still shaking from earlier, so suggested to our group that we should eat lower down the hill. I am not great at hiding emotion and they knew I was nervous despite not being worried themselves and thankfully, as good friends do, they readily agreed. I *was* the tour leader, now I was the tour millstone. I held my nerve for a few photos though, I hope they do the view justice.

Another group joined us at the top having come up the Ptarmigan route. They looked knackered and cautioned us not to go down that route as it was very steep. We were pleased that we'd chosen the tourist route after all. I wasn't keen to go down anything too steep due to my recent scare and neither were the other three, so we agreed to go back the way we'd come. Most of those at the top did the same.

Back at the plateau (after navigating the scary path again) we finally had our lunch in the sunshine. Jane's sandwich bag caught in the wind and went flying across the moorland with me in hot pursuit, much to the amusement of Pete and Ali.

As a Nepal tip, I was still learning. My phone was out of battery and I had been trying to charge it using my powerbank for the last hour, but the wire was damaged, and I wasn't able to record the route properly. I must remember to take a couple of spares to Nepal. I don't want anything stopping me from recording my journey there. Ali had taken over as official photographer and most of the photos on here are hers.

Looking back down the path to the start point.

WALK 10: BEN LOMOND. LOCH LOMOND. LOWLANDS. SCOTLAND

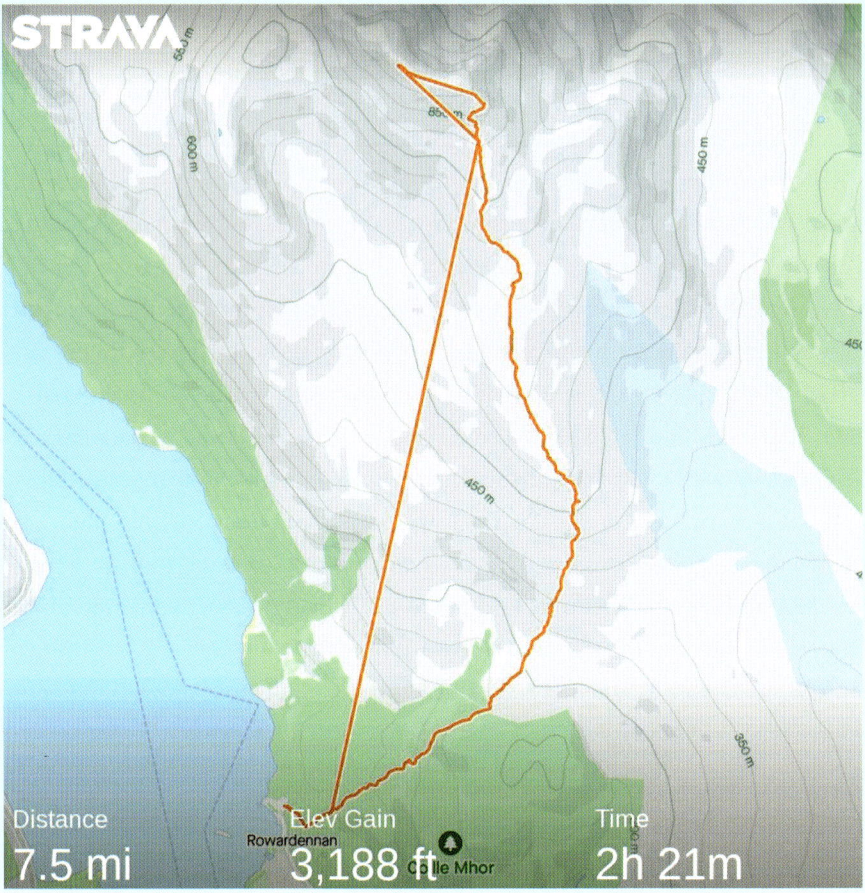

Distance: 7.5 mi
Elev Gain: 3,188 ft
Time: 2h 21m

Elevation

Elevation Gain	3,188 ft
Max Elevation	3,115 ft

Pace

Avg Pace	18:50 /mi
Moving Time	2:21:17
Avg Elapsed Pace	49:38 /mi
Elapsed Time	6:12:28
Fastest Split	3:51 /mi

In theory, we knew what we were in for on the descent as we just retraced our steps back to the car park, but it seemed to be steeper and longer than we remembered. Jane commented on a couple of occasions that if she'd have come downhill first, she wouldn't have gone up in the first place. Funny how tiredness can impact the memory as she had been fine going up – even with her 'legs not working'. They did joke with me that that I must have a short memory and forget the things that are tough quickly and only concentrate on the good things that have happened. That's being an optimist as far as I am concerned. Maybe they have a point and that's why I don't get bored easily on my solo training walks – I'll take it as a positive.

Out of the four of us, Pete actually struggled the most on the way down. Despite being a veteran of many hill walks, it was always the downhills that impacted him most, and here it was no different. By the end he was glad to get back to the car park. There were many false dawns for him too, especially through the trees when we couldn't see where the path ahead was going more than a few metres into the distance. These false dawns can really impact the psyche – it is similar to reaching the crown of the hill going up, and realising it isn't the top. Another good lesson for me here – to not judge others by how I am feeling. I was okay going up and down, but not at the top. None of the others had the same experience. We all have different highs and lows in mood, fitness and resilience and it is important to remember that in groups someone will always be in a better mood, or will want to go faster, or will be the least prepared. It is easy to think that everyone should be like you, but what if it is you who are the slowest, or in the worst mood or the least prepared? You would want understanding and empathy. I got it at the top from the others when I was scared and I gave it to Jane going up and then Pete coming down, despite me wanting to go faster.

At the bottom, we congratulated each other and reflected on what we had achieved. Pete had loved the views. Jane commented on the sense of achievement. Ali said she now understood why midget gems were the currency of the mountain.

A lovely day with fabulous friends. What I don't understand is why they don't want to do another mountain next year!

WEEK 11
Monday 29 August – Sunday 4 September – Three weeks to go
Weight at start of week: 107kg
Weight at the end of week: 106.8kg

Cumulative weight lost: 7.7kg
Steps completed in week: 121,968
Cumulative: 1,433,271
Fundraising total to date: £422.19
Coke watch: Four cans of Diet Coke
Booze watch: Zero

It is now getting close. Only 16 days to go at the end of this entry. I have decided to really cut back on my training. The gym is boring, even with my earphones in, and with other commitments at work, I am not getting as much time to go on two-to-three-hour walks. I can feel the energy inside me bursting to get out. I may get one more full-day walk in, maybe go back to the Edale Skyline with one of the kids.

I bought a new pair of Gelert walking shoes for £30 from Sports Direct this week as back up, so I needed to wear them in. A 30-mile walk on Wednesday around the local area (a new record) tested them to the full and the aching feet and Compeeds showed me that I need to try them again, with a second pair of socks. It was a good workout though. Not especially quick (see training walk section) but a lovely day and a chance to catch up on some podcasts which I have missed. Isn't it funny that I can walk in the fresh air for nine and a half hours and not get bored, yet 30 minutes in the gym leaves me desperate to leave.

I have now got everything I need (I think). I took everything out of my case to check what I had and to transfer the contents into ziplock bags for the trip. Then packed it all up again. With most things packed (excluding things for hand luggage) I was on 15kg. Way below my airline limit of 30kg, but right on the edge of the porter/day pack limit. I may have to leave some stuff in Kathmandu and wear the same pants for three days, rather than two – eeugh. It is a shame in a way that I have everything, as I do enjoy buying walking gear – as Jane and my credit card bill will attest.

Money – I have tested my Revolut bank card and app, so that I can transfer money easily into US dollars. From my reading it seems that this is the currency of choice after the Nepalese rupee. I am not keen on taking $2,000 in cash to Nepal (I haven't even paid for the trip yet, just the deposit), so this gives me some peace of mind.

I have saved my attempts at dieting to the end, as I have finally dropped below 107kg on a Monday morning weigh-in, but I am way behind my goal of 100kg by the time I leave. Even optimistic me doesn't think I will lose a stone in a fortnight, so I will just keep trying to be good. Since Scotland, I have decided not to drink, so no booze this week, despite two meals with friends, and a real reduction in my Diet Coke intake – just four 330ml cans. I would probably drink this amount in a day usually. Good for the bank account too, less so for the shareholders.

I am nearly on 1.5 million steps, hoping to go well above that next week.

Training Walk 11
01/09/2022 – A 30 mile local walk
I was debating whether to do another training walk. After Scafell Pike and Ben Lomond within a few days of each other I knew I had the uphill walking skills and stamina that I would need. I found them reasonably easy. Another long-distance trip from home would only serve the purpose of seeing a different landscape. Tempting as that was, I decided to concentrate on the gym – especially running on the treadmill. But after a few goes, I was bored. As they were only 30–45minute sessions as well, they would increase stamina but not necessarily endurance.

I had the excuse I needed to get back on the road. I bought a new pair of walking shoes – only some cheap Gelerts from Sports Direct – but they would be a good backup for my comfy boots. I just needed to break them in.

A quick look at the weather and Thursday 1 September was plumped for. Blimey, I was now in the calendar month of the trip. I decided on a long endurance walk, with the initial plan to walk for 12 hours. There wasn't a really fixed route planned, just a general idea to do some of the original training walk, but to add extensions.

I won't bore you with the mile-by-mile description as some of it was on roads, and some has been recorded already. You can see it from the map at the end anyway. There were some findings though.

I was glad I took my Compeeds. The shoes were slightly too big and there was rubbing. Within ten miles I had them off and applying my magic plasters. I will definitely need another long walk in them, this time with an extra pair of socks.

I took it a lot slower, with more breaks. In all I did 30 miles, with about 400m of elevation, and it took me nine and a half hours, with an hour's break across several stops. It would have been a strange sight for passersby as I sat on park benches to rest, while whipping off my socks and shoes to allow the air to cool them down. Don't worry, no one else was on the benches with me. I would normally not have

WALK 11: A 30 MILE LOCAL WALK

Distance: 30.0 mi
Elev Gain: 1,260 ft
Time: 8h 29m

Elevation

Elevation Gain — 1,260 ft
Max Elevation — 433 ft

Pace

Avg Pace — 16:58 /mi
Moving Time — 8:29:22
Avg Elapsed Pace — 19:02 /mi
Elapsed Time — 9:31:20
Fastest Split — 14:47 /mi

these small breaks, but I found them really valuable. When time isn't an issue, as it won't be in Nepal, then the usual desire to go quickly is not only not needed over there but actively discouraged. Luckily, my feet meant I followed this to a tee.

I had a final test run of all my 'pills'. With the SIS electrolytes and water purification pills in my water bladder, and half a Diamox taken before, I am now confident that they:

Do not give me the runs. Do not give me any allergic reaction. Do make me need to wee (three times in the first two hours).

I can keep this in mind in Nepal, but without worry that something awful could impact me. I did drink nearly five litres of water on the walk, so I may need to think of plan B in Nepal. I only have a three-litre bladder, so I may need a reserve too. Heavy to carry at 4kg but I am determined not to get altitude sickness through my own fault. If I get it physiologically, I can live with that, but not through lack of precaution.

As home approached, my Strava said that I was going to be just shy of 30 miles, so I walked straight past the front door and round the block to make sure I hit the milestone. Then it was straight into the garden, and immediately putting my feet into a bucket of cold water. It certainly helped. Jane was going out with her pals for tea, so being lazy, I just went to the chippy rather than cook. They were lovely.

WEEK 12

Monday 5 September – Sunday 11 September – Two weeks to go.
Weight at start of week: 106.8kg
Weight at the end of week: 105.9kg
Cumulative weight lost: 8.6kg
Steps completed in week: 73,004
Cumulative: 1,506,275
Fundraising total to date: £652.19
Booze watch: Three bottles of Ghurka (plus a cheeky pint of Birra Moretti)

* * * * *

A really sad week for me and 65 million Britons as we mourned the loss of Queen Elizabeth II, our monarch of 70 years. Whether you're a monarchist or republican, there is no doubt that she was a remarkable lady. RIP Your Majesty, you'll be badly missed.

We also had a new prime minister appointed as the Tories finally chose Liz Truss. Let's hope she manages to steer the country through a very tricky period.

* * * * *

With only a fortnight to go, and with a lot of watching the rolling news about The Queen, the training intensity trailed off. I did two gym sessions – one hour on the stepper in each one, and two mid-distance walks, ten miles and six miles (both on the flat). I also broke through the 1.5 million steps barrier – very satisfying. It is now just about keeping some movement in the legs and some energy in the body before I fly on the 20th. The Coke consumption is also back under control – for now.

I read a couple more books and I have realised that I have overpacked. I am now on 20kg, before hand luggage. I am allowed 30kg on the plane to Nepal, so no worries about getting to Khatmandu, but after an email chat with the tour operator Raj, he confirmed that I can only take 15kg max on the plane to Lukla. I may just take what I have to Khatmandu and make a call there about how to repack for the actual trek. After all, I am going to be in the capital for six days either side of the Lukla flights so I do need some home casual clothes. I'm sure I will find a left-luggage store while I am away.

I was checking my documents and realised that I need to download and fill in the Nepalese International Traveller Arrival Form at https://ccmc.gov.np/. It is easy to do as the website can be viewed in English, but it comes out in printed form in Nepali, so it could say anything. If I'm arrested at the airport, you'll know why!

I have also upgraded my phone to a Samsung S22. I asked for fast charging and a great camera. I have tested it slightly so far and it seems fine, but just in case, I will take my old one as well. I don't want to be short of photos/video, so the more backup I have the better.

Another app I downloaded was an altitude app. I can get altitude from Strava, but unless there is an internet connection there may be a lag of seeing how high I am. The app doesn't need the net, so I will get real-time information.

On the BBC Weather app, I have plugged in Kathmandu, Bhaktapur and Namche Bazaar. At the moment, the long-range forecast for my first four days in Khatmandu is partial raining, and in Namche it is light clouds. Imagine I get to the Himalayas and I cannot see the mountains because of the cloud. The trip will still be life-changing, but…The final preparation this week was a curry with a load of good friends at the Yak and Yeti in Beeston, Nottingham. Yes you guessed it, I wanted to try some Nepalese food. It was a great night and I even had dal for the first time. As dal bhat is heavily trailed by all the books I thought I'd try it. It was okay. I'd hope to get some veggies in there in the hills. I also broke my sobriety. I vowed that I would only have another drink if it was Nepali, so while others had the pints of Cobra, I had three bottles of Ghurka lager. Delicious, and I am looking forward to trying it again in its native country.

Finally, a good weight week. I finally broke below the 105kg barrier on Friday, until the curry and beer took me back over, but after hovering in the 105s–107s range for a few weeks, it was a good feeling. I have changed my target (which was 99.9kg) to under 104kg. One week to go. Maybe eating a diet of dal bhat for 11 days, plus the hiking, will get me below the 100kg mark.

*****

WEEK 13

Monday 12 September – Monday 19 September – Final Week.

Weight at start of week: 105.9kg
Weight at the end of week: 106.2kg
Cumulative weight lost: 8.3kg
Steps completed in week: 85,528
Cumulative: 1,591,803
Fundraising total to date: £792.14
Coke watch: Five litres, after a late-week lapse
Booze watch: Two nights of light beers with family

A slightly extended diary this week as I leave the UK on Tuesday the 20th (the day I am writing this). An extra day has been added on to include Monday the 19th, the Queen's funeral, a day of great sadness, but full of pomp and ceremony that the British do best.

To repackage an earlier analogy, Christmas has come. The decorations are up, the presents have been bought and Santa has been down the chimney. I am sat waiting for the time to go to Manchester with two suitcases (combined weight 28kg) and a backpack (5kg). I know I am only going to be able to take 15kg on the plane to Lukla, but I will have almost a week at the end of my trek in Kathmandu, so I am going to take everything I want, see what I get from the trekking company (sleeping bag and jacket) and then figure out what I can take to Lukla. I'll just leave the rest in Kathmandu for my return. I have done some basic division and I reckon I am about 5kg too heavy for Lukla at the moment, so I will have to downsize, or carry loads on my person!

The really big news of the week is that I have a pal. Raj from Outfitters Nepal emailed me on Monday asking if I could fly to Lukla on the 22nd instead of the 26th as someone has booked the trip for that slot. The 'computer said no' initially (for non-UK readers, this is a catchphrase from a superb comedy series, *Little Britain*) but after some thought, I agreed. It would leave me plenty of room in the schedule later for bad weather and flight delays coming back from Lukla. I have rearranged my golf round (it was the 23rd) and mentally prepared myself for flying to Lukla less than 24 hours after landing in Kathmandu. I need to change money, get my new SIM and arrange any visas/permits, but it should be doable. The weather in Kathmandu for the next few days is also a little sketchy, warm but rain spells, whereas Namche Bazaar is light wind and light cloud, so another reason to go earlier. My walking buddy is a 38-year-old German called Anton. That's all I know. I hope he isn't a manic alpine climber as he has 14 years on me! If he is a footy fan, I know we'll get along. Watch this space.

Not too much else to report. Only a couple of walks on the flat this week (eight miles and six miles), plus day-to-day pottering, so I am bursting at the seams with energy. I hope I have this correct as I haven't climbed a big hill since Ben Lomond at the end of August. I am banking on some serious muscle memory to get me going.

My pal Ash lent me his large powerbank – I now have two, so there should be no way I am running out of juice now.

Four meals out this week, hence the lack of movement on the weight front. On Wednesday, it was virtually the whole family as my parents and my brother and sister's families all met up to say farewell to Jim, my eldest son who goes backpacking while I am away. I will miss him terribly and also Matt (middle son) who goes in the same direction in February. They will both get a one-way ticket to Bangkok and I am sure that they will not be back for 12 months minimum. Thank you 'big tech' for video calling now. When Jane and I went on our similar trip back in the 1990s, we were away for 17 months and our parents had a two-minute phone call every Sunday to find out we were safe and well. Have a great time Jim. The hardest part for me will be that I am not at home when he actually goes, so Jane will have to cope with the empty house alone. Sorry Jane.

Jane and I also went to another Nepali restaurant (yes, I know I am obsessive), the Ghurkha Express in Beeston. A really nice atmosphere, but this isn't just a plug. On the wall was a picture of Everest taken from the top of Kala Patthar. It was incredible. Of all the books I have read, certainly the personal accounts, not one of the authors made it to the top. Two got halfway; the rest were either too ill, or too tired to go. I started to feel despondent about ever getting there after reading these accounts, but just seeing this picture invigorated me. When I am waking up in Gorakshep, and the choice is stepping into the freezing cold for an optional climb at 4am or staying in bed, then descending back towards Namche, I will think of this picture and hopefully get out of bed and clamber up the hill. It could be the best view I have ever seen, and ever likely to see, and I don't want to miss it.

So that's it. Thirteen weeks of training, two cancelled trips due to Covid, lots of research and reading, two large bags of kit, 500 miles and 1.5 million steps of training and nearly a stone and a half in weight loss. I am ready. Manchester, Doha, Kathmandu, Lukla and EBC here I come!

BOOK REVIEWS:

These reviews are written in the order I read the books, not in order of quality or recommendation.

One Step at A Time – My Journey to Everest Base Camp
Paul Tallett – 9798695554681 - £8.99 – 156 pages
https://www.amazon.co.uk/One-Step-At-Time-Journey/dp/B08LNL4DYL/ref=sr_1_1?crid=28U09R9MZSJJZ&keywords=paul+tallett&qid=1656930268&sprefix=paul+tallett%2Caps%2C73&sr=8-1

If you are after a book that has every last detail in – full kit lists, itineraries, helplines, details about insurance, visas, inoculations, permits – then this is not the book for you. If you are after a heartfelt, honest account of the author's trip, including the downsides, then give this a go.

Tallett briefly goes into his back story which sets the scene and then talks about his training in the hills of Scotland. I would have liked more of this (especially length of days) as it would help me understand more about his level of mountain fitness.

The trip to Base Camp is well documented; he clearly took notes while out there rather than trying to remember it all on his return. There are some interesting photos too.

I would have liked to know a bit more about the other characters in the group. Although they were mentioned in passing, I never really got the feel about how they helped him, or he helped them, to overcome the arduous nature of the trip.

There are some nice tributes to the Nepalese people who helped him along the way, and some of the facts about Nepal and some of the sights he saw also give a good flavour of what to expect while you're out there.

The writing was basic, and the word count was a bit low. Even though it was 158 pages, there cannot have been more than 30,000 words in there. It took less than a day to read it.

But at £8.99, it is worth it. Taking a lot of different aspects of the trip can only make your experience either more prepared or more anticipatory.

* * * * *

Concise Guide to the Everest Base Camp Trek. How to Prepare, What to Take and What to Expect

Katherine Rock – 9798611052174 - £7.99 – 79 pages

https://www.amazon.co.uk/Concise-Guide-Everest-Base-Camp/dp/B084D-PHY8K/ref=sr_1_1?crid=2WLHRBXYNFXSO&keywords=katherine+rock&qid=1657535586&s=books&sprefix=katherine+rock%2Cstripbooks%2C54&sr=1-1

This is a book I read in an hour. It must only be about 10,000 words, so from a value-for-money perspective, it is on the edge of whether it is worth it. The author is an Aussie who travels solo on the luxury package, something that most people do not consider due to the price. As a result some of the information is not relevant, but there are some interesting contrasts between the two types of trip. As a traveller you need to consider whether you want that extra home comfort.

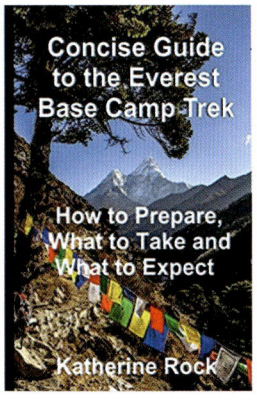

There are some decent things in there, over 60 per cent of the book is the actual practical guide, and I definitely added a few things to my list of things to buy and take. The biggest disappointment was the blog of the trip itself. I really want to get a feel of what it is like, but it was scant, and a lot of it doesn't describe the experience that I will have. E.g., the author likes travelling alone and she doesn't really want to join conversations with other travellers. If you want a packing list, you can get this online, if you want a book that really describes the experience, then this falls well short of the mark. At £8 I bought it because I wanted as much research as possible, but if money is tight, you can get most of this for free elsewhere.

Kathmandu and the Kingdom of Nepal (Lonely Planet) 1983
Prakash A. Raj – 9780908086467 – 144 pages
https://www.amazon.co.uk/Kathmandu-Kingdom-Nepal-Prakash-Raj/dp/0908086466/ref=monarch_sidesheet

What a treat this was to read. While travelling around Asia in 1996 and '97, the Lonely Planets were 'must-have' guides, and although I have a more up-to-date version (see later review), I couldn't resist buying this in one of the local charity shops.

The book itself is obviously dated, it is nearly 40 years old after all, but the early history and general geography won't have changed. Some of the descriptions of Nepal, the customs and the people were great. It will be interesting to see how much it has changed when I get there.

There is a really good section on the EBC trek and some of the stats are scary. At one point, Raj says that the up and downs on the trek is the equivalent of climbing Everest twice. I think he was talking about the trek from Kathmandu to EBC, rather than from Lukla, but it was still a sobering thought and did change my training schedule.

There are also some good descriptions of towns around Kathmandu, including Patan, Bhaktapur and Nagarkot – places I may now try and visit – or in the case of Patan, revisit.

A lot of the book is irrelevant as it talks about other parts of Nepal, so if you want to stay focused on the EBC trip only, then such a broad guide may not be useful. I certainly wouldn't go out of your way to buy this edition, but if you come across it in a charity shop, a car boot sale or just surfing the net, settle back and enjoy some nostalgia.

Trekking the Everest Base Camp – The Day to Day Guide and what isn't in the guide books

Ta Hiron – 9781095937587 – 70 pages

https://www.amazon.co.uk/Trekking-Everest-Base-Camp-guidebooks/dp/1095937588/ref=sr_1_4?crid=25VZV1B3Q5HSK&keywords=ta+hiron&qid=1658406597&sprefix=ta+hiron%2Caps%2C88&sr=8-4

This took about an hour to read. The text is large and the word count is miniscule. It is a book version of an ebook and no care has been taken to adapt it to the printed format. For example, it says things like, '*if you want to watch the video click HERE*,' which you cannot do in a printed book of course. At only 80 pages (of which ten pages are just single pictures and captions), it is very poor value for money if you pay full price, even at £6.99.

There is very little in this book about the trek itself, it often just seems to be an account of what they ate on the way and a bit about how they felt. Nothing about the terrain, how difficult it was, the landscape, the people, the customs, the history. If you want another list of things to take then go for it and you will find a nugget or two in there that you haven't found elsewhere.

I do like the way that the couple describe their difficulty level each day and their subjective opinion of their altitude sickness. They also give some detail about the quality of the toilets. The other nice touch is describing the kit in terms of what they used and didn't use and what they wished they had more of.

The title says it is a guide of what isn't in the guide books, but there isn't that much extra. Swerve this book if you're short of cash, or if you're after lots of content published professionally, but if you just want another confirmation of what you should take then give it a go. Or even get the ebook so you can download the links.

The Best Little Guidebook for Trekking the Everest Region
Alonzo Lyons – 9781502421340 – 133 pages
https://www.amazon.co.uk/Guidebook-Trekking-Everest-Insider-Editions/dp/1502421348/ref=sr_1_2?crid=KAWJLEXNIOSG&keywords=alonzo+lyons&qid=1658408252&sprefix=alonz+lyons%2Caps%2C82&sr=8-2

This is a self-published title from Amazon and its layout is terrible, but I have a really soft spot for it. At 133 pages of quite small text, it packs a lot of information in. There are some of the usual things in this type of book such as kit lists, but they are by no means the bulk of the text. There is language, money, customs, maps – even attitudes to gender.

However, where the book really holds the attention is the detail of the walk itself, including directions for the independent traveller and some really good information on the towns along the way. E.g., the section on Namche Bazaar talks about what to do there as well as the basics. The walks are described as if you were walking them – turn left here, go right there – and it describes whether there are uphill sections or downhill ones, as well as intermediate heights and distances (again, just in hours which is frustrating). The author also takes you on little side trips – useful if you're independently trekking, but the way he does this is let down by the design, as you are unsure where the side trip description ends and the main walk continues. I suspect it would be a lot clearer when you are actually following the instructions, but as most people will have guides, then directions are not to be worried about.

A useful addition to the Base Camp library that is not written as an 'experience' book, but rather as a genuine guide.

Everest: A Trekker's Guide: Base Camp, Kala Patthar and other trekking routes in Nepal and Tibet
Radek Kucharski – 9781852848361 – 320 pages
https://www.amazon.co.uk/Everest-Trekkers-trekking-International-Trekking/dp/1852848367/ref=sr_1_3?crid=3SPL4CQT5OWKV&keywords=Radek+Kucharski&qid=1659342900&sprefix=radek+kucharski%2Caps%2C98&sr=8-3

This is my favourite book so far, and the most useful, especially if you are looking for the practical side of the walk. The author has travelled in the region many times, and this is a detailed look at the trek itself. Written after the earthquake, it is up to date and authoritative.

Published by Cicerone, it is not cheap, RRP £17.95, but it is worth every penny. In full colour, with a protective plastic sleeve and over 300 pages of content, you get 75 pages of general information – visas, weather, health, communication, budget, cultural interaction, drinking water to name just a few categories. The rest is about individual treks in the region, including EBC. All the books covered so far in this review section discuss some of these things too, but this is really clear, well-written and easy to reference due to a comprehensive contents page and layout.

There are maps of the region and lots of additional info not seen in other books, e.g. things to do in Namche Bazaar.

But the real value of the book for me is detailed discussion of the walk itself, including times taken, things to see on the way and the elevation gained and descended during the day, something I have been after all along. E.g., 'Namche to Tengboche. 6.25 miles, 5hr-5.5hr. 875m of ascent, 425m of descent. 450m between the two places.' In most books it only gives you the time and the overall elevation gained.

If you are an independent traveller, then this guide would be brilliant for you. If you are with a guide on a group walk, you won't need to know directions, but knowing what you are looking at taking on each day will help manage your expectations and reduce doubt that you are capable of achieving the task ahead.

The downsides – it is small writing. As a man of a certain age with an astigmatism, reading it in bed at night with artificial light, it was sometimes tricky to get it first time, but in the day it is fine. It is also a guide only and not a personal view of the trip – you would need to get this from some of the other books mentioned here. The other downside, and an inevitable one, is that he talks about other treks in the Everest region, so 100 pages or so are not needed if you purely want a book on EBC. Of course if you are an independent trekker, or you want to go on a different trip in future, then the whole content would be good for you.

But don't let these downsides put you off. This is a terrific book, really useful, well produced and authoritative. I will read it again a fortnight before I go and I will be taking it with me so I can prep for each day as I walk to EBC.

Lonely Planet – Trekking in the Nepal Himalaya

Bradley Mayhew, Lindsay Brown and Stuart Butler – 9781741792720 – 375 pages

https://www.amazon.co.uk/Lonely-Planet-Trekking-Himalaya-Travel/dp/174179272X/ref=sr_1_1?crid=30ANT198Y3G1F&keywords=978-1741792720&qid=1659949456&sprefix=978-1741792720+%2Caps%2C92&sr=8-1

This was published in 2016, and I bought it for my first planned trip in 2020, so it is slightly out of date now. There is a newer version which hopefully irons out a lot of issues with this edition – primarily, the book was based on Nepal before the earthquake. There are references to it, as it was released slightly after the event, but it hadn't been researched and updated fully. It left me feeling short changed.

There is the usual Lonely Planet information in there, and it is a well-produced publication, with some colour photography at the beginning and two-colour printing throughout the rest of the book. As I am not travelling independently, a lot of the information about places to stay is not needed, and as it covers the whole of the Himalaya, a lot is unsurprisingly not needed.

There are some descriptions of the walk, and the things you will see each day, and the 'Understand Nepal' section at the back is useful, further confirmation of things I have read already.

There are some nice things in there, which took me back to backpacking in the 1990s when there was no internet to refer to and Lonely Planets were the bible of backpackers throughout the world. The street maps of Kathmandu and Namche Bazaar will come in handy for exploring on foot and some of the tips are good.

However, as a guide I found the previous one I reviewed, *Everest: A Trekker's Guide: Base Camp, Kala Patthar and other trekking routes in Nepal and Tibet*, so much better. I will probably take the Lonely Planet in my suitcase for Kathmandu, but I won't take it on the trek. Maybe if I had read this book first, I would be raving about it more, but as it is mainly a confirmation book of things I know already, it is not so useful – for me anyway.

Himalaya

Michael Palin – 9780297843719 – 286 pages

https://www.amazon.co.uk/Himalaya-Michael-Palin/dp/0297843710/ref=sr_1_1?crid=217AZQQ6GFW6S&keywords=0297843710&qid=1660549940&s=books&sprefix=0297843710%2Cstripbooks%2C109&sr=1-1

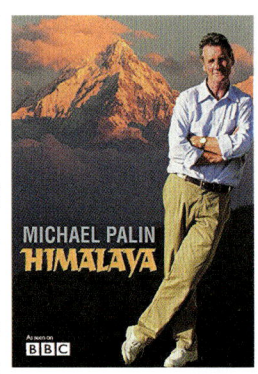

Another one I saw in a charity shop for £2 which I thought I'd have a read of. As a Monty Python fan, there is always that goodwill towards anything Palin does and I remember the travel documentary series that he produced. This volume was after *Around the World in 80 Days*, *Pole to Pole* and *Sahara*, and covers his trip to the Himalaya in 2004, so well before the earthquake, and during the Maoist rebellion in parts of Nepal. It is a full-colour, A4 hardback – a classic coffee table book with excellent production values.

I didn't read all of it, just the section on Nepal, and as it was written in a diary format, there were many things he did due to his position as a famous BBC TV documentary maker that wouldn't happen to a 'normal' traveller. For example, he met the King and was present at Ghurkha selection training – it'd be nice but unrealistic. But some of the descriptions of the mountains, as well as the cities of Kathmandu, Patan and Bhaktapur were very engaging and inspiring.

The photography, as you would expect, is excellent and really brings the country to life.

Unfortunately for my research, he travels to Annapurna base camp, not Everest, but some of the issues are still there for him, and at one point he became really ill. And then almost straight away, got his mojo back and carried on. I think if I start to see signs of altitude sickness, then this heartens me as the body gets acclimatised. The words 'descend, descend, descend' loom large in this section. He had also had a beer while at altitude which may have contributed to his sickness, something that his guide advised against, as do all the books read so far. His TV crew were helicoptered off the mountain to keep to their schedule (not for illness) and this is certainly not an option for most travellers.

So if you are looking for something that gives you a feel for the country, then have a read. If you want a book to describe what you are likely to experience, then probably not.

For me it was £2 well spent.

A Guide to Trekking in Nepal

Stephen Bezruchka – 0898860032 – 256 pages

https://www.amazon.co.uk/guide-trekking-Nepal-Stephen-Bezruchka/dp/0898860032/ref=sr_1_1?crid=2MB4X85O5AQ13&keywords=0898860032&qid=1662110299&sprefix=0898860032%2Caps%2C89&sr=8-1

Another retro book bought in a charity shop for £2. First published in 1972, this edition was from 1983. Looking on Amazon, there are many more modern editions, and based on the content in here, it may be a decent one to have a look at, although the latest is 2011, so before the earthquake.

According to the author, this was the first definitive guide to trekking Nepal, and it is detailed. It has an interesting forward from Sir Edmund Hillary but he gets very preachy later on about the destruction of the environment by trekkers which I am sure is not so relevant today. It is nice to hear his voice though. There is some really good information in the book about preparation, culture, health and language, but I have got a lot of this from some of the other books I have read. Due to the date, a lot of the information is no longer valid. I did love the health section where he advises moleskin for dealing with blisters – I think I'll stick with my Compeeds. It was also interesting how Diamox was also around even back then.

The best section is on 'Interacting with Nepal' which gave me real food for thought, especially some of the don'ts, e.g. never put anything in a Nepali fire, even paper litter. I will have a quick re-read of this section before I go just to make sure I don't make any faux pas while I am there.

Like all the guidebooks reviewed so far, there is a lot not needed for this trip as he discusses the Terai and the Annapurnas. The section on the Khumbu region and the walk to Base Camp was surprisingly short and didn't add anything to my knowledge. In fact, it just confused me, so I skipped the end.

It was worth the £2, and I am glad I bought it.

Doofus Dad Does Everest Base Camp
Mark E. Johnson – 978057821289 – 190 pages

https://www.amazon.co.uk/Doofus-Does-Everest-Base-slightly-less-than-epic/dp/0578212897/ref=tmm_pap_swatch_0?_encoding=UTF8&qid=1662622149&sr=1-1

I bought this book two years ago and read it in a couple of days. Then my trip got cancelled twice so I came back to it. I remember enjoying it then but wondered whether it would have the same effect on me as I have now read other accounts.

I shouldn't have worried. I read it in two days – again. And I thoroughly enjoyed it – again.

It is a well put-together book – nicely edited and designed with a cartoon-style jacket. It isn't just a cheap, thrown-together self-published blog. At approximately 200 pages, there is plenty of content. Like anything printed digitally on 'reading book' paper, the quality of the pictures is not great and you cannot really see a lot of the detail in them. Maybe he needed to just make the pictures bigger. At $19.99 for 200 pages it is not as cheap as some of the others, but it is worth it as it really captures the essence of the trip, but with humour.

The author is an American, so we do come at this from different angles, but some of the humour is straight out of popular US sitcoms so it sort of translates to the UK reader. Some of it seems a little contrived and I suspect certain artistic license has been taken to describe some situations, but that didn't worry me. I know I would get on with him if we met in real life which made me much more lenient towards him. Even more so as he is 52 in the book, exactly the same age as I am when I go and it was interesting to see what physical issues he faced. As an organiser of his group he had added responsibility for his clients (which included his wife and friends) and you could sense the relief as they got back to Lukla that that responsibility had been lifted.

The style of the book is first-person as it is a narrative, but it is nowhere near a guide book, so if you're after a history or geography lesson, then you won't get it here. What you do get though is an honest account of the trip with some geography and social commentary thrown in. He is a writer by trade and you can tell. The sentences flow well and he brings in well-honed writer's skill at setting the scene and describing the events within that context.

There are some low moments, so if you don't want a spoiler alert, skip this paragraph. Two of his party, including his wife, are airlifted from the mountain, neither of them for altitude sickness. I was frustrated with this. I am determined not to go off unless my life is in danger and cannot afford the thousands of pounds to just get a chopper out. Obviously this party could.

There is a real affection for the Nepali people, their culture and their diet and I hope to encounter a lot of this.

Looking at some of the walking stats, and a very brief section about the training, I am satisfied that I have done enough to meet the physical challenges. It is just the mental and physiological ones I need to be aware of now. He did give one great tip, to eat garlic soup every day – an old Sherpa trick apparently. And there was I thinking it would be dal bhat twice a day.

There is a kit list, and some walking stats but it doesn't dominate. In fact, I barely read it at this point.

I would recommend this book to anyone who wants to look past the usual guidebook. Along with the first book I read by Paul Tallett, this is one to get you in the mood for the trip.

How Not to Trek to Mount Everest

Cory McLeod – 9781710964929 – 88 pages

https://www.amazon.co.uk/How-Trek-Everest-Cory-McLeod/dp/1710964928/ref=sr_1_1?crid=NVKAWU6RIGHN&keywords=cory+mcleod&qid=1662895348&sprefix=cory+mcleod%2Caps%2C77&sr=8-1

I have a declaration before I write this review. I have a professional relationship with Cory as we are in discussion to publish a book about his life. Saying that, I am not here to give faint praise.

The book is really short, only 88 pages, and with no more than 15,000 words, I read it in about an hour. At £10.05 it was expensive for such a small amount of content, but out of professional curiosity I bought it anyway.

The major upside is that all the photos are in colour, which none of the other eye-witness books have. This probably explains the costs. It is nice to see the hills and prayer flags in a recognisable way. The downside is the photos are far too small and with pages to spare, these could have really helped to excite the reader much more if they were bigger.

The style is engaging, one of the reasons I am interested in his other stories, but it all seems a bit rushed, something he admits to in the book. It is more of a blog, rather than a well-constructed book and some of the layouts could show more technical skill; it feels like a print of an MS Word doc sometimes.

But what it does do is give you a little of the other side. He mentions in the title how NOT to trek Everest and there are plenty of examples of this – lack of money, no sleeping bag, bad timings etc, which obviously gives the reader a chance to learn from his mistakes.

What struck a chord with me is his solo travel, and sometimes the loneliness seeps through. He was desperate to meet others on the way, and I am sure I will be in the same position. We sound similar in our need for human contact, and some of the tips about keeping in touch are good. A relationship forged higher up the hill paid dividend for him later. Travelling solo means you are forced to mix with people outside of your 'tribe', as long as they let you into theirs. (NB – since originally writing this, I do now have a companion)

Cory also mentioned the garlic soup tip. Two recommendations are enough for me.

If you're short of cash, don't bother, but if you want to get as much info about the experience as possible, then give it a go.

Adventure to Everest Base Camp

Karl H. Myers – 9781541379169 – 225 pages

https://www.amazon.co.uk/Adventure-Everest-Base-Camp-Myers/dp/1541379160/ref=sr_1_1?crid=25IO2CY44AZ5C&keywords=9781541379169&qid=1663402360&sprefix=9781541379169%2Caps%2C79&sr=8-1

This is the final book I read before my trip, finishing it on the Friday as I fly on the Tuesday. It is longer than some of the 'eye-witness' books I have read and like the others it offers a different perspective.

The author flew in from the States, didn't even leave Kathmandu airport before going to Lukla, then on the way back, did the same. He never even saw the city at all. The perils of only having two weeks' holiday I suppose. I have made sure I have plenty of time for the whole 'experience'. This made the book solely about the hike.

I suppose after reading so many, this was fine for me, but if you want more about Kathmandu, then go elsewhere.

The book is black and white and is self-published through Amazon like a lot of these are. The author is a court reporter in the States and you can tell by the writing style. There are lots of one-line paragraphs, and with the large text and generous spacing, it looks like you're reading a photocopied book created on MS Word. However, the book is relatively cheap, only £8 on Amazon as I write, so worth a go.

One thing I really like about the book is the number of pictures. They are littered throughout and they really give you a feel for the things he is describing. At a generous size too, you can make out the content, even with the print quality not being great. Some of the pictures are of the scenery and some of the people and buildings he encounters.

I enjoyed the book. He goes into great detail about certain things, e.g. trying to leave Lukla which turns into a little French farce – I do hope the weather is clear for me. He also has some good descriptions of part of the walk and his feelings – he doesn't hide when he is annoyed. Later on, you can tell he is tired and his journal becomes more sketchy, e.g. he doesn't describe his walk back to Lukla from Namche Bazaar which has been featured in most of the books I have read.

I do get frustrated that he seems to spend most of his time in the lodges, mainly in his room. However, he travels alone with a guide, and I think this definitely affected his sociability and therefore his mood. There were people along the way to encourage him, but that camaraderie was missing from his trip. He doesn't seem to have much fun. Until four days before reading this, I was due to travel alone, but now have a walking partner (see main text), and after reading this, I am glad I have. I think in some of the darker moments, having a constant backup will be vital.

As of yet, I have not read any first-hand experiences of anyone who has actually climbed to the top of Kala Patthar to see the sunrise over Everest the morning after reaching Base Camp, and Myers was no different. I have been very sure that I was going to do it – after all, I am never going to this region again, but reading about everybody's failures is putting doubt in my mind even before I start. I hope my guide and new walking companion want to do it so FOMO kicks in and I slay the doubt with my imaginary sword.

I was very disturbed by one of Myers' 'facts', saying that Lukla has four plane crashes a year. It was anecdotal so I looked it up. He did go in 2014, versus my trip in 2022, so timings may have changed the figures. In the last ten years, there have been ten crashes across the whole of Nepal – the most recent as I write was on the flight from Pokhara to Jomson in May 2022. Terrible news for those on board and their families of course, but oddly reassuring that I wasn't taking as big a risk as the author reported. With 40,000 people travelling to Base Camp each year, that is a massive amount of flights that are successful.

In summary, the overriding message from this book is that it is going to be cold and hard. I go six weeks earlier in the year to the author (late September rather than mid-November) so hopefully the cold will not be as bad for me, but I am not ditching my fleece sleeping bag liner now, despite the bulk. As for the hardship, I am ready for it. I know it is coming, I just need to get through it.

Other books to mention which I have read:

***Beyond Possible* by Nimsdai Purja, 9781529312263** – this is the story of one man's dream of breaking the record for climbing all 14 mountains that reach above 8,000m. It is also a Netflix documentary, *14 Peaks*. If you want a story about great perseverance, mountaineering skill and teamwork set in some of the most inhospitable landscapes on earth then read this or watch the Netflix show. He is incredible.

***The Ascent of Everest* by John Hunt, 1954** – Hunt was the expedition leader on the first successful climb of Everest. Sir Edmund Hillary and Tenzing Norgay took the plaudits, rightly so, but it was Hunt that was the brains behind the organisation. Without bad weather, Hillary wouldn't even have been the first on top, as he was the second 'foreign' summiteer chosen – the first had his attempt curtailed and it just shows how history judges you as I cannot even remember his name. I read it 20 years ago, and was riveted. Definitely worth adding to your list.

***Annapurna: The First Conquest of an 8,000-Meter Peak* by Maurice Herzog, 1953 – 9780005212158** – another one I read many years ago and still remember vividly. It is bleak and inspiring. Herzog describes the difficulties of going into the death zone brilliantly. With all we know about kit now, it is almost beyond belief how these pioneers went into their expeditions with such limited clothing technology. The ending is sad (he loses his gloves on the descent with all the issues associated with that) but ultimately he gets down to tell the tale. I was gripped.

THE TRIP

20 AND 21 SEPTEMBER 2022
DAY 1 AND 2: MANCHESTER TO DOHA, THEN TO KATHMANDU

So the day had arrived and I wasn't going to cut it fine. Jane had a busy day's work so we agreed to set off at 8.30am, to arrive in Manchester before 11am, giving her time to get back and get on with her day. It was four hours before my flight at 3pm but there was plenty to do. Some last-minute checks – money, passports, hand luggage and we were off. It was really bittersweet as Jim got up early to come and see me off. It was a weird feeling knowing I was going on a great adventure, yet I said goodbye to him for the last time before he jets off for at least a year on an even greater one.

We arrived at Manchester airport with almost perfect timing, just as the second contestant had finished on Radio 2's PopMaster quiz. Everything stops for this and it probably made the final 15 minutes with Jane easier as we weren't concentrating on saying our final farewells for our longest time apart in the 30-odd years we have been together. It was a really tender moment at the concrete drop off zone. I will miss her immensely.

It was an uneventful time in the airport. The usual hour or so to go through bag drop off with Qatar Airlines and security and I could relax for an hour before the gate was called. It was getting very real.

As we were all sat around at the gate waiting for the call to board, one of the cabin crew was handing masks around. I politely declined but he insisted they were mandatory. I cannot believe this Covid theatre is still playing out. What are they trying to prove? That they are more caring and virtuous than other airlines? After a very stroppy text to Jane, ranting about my holiday being ruined, she rightly told me to calm down. Even though she wasn't there, she still called it right. So at the boarding gate, I told them that masks made me very anxious and could I have an exemption. It wasn't far off being correct, but the anxiety is caused by the thought of having to wear one rather than the physical claustrophobia that I claimed. The check-in staff member said he'd call the company doctor but after a couple of phone calls and no response, he marked me down as not needing one and he printed off new boarding cards with the magic words, 'mask exempt'.

The journey itself was long, over six hours. It was pleasant enough though. No annoying kid behind me messing with the tray table, and a pleasant Thai girl and Filipino lady in the same row. There was no desire from anyone to chat for the whole journey, but enough to keep the solitude at bay. I thought I'd be fine for six hours. I am not bored easily, but it did drag. I even resorted to watching *Les Misérables* for the final part of the flight. A good, long, enjoyable film to pass two and a half hours. Looking around the flight, most people had their masks off completely or below their chins.

Doha airport is massive. Nearly everyone I spoke to was transiting through – Bangkok, Bali, somewhere I'd never heard of. Our flight was 30 minutes late arriving but I still had plenty of time, nearly two hours. But I panicked. On the airport departures board was a flight to Kathmandu an hour earlier than I had thought. Had I misread it? I legged it the half a mile to the gate, catching up with a guy I recognised from my flight who had done the same. We compared tickets as final boarding was called. Mine was a different flight number. After a wait for the departures board to flick round, it was confirmed, I had another hour. There were two flights to Kathmandu. Phew. Especially as I needed the loo. I also had time to take in my surroundings. There were many shops, restaurants and bars – there was even a small WH Smith, a staple of British airports for many years.

The flight was on an older plane with less legroom but I was near the doors so an easy exit in an emergency (you always have to look). Except there was an elderly Nepalese couple next to me. Lovely people but not going to leave in a hurry. Maybe my experience at Kathmandu airport in 1996 was still uppermost in my mind.

The highlight of the flight, and possibly of any flight I've ever taken, was as dawn broke. I had deliberately picked the left side of the plane as I assumed we'd fly directly west to east and it paid off. We were flying at 40,000ft, just to make sure we were above the Himalayas, and as we passed alongside the mountain range, Dhaulagiri thrust out of the clouds like Poseidon (or Godzilla if you're into monsters) rising from the depths of the oceans. It wasn't just Dhaulagiri though; Annapurna 1, Manaslu and a few others showed their majesty. Truly stunning.

After a holding pattern of at least 540 degrees we plotted a course between the foothills and the ground changed from steep-sided paddy fields to the flat plain of the Kathmandu valley and we landed.

It took about an hour to get out of the airport. After hearing horror stories about the queues it was simple. Go to the automated kiosks to apply for your visa, take the receipt (or photo of the screen) to the payment counter, pay your US$50 for the visa and then through passport control. I am never in a great hurry, so was one of the last to complete this process and it was fun to get to the luggage belt and seeing everyone who had rushed through still waiting. I think I got my two cases before most people. Classic hare and the tortoise.

My tour company, Outfitters Nepal, had arranged for pickup and I was greeted by Indra, who turned out to be my guide. I've never had my name on a greetings board at an airport before. The taxi took 40 minutes as the roads were

With NG at the Outfitters Nepal offices in Khatmandu.

View from the small balcony next to my room at the Moonlight Hotel.

rammed with cars, buses, motorbikes and people. A few policemen seemed to be in control of the junctions, but it was hard to tell. I did love it though. No one gets angry as everyone drives the same so they go a lot slower. Our really structured road system could learn something from this.

A quick check into the terrific Moonlight Hotel and Indra took me to the Outfitters offices to meet Raj and the chairman, NG. After months of emailing, the chance to meet in person was lovely. It is a small operation, but very professional and highly recommended – so far. Indra then took me to get a Nepalese SIM card. That took longer than getting out the airport. Make sure you leave time for this if you're on a schedule. The guy organising it had to keep phoning his dad for advice. It's good to see dads are useful, wherever in the world we are.

The rest of the day has been settling into Kathmandu life. It is hot, bustling, in your face mayhem, but as a contrast to everyday life in the UK, it is fabulous. After having lots to eat on the planes, I didn't fancy any food, so a power nap, walk around Thamel and Durbar Square, my last two beers for a fortnight (Everest lager of course) and it's back at the hotel writing this and getting ready for a 5.30am leave time for the main event, the flight to Lukla at 7.30am. I'll describe Kathmandu in more detail on my return, but I know I'll enjoy myself.

Thamel, the tourist area of Kathmandu.

Bustling Kathmandu.

22 SEPTEMBER 2022
DAY 3: KATHMANDU TO PHAKDING VIA LUKLA

After three years of planning, training, packing and delays it was D-Day. And it was either going to be exhilarating or terrifying as the trip involved a flight to Lukla, the 'most dangerous airport in the world'. I didn't sleep well, probably still on UK time or just nervous energy, yet I was jolted by the 4.45am alarm call. At least I slept a bit it seemed. I was down in reception waiting for Indra and the taxi by 5.15am, for a 5.30am pick-up of Anton who was staying in a different hotel. I asked Indra if my bag was too heavy. It seemed it but my scales had broken so I couldn't weigh it. He assured me it would be fine. It nearly wasn't. The rest of my stuff was left in the hotel for free, awaiting my return.

We retraced our route the previous day back to the airport. So much less busy at 6am than at peak rush hour. The streets were just coming to life but were still relatively empty and you could see the rebuilding that was going on after the earthquake. There was a debate between the driver and Indra about where Anton's hotel was, it shows that blokes the world over like nothing more than a discussion on the best way from A-Z. Anton got on the minibus after a confusion over where the actual hotel was (it seems neither of them were right). I immediately knew we'd get on. Although not a football fan, we do have magical scenery to discuss. I'm sure we'll be fine.

At the airport, we went to the 'small plane' terminal. My moniker, but pretty accurate. With names like Buddha Air, Yeti Air and Tara Air, these weren't your big international jet engine planes. Check-in was also a little more chaotic. We were over the luggage limit and Indra spent a couple of minutes haggling. As my bag was 15kg and not 10kg, I stumped up the 850 rupees to make sure it stayed on the plane. It sounds a lot, but it was only £6 or so. Well worth it. The compromise apparently was that Indra's bag was going to come on the next flight.

THE TRIP

At the 'small planes' terminal in Kathmandu with Indra and Anton, waiting for the flight to Lukla.

Getting on the flight to Lukla.

We eventually boarded ten minutes after the flight take-off time passed but there was no long settling-in period. Indra also noticed that his bag made it after all. A quick safety brief from the stewardess which I couldn't hear and we were off. The plane was a twin prop with room for about 16 people. It was not quite full, probably why the bag made it. I got a window seat on the right at the front – lucky you think – but only four seats weren't window. I was right by the propeller and as we taxied down the runway, the noise and vibrations started to intensify. As we stopped ready for take-off, the engine revved to maximum and the brakes were released. Imagine a rollercoaster starting, or a Grand Prix car at the front of the grid. We were pushed back into our seats by the G-force and after a short time on the ground we lifted into the air. I was pleased that is was calm and relatively clear weather as the plane vibrated through the low clouds. What a trip though. Flying at only 3,500m, the detail of the landscape below was easy to make out, much more so than the journey in.

I thought it would be a flight where I would be dreading the landing but as the plane darted between the brooding foothills that towered above us, I found I was looking forward to it. It would have been nice to have been on the left-hand side

Safely landed at Lukla. The small Tata Air plane kept below the highest hills and landed very smoothly.

THE TRIP

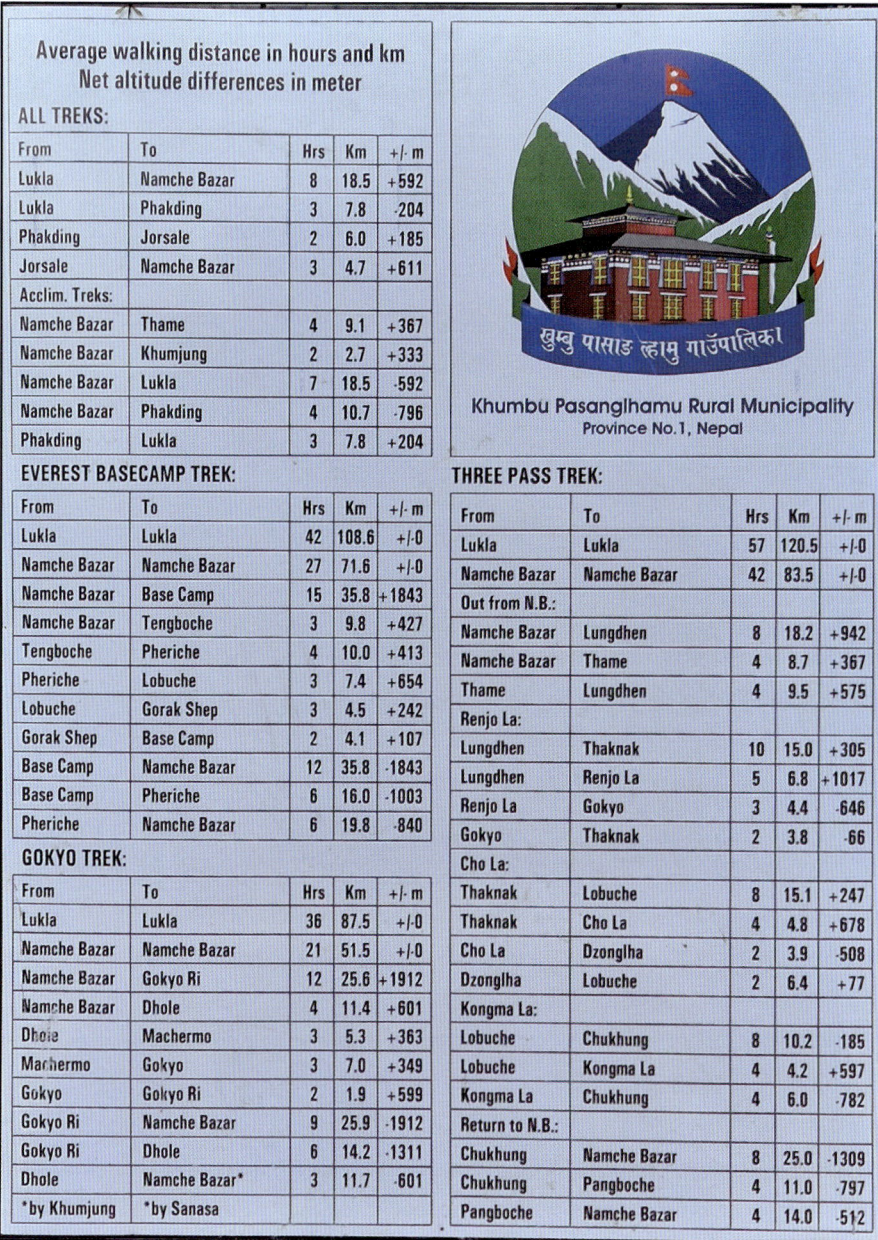

Average walking distance in hours and km Net altitude differences in meter				
ALL TREKS:				
From	To	Hrs	Km	+/- m
Lukla	Namche Bazar	8	18.5	+592
Lukla	Phakding	3	7.8	-204
Phakding	Jorsale	2	6.0	+185
Jorsale	Namche Bazar	3	4.7	+611
Acclim. Treks:				
Namche Bazar	Thame	4	9.1	+367
Namche Bazar	Khumjung	2	2.7	+333
Namche Bazar	Lukla	7	18.5	-592
Namche Bazar	Phakding	4	10.7	-796
Phakding	Lukla	3	7.8	+204
EVEREST BASECAMP TREK:				
From	To	Hrs	Km	+/- m
Lukla	Lukla	42	108.6	+/-0
Namche Bazar	Namche Bazar	27	71.6	+/-0
Namche Bazar	Base Camp	15	35.8	+1843
Namche Bazar	Tengboche	3	9.8	+427
Tengboche	Pheriche	4	10.0	+413
Pheriche	Lobuche	3	7.4	+654
Lobuche	Gorak Shep	3	4.5	+242
Gorak Shep	Base Camp	2	4.1	+107
Base Camp	Namche Bazar	12	35.8	-1843
Base Camp	Pheriche	6	16.0	-1003
Pheriche	Namche Bazar	6	19.8	-840
GOKYO TREK:				
From	To	Hrs	Km	+/- m
Lukla	Lukla	36	87.5	+/-0
Namche Bazar	Namche Bazar	21	51.5	+/-0
Namche Bazar	Gokyo Ri	12	25.6	+1912
Namche Bazar	Dhole	4	11.4	+601
Dhole	Machermo	3	5.3	+363
Machermo	Gokyo	3	7.0	+349
Gokyo	Gokyo Ri	2	1.9	+599
Gokyo Ri	Namche Bazar	9	25.9	-1912
Gokyo Ri	Dhole	6	14.2	-1311
Dhole	Namche Bazar*	3	11.7	-601
*by Khumjung	*by Sanasa			

Khumbu Pasanglhamu Rural Municipality
Province No.1, Nepal

THREE PASS TREK:				
From	To	Hrs	Km	+/- m
Lukla	Lukla	57	120.5	+/-0
Namche Bazar	Namche Bazar	42	83.5	+/-0
Out from N.B.:				
Namche Bazar	Lungdhen	8	18.2	+942
Namche Bazar	Thame	4	8.7	+367
Thame	Lungdhen	4	9.5	+575
Renjo La:				
Lungdhen	Thaknak	10	15.0	+305
Lungdhen	Renjo La	5	6.8	+1017
Renjo La	Gokyo	3	4.4	-646
Gokyo	Thaknak	2	3.8	-66
Cho La:				
Thaknak	Lobuche	8	15.1	+247
Thaknak	Cho La	4	4.8	+678
Cho La	Dzonglha	2	3.9	-508
Dzonglha	Lobuche	2	6.4	+77
Kongma La:				
Lobuche	Chukhung	8	10.2	-185
Lobuche	Kongma La	4	4.2	+597
Kongma La	Chukhung	4	6.0	-782
Return to N.B.:				
Chukhung	Namche Bazar	8	25.0	-1309
Chukhung	Pangboche	4	11.0	-797
Pangboche	Namche Bazar	4	14.0	-512

Only 108.6km to Base Camp and back.

as the white tops could be seen, but the scenery was still dramatic. As the small landing strip appeared amid the small town visible on the hillside we prepared for landing, and a few seconds later we were down. It seemed to stop really quickly, but very smooth. Like a lot of things in life, the anticipation was worse than the actual.

Indra took us for a cuppa and some food, and I sampled garlic soup for the first time. Not quite warm enough but tasty and enough to sustain me until lunchtime in Phakding – our destination for the day. I also took half a Diamox, which later necessitated a couple of inevitable loo stops along the way.

We met our porter, Sontos, and he started to strap all the kit on to his back. It must have weighed 30kg at least but he didn't seem to mind. We set off leaving Sontos chatting to a friend, but he soon passed us.

Exiting Lukla, through an arch dedicated to Pasang Lhamu, the first female Sherpa to climb Everest (https://en.wikipedia.org/wiki/Pasang_Lhamu_Sherpa), we passed a permit hut and police checkpoint which Indra sorted for us and we were off. A sign on the wall indicated distances to all the stop-off points and the extent of the trip became fully apparent.

I'd read a lot of books about the trip and I knew it would be downhill to begin with. I was surprised though that it was not as steep as I imagined. Having climbed lots of hills in my training, you know that steps indicate steepness, but most of the trip was on flatter paths. It was downhill for the first hour or so but nothing about the return trip worried me – but I did recognise I was feeling fresh and excited; would I feel the same on the way back up? We passed many prayer wheels, spinning them clockwise for good luck (always with your right hand, with the wheel on your right), and numerous Buddhist stone memorials to the dead, all ornately decorated with prayers. The daily Nepali life was going on around us. Donkeys carrying produce (mainly potatoes it seemed) were driven on by increasingly younger herdsmen. Farmers in the fields were tending their crops, and we even saw a young calf suckling on its mum in a field next to the path.

Indra was in no hurry and neither were we. The whole estimated time to Phakding was only three hours, so Anton and I took the opportunity to take lots of photos. It was slow going, but that was intentional. As we were getting to know each, Anton was calm and deliberate. He is an engineer and a German and we all know the typical stereotype about that. He didn't disappoint as he seemed to be weighing me up. After a while, he seemed to relax and I felt it wasn't just a one-way conversation. I was probably annoying him with my constant babble, but he was too polite to mention it if he felt it.

The path was generally downhill but there were a few undulations. I didn't find them difficult at all. Even at more than 2,500m it was fine, maybe all the training really was working. It was interesting to notice that different sections

THE TRIP

The animal porters on the way to Phakding. The path is not as steep as I had expected.

of the walk reminded me of different training walks. Dovedale in parts, Yorkshire Three Peaks in others. I suspect I will also draw on this experience on the steeper, longer parts.

There was never a major distance between lodges, shops, schools and prayer wheels. Life really is abundant up here. I felt for the places near Lukla, too close for us to stop when going downhill, too near for people to stop on their last section of their 11-day journey.

We eventually stopped for a cup of mint tea at Thadokoshi, approximately halfway. The views were incredible, and we hadn't even seen any mountains with snow on yet. I can't wait until we get higher and they become the backdrop. Anton noted that if you listened to the river and looked at the scenery, you could be in Italy.

What a start though. Indra explained the meaning behind the name of the river, Dudh Koshi, which stood for milk river. It was obvious why. The speed of the water cascading down from some of the highest peaks was churning the water so much it was just white foam on the surface. In places it would have been tempting to jump in for a cool off, but that would have been just silly – oh and life-threatening.

The weather started to break, and after extra sun cream in Thadokoshi, it began to rain slightly. Not enough to take out the waterproofs, or even to add a layer, but it does demonstrate how quickly the weather can change at this altitude.

Before we knew it, we were in Phakding, our destination for the day. It was only 1.15pm. Indra took us to the Trekkers Lodge, one of many ski chalet style lodges/

A picture which encapsulated Day 1 of the trek. Fantastic views, the Milk River below, a Buddhist Stupa and flag and a memorial to the dead.

The first night's stopover.

restaurants along the way and our destination for the night. It is common custom to eat where you stay so we ordered lunch. I had fried potatoes in, you guessed it, garlic. Delicious.

With a few hours to kill before dinner at 7pm. Anton and I went to our room and started to unpack a few things and have a hot shower. I will be trying to get as many of these as possible, until it becomes impossible, but it felt good. After rigging up the chargers into the electric socket with some insulation tape (great tip from one of my books) we replenished our phones and powerbanks before a walk around the village. From end to end it took about ten minutes. There was an Irish bar (there's always an Irish bar) and even a snooker hall, but neither of us were tempted.

So for the rest of the day it was spent relaxing. A couple of Scottish guys, Mark and Keith, were on our plane, and they are in the same lodge, so we chatted a lot to them. Then it was time to write this before dinner. With completion after the meal.

Stats for the day. Approximately 15,000 steps from Lukla to Phakding. A 200m descent over 4.8 miles, and my blood O_2 reading fluctuated from 97 per cent in Kathmandu to as low as 89 per cent at our halfway stop. After a couple of hours in

Phakding. The colour is everywhere in this region.

Phakding, it's back up to 93 per cent. I don't ache, even from the heavy day pack (about nine kilograms), and there are no signs of any altitude sickness symptoms. Anton is the same. I have drunk four litres of water plus about five cups of fruit tea. My target was five litres, so bang on track.

We'd ordered dinner straight after lunch and there was no doubt what either us were having. The dal bhat. Indra was our waiter, for the main course, the seconds (unlimited if you want it) and the dessert. Dal bhat is lentil soup and rice. With veggies and very spicy pickles it was really tasty, and even a few hours later writing this, my hunger is very satisfied. At the airport, Indra had been carrying a cardboard box and it was intriguing what was in it. We knew the answer when the dessert arrived – fresh sliced apple and pomegranate seeds. The porter had carried them all the way from Lukla, so at least his load will be slightly lighter tomorrow. Indra also briefed us on the day ahead. After an easy day today, it was going to get tougher.

I went outside in the hope of seeing a clear, starry night but the cloud cover put a stop to that. A WhatsApp video chat with Jane and Dan (who was home) and it was almost bed time. Some of the other trekkers were still chatting in the lodge, mainly to a couple who had come down from Base Camp and who were very keen

DAY 3: LUKLA TO PHAKDING

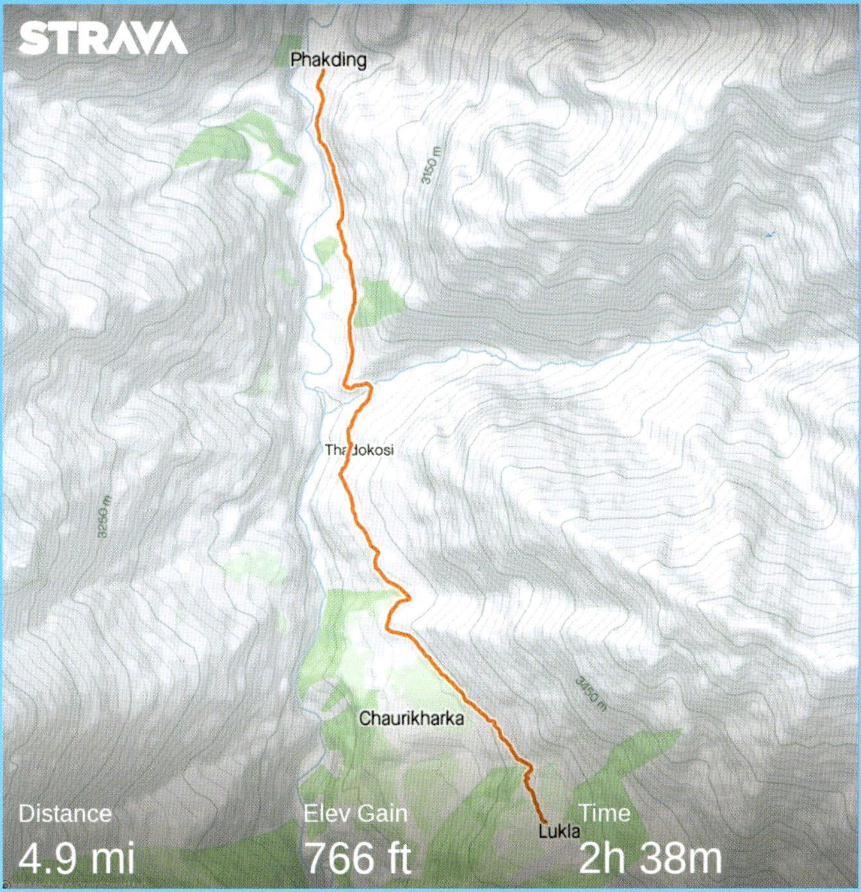

STRAVA

Phakding · Thadokosi · Chaurikharka · Lukla

Distance	Elev Gain	Time
4.9 mi	766 ft	2h 38m

Elevation

Elevation Gain	766 ft
Max Elevation	9,379 ft

Pace

Avg Pace	32:13 /mi
Moving Time	2:38:30
Avg Elapsed Pace	42:20 /mi
Elapsed Time	3:28:21
Fastest Split	29:09 /mi

The room at the Trekker's Lodge, basic but comfortable. Note the makeshift plug combination and Indra's mysterious box.

to tell their story. I wanted to experience it live so didn't get involved. Neither did Anton. So we said our farewells and bunked down for the night. There are three beds, so like proper blokes we have left the one in the middle free. I wonder who is going to blink first and go for the spare duvet and pillow.

It is going to be about eight degrees celsius tonight, so I have wrapped up in my skiing long johns and shell jogging trousers on my legs, and long-sleeved skin and long-sleeved top for my body. And socks of course. I am currently in my fleece sleeping bag liner, but not yet in my Outfitters supplied down sleeping bag. I'll leave it until/if I get cold or maybe I'll blag the spare duvet. I'll report tomorrow on whether it was a good tactic.

If Anton doesn't snore (he says he doesn't) I should sleep well after two nights of broken sleep.

It is only 9.30pm. It is classic early to bed, early to rise in the hills. Breakfast at 7am.

23 SEPTEMBER 2022
DAY 4: PHAKDING TO NAMCHE BAZAAR

When I first started teaching at Loughborough University, I was shown how to moderate a business game from Harvard which was designed to test students' communication and decision-making skills. In teams of five they had to climb a virtual Mount Everest. As part of the induction to the game there is an interview with an American mountaineer who has summited Everest and talks about his experience. Having watched it nearly a dozen times, the one part of his trip that fascinated me the most was his stop-off in Namche Bazaar. Today I was finally going there. Although it promised to be a demanding day (according to all the eye-witness books), I was really looking forward to the walk.

Having gone to bed so early and after little sleep previously, I thought I'd sleep like a baby. I did, only this baby was teething or had intermittent bouts of colic. Anton had no such worries; he fell asleep immediately and only woke up because the alarm started over nine hours later. According to Fitbit, I hit seven hours, but it didn't feel that much. It wasn't cold though. I didn't even use the sleeping bag provided or spare duvet.

Looking out the window it was overcast higher up but not too bad lower down. The forecast was light cloud and light breeze. Fingers crossed.

Breakfast was at seven so we could get going early on our seven-to-eight-hour day. Most others had the same idea. I had a Nepali breakfast, which had some chapatis, jam, fried potatoes and vegetables. I didn't quite know what to make of it as a combination, but it tasted okay if eaten separately.

After packing most of our gear the previous night, it didn't take long to be ready to go, so instead of an eight o'clock start, we were actually out 20 minutes early. Much to our delight, the weather was lifting and blue sky was starting to become the dominant colour above. My O_2 measure was 88 per cent, Anton's was 98 per cent. He really is a machine.

What a lovely day to wake up to. And our first suspension bridge to cross. There were many more to come.

The first half an hour was steady, with some up-and-down walking but nothing to bother us. Like day one of the trek, there were tea houses everywhere and even a very plush-looking German hotel complex. Anton seemed a bit bemused by this actually as everything else so far had been in English.

We followed the milk river again, and before the hour mark, a dark, menacing peak loomed across the river. I didn't fancy climbing that. A few more metres and a second peak appeared on the same hill. Imagine getting to that point and finding another higher one. Then there was a third, then a fourth, and then it appeared. At just over 6,600m high, Thamserku's white-topped peak sparkled in the morning sun. It was magnificent and could well have taken 'highlight of the day' there and then. The main reason for coming to Nepal was to see these colossal sights for real and Anton and I just stood transfixed for a few moments before realising we had to get good camera footage of it. I did try and plant it in my own internal memory bank so I wouldn't have to rely on the photos and videos – something I am conscious of.

Opposite and following page: Our first white-topped mountain of the trip. This is what we had come for and hopefully it was a taste of things to come.

We weren't walking especially quickly, just repeating the routine from the day before. No rush, lots of photos, going at each other's pace. Indra seemed to think we were going well though.

Round the next corner was one of many waterfalls that just appear from nowhere. There certainly isn't a lack of water in this part of the world. The difference with this is we were really near the bottom. It was within touching distance and the water was shallow enough to walk to. So of course I did. I thought I'd be able to

Getting close to the waterfall, lots of spray stopped me getting closer.

get my hand under the main stream but the invisible spray from an overhanging rock was very tangible as it sprayed me before my destination. It was so refreshing. Just up the hill were a couple of lodges and if I'd have been staying at one of them, I would have been (nearly) stripped off and gone under fully.

As we descended again from the lodges, Keith and Mark caught us up, Keith in his kilt. That's the Scots for you. He is trekking for charity too, and the kilt is part of it. They are becoming a much bigger part of our experience which is good for both of us. They are similar age to me and they met as recruits in the Marines years ago and have kept fit ever since. Keith is even doing a half-ironman in about a week after he gets back. I trained for the walk, he joked he is using the walk as training. Just as they were about to speed past us, we spotted a big pile of rubbish near the river, and being ignorant of Nepali ways we cursed the environmental impact. Indra explained that it is collected in a big pile and then when it is big enough it is burnt. On second look, there was a wall round it, obviously indicating a deliberate, self-contained pile. With no weekly rubbish collections we're so used to, this was a practical solution.

Another exciting thing to report was that I have started to look forward to the suspension bridges, even with my fear of heights. There are many of them along the way, and with this fear I thought I would be clinging on for dear life, probably with my eyes shut. They don't bother me, and I can even look through the metal strips underfoot now. Mind over matter of course. I may try and channel that when things get really tough.

Another piece of Nepali engineering was at the side the milk river, but a particularly ferocious stretch. A small water mill had been built to harness the power to grind the buckwheat being grown in the region. It must have been going like the clappers such was the speed of the water.

After another uphill stretch we reached the village of Monjo at 2,850m. I took my pack off to look for my reading glasses and couldn't find them. I had had them that morning, and was sure I'd packed them. It is going to be a small issue, especially writing this journal which I am doing through a little blurring. I will definitely need to check names in the edit. Jane says I lose things all the time, and I always fight back saying of course I don't. Maybe she is right after all (my parents, children and friends are also nodding at this point).

Just after Monjo was the entrance to Sagarmatha National Park. It is 3,000 rupees for foreigners, about £20, but as it was part of the trip price, Indra dealt with it. While waiting for the admin, I read the board which detailed the prices for sports inside the park's boundary. They were really cheap, including banjy (sic) jumping for only seven dollars. Not sure where the elastic would be attached though.

A grand archway led us into the park and an immediate steep but short descent, before another suspension bridge. As a village loomed ahead, we suggested to

THE TRIP

The entrance to the Sagarmatha National Park. Very untroubled and relaxed.

Loads to do, including Banjy Jumping.

SAGARMATHA NATIONAL PARK ENTRY FEE

S.N.	Details	Fees		
		Nepalese Citizen	SAARC Countries Citizen	Other Foreign Citizen
1	Entry (Admission) Fee (per person) (Inclusive of VAT) Note: The minor below 10 years of age shall not be charged	NRs. 100.00	NRs. 1500.00	NRs. 3000.00
2	Entry Fee for Tourist Porters (Inclusive of VAT)	NRs. 25.00		
3	Guide License Annual Fee (Inclusive of VAT)	NRs. 1500		
4	Helicopter landing Fee (Inclusive of VAT)	NRs. 3000		
5	Helicopter Hovering Fee (Inclusive of VAT)	NRs. 3000		

Sagarmatha National Park Adventure Tourism Activities Fee

S.N.	Details	Unit	Fees		
			Nepalese Citizen	SAARC Countries Citizen	Other Foreign Citizen
1	Sky Diving	Per person	NRs. 500/-	NRs. 2000/-	USD 100/- or Equivalent NRs.
2	Hot Air Ballooning	Per person	NRs. 500/-	NRs. 2000/-	USD 100/- or Equivalent NRs
3	Microlight Flight	Per person	NRs. 500/-	NRs. 2000/-	USD 100/- or Equivalent NRs
4	Paragliding	Per person	NRs. 250/-	NRs. 1000/-	USD 50/- or Equivalent NRs
5	Para Motoring	Per person	NRs. 250/-	NRs. 1000/-	USD 50/- or Equivalent NRs
6	Skiing	Per person	NRs. 200/-	NRs. 1000/-	USD 50/- or Equivalent NRs
7	Rafting/Canoeing	Per person	NRs. 500/-	NRs. 2000/-	USD 100/- or Equivalent NRs
8	Bangy Jumping	Per person	NRs. 100/-	NRs. 200/-	USD 7/- or Equivalent NRs
9	Mountain Biking	Per person	Free	NRs. 200/-	USD 7/- or Equivalent NRs
10	Football, Volleyball and Other Athletics	Per person Permission period	Free	NRs. 200/-	USD 7/- or Equivalent NRs
11	Camping	Per person Per Entry	NRs. 100/-	NRs. 1,000/-	NRs.1,500/-
12	film & documentary Shooting		Nrs. 10,000/-	NRs. 50,000/-	USD 1500/-

N.B. In case of shooting the cinema (documentry, film) using drone, additional 25 (twenty five) percent fee shall be levied.

Use of drone (UAV) is prohibited inside National Park

Indra that we'd like to stop for a cuppa. No need, it was the pre-planned lunch stop. We'd taken two hours 40 minutes to get there, quicker than the three and a half to four expected by Indra. He had based his estimate on our speed yesterday. Now we were in our stride.

At the restaurant in Jarshelle we sat near a young couple from our plane so we had a brief chat with them. In fact the whole day had been a lot busier. As planes arrive in Lukla every hour or so, everyone sets off at different times. On this leg, everyone leaves Phakding about the same early time. It was a much better atmosphere throughout the day. After another garlic soup for me, it was time to relax and enjoy the view in the blazing sun. More sun cream was applied and the next part of the trip discussed. Five minutes later we were inside putting our macs on as the rain came. Five minutes after setting off, they weren't needed any more. A really quick downpour luckily. I didn't fancy the climb to Namche in the pouring rain.

We were at 2,800m in Jarshelle, so had a 600m ascent to go. Less than one of the Yorkshire Three Peaks. I was confident I could do it, but was bracing myself for an horrific slog. Most of the books had talked about how difficult this would be. I braced myself for counting 100 steps before each rest. We predicted how long it would take us to get to the lodge in Namche. Indra, with inside knowledge had to go first and said 2.10pm – only six and a half hours from start to finish with a long lunch. He must have been impressed. I was optimistic as usual and went for 2pm, Anton 2.30pm. They're getting used to my silly games. We even had a bet on what colour the roof of our lodge was in Namche. Indra wasn't allowed to enter. Neither of us won.

After a pleasant 20-minute stroll along the river's edge, a stone staircase started upwards. This was it, the two hours from hell. I made a short video declaring it, full of melodrama expecting it to wind upward for 600m. After about 100 steps it was over and the path went down again. Doh!

After seeing the snowy peaks earlier, the next real excitement for me was crossing the Hillary bridge, suspended high above the river. Surely the scariest one yet. There was another steep climb to reach it, so at the top, as an excuse for a rest we waited for about 20 donkeys to cross. They weren't scared, or at least they never let on. They raise them tough in the mountains. Keith and Mark caught up again and without a rest, crossed just before us. It wasn't scary and it was another experience knocked off my EBC to-do list. Surely I cannot be enjoying myself this much.

With Anton on the way to the Hillary Bridge (the highest one). The climb to Namche was near.

https://goodkarmatrekking.com/travel-news-and-updates/hillary-suspension-bridge-on-the-way-to-namche-bazar

https://www.youtube.com/watch?v=lgEx6Y0akw8

After the bridge, the real climb began. After seeing us climb the steps and then up to the bridge, Indra was impressed and said we'd be a lot quicker than he thought. At 2,935m we were close to my highest point ever in Nepal, and only another 500m of ascent to go. Surely this was where it would get painful now.

The donkeys crossing the Hillary Bridge. If they could do it, so could I.

It was relentless but it wasn't steps for most of it. The path switch backed every 20m or so and I called when I needed a break. Anton is only 70kg and a highly fit semi-pro motor sports driver. He has 14 years and more than 30kg on me. Indra never needs a rest. In fact, without me I don't think they would have stopped at all. I think I deserved to be the one calling the shots for stopping. Anton was great, very patient, and after a while he even intuitively knew when I'd be ready.

But my training was really paying off. The breaks were short and I got my breath back easily, even as we crossed the 3,000m barrier when oxygen falls to 70 per cent of sea level. I do breathe heavily and sweat a lot on hills, so although I felt fine, Anton kept looking at me as if I was going to keel over at any time. After today, he may look past the fat boy outward impression and know I am very capable of the endurance needed for this walk.

It carried on like this for only about 40 minutes when the viewpoint for the first sight of Everest appeared. You had to look between the trees and here it was – a completely cloudy sky. Tomorrow maybe, at the appropriately named Everest View Hotel on our acclimatisation hike, we'd have our first view of the top of the world. Our new Scottish friends were there also. Another short walk and another checkpoint. It had been steep, but nowhere near as bad as I'd imagined. Maybe the other eye-witness accounts were over egging it for dramatic effect. Or maybe all my training really was working wonders.

As I pondered how far Namche would be from the checkpoint, a fellow hiker pointed it out through the trees, just around the corner, about 300m away on a relatively flat path. We'd made it. Was that it? It had been no worse than the first part of Scafell Pike in the Lake District, and I had been up there eight times. I didn't need to run or lift weights to be fit enough for this part. I just needed miles in the legs and I'd certainly done that.

Namche was everything and more than I could have hoped for. Colourful, vibrant and beautiful. It was built around a basin with layer upon layer of lodges, shops, bars and local houses. It was even home to the world's highest dentists. The eyewitness accounts talked about the trudgery of more steps to get to the accommodation, and there were some it's true, but another overblown scare story as far as I was concerned.

At the entrance to the village was a large stupa, next to a volleyball court where locals seemed to be using it consistently. Next to snooker, was this the national sport?

Indra took us to our lodge, the 8,848m lodge, so named after the height of Everest. It was only 1.40pm. What an achievement! Mark and Keith were there too. After a plate of fried potatoes and a pot of lemon tea, Anton and I went for another hot shower and changed for a wander round Namche. I was keen to go to the top of the town – sleep lower than your highest point has always been a mountaineering mantra, and Anton joined me. As we headed up, the full scale

The path to Namche, long and uphill, but not too difficult. Mark and Keith on the left of the picture. Keith in his kilt.

of the town became apparent and we zig-zagged around the layers. We estimated we'd added at least another 50m to our ascent for the day. While walking we saw a new building being erected. There was a constant tap, tap, tap sound as many people were chipping away at stone blocks to make them the right size for the construction. It was a constant sound, and strangely reassuring. Another reminder though how life in the hills was not conventional; no pallets of bricks here, it was done by hand.

There will be time for shopping on our way back through Namche on the return journey so we just browsed mainly, mentally ticking off presents and memorabilia we would buy on our return. I bought a toothbrush as I'd somehow lost that too (go on, say it). I did buy an Everest Base Camp baseball cap for £3 to wear from now on. I know I'll have to bin it if I don't get there, but I really think it adds to my experience and integration into the landscape. Small things, but nonetheless…

Back at the hostel, Keith was not in a great place. Lack of appetite, headaches and nausea. He'd hardly drunk any water, about one and a half litres. Could he have altitude sickness? His guide was really concerned and put a large flask of water and a lemon tea in front of him. The O$_2$ reader showed a healthy 90-plus which was some comfort, but the nagging feeling was there. My friend from home, Reg, had read that altitude sickness was not just physical but could be contagious, so despite drinking five litres of water, I felt a slight throb of the head. As soon as Keith went for a nap I felt no effect at all. Maybe Reg was right.

As a quack doctor I think he actually has sunstroke as he didn't wear a hat or drink enough. Let's hope that's true. He couldn't manage dinner, another delicious and plentiful dal bhat. At around 8.45pm everyone packed off to bed and while

The entrance to Namche, the many layers built into the hills.

Namche at dusk from our hotel balcony, a beautiful sight.

Anton checked his phone I began today's entry. I'm on an iPad and I am typing with one finger. Anton hates it as it isn't efficient. So German. He has a point. It's taken me ages tonight.

A shorter day tomorrow so an 8am breakfast. Oh and my new toothbrush broke in three places before I'd even used it.

Stats for the day: 33,290 steps. Five litres at least of water. Closing O_2, 88 per cent. Not aching at all, and no sign of altitude sickness. Same for Anton. we climbed 3,938ft in total with all the ups and downs. It took five hours 53 minutes from start to finish and we're now at an altitude of 3,400m.

DAY 4: PHAKDING TO NAMCHE BAZAAR

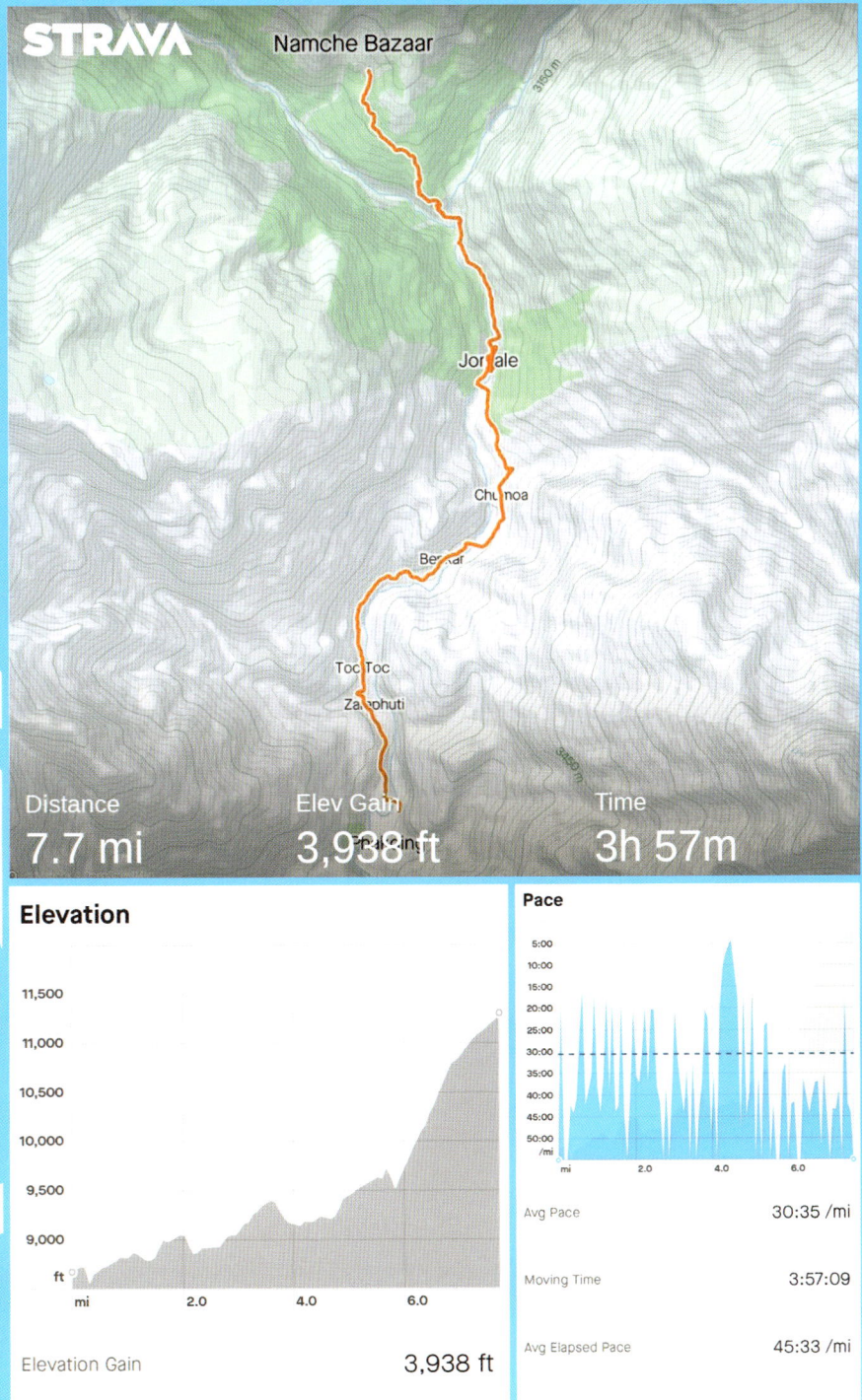

STRAVA

Distance: 7.7 mi
Elev Gain: 3,938 ft
Time: 3h 57m

Elevation

Elevation Gain: 3,938 ft
Max Elevation: 11,303 ft

Pace

Avg Pace: 30:35 /mi
Moving Time: 3:57:09
Avg Elapsed Pace: 45:33 /mi
Elapsed Time: 5:53:16
Fastest Split: 19:34 /mi

24 SEPTEMBER 2022
DAY 5: ACCLIMATISATION HIKE FROM NAMCHE TO THE EVEREST VIEW HOTEL

When I was in junior school, so aged ten or 11, I read *The Starlight Barking*, Dodi Smith's follow up to *101 Dalmations*. It was about how dogs have a sort of dog telegraph system where one starts barking a message, the next one then repeats it, then the next, until the message reaches its intended target. I thought it was so lovely and hoped it was true. Last night, I could have easily strangled the one below our hotel that was obviously dictating the dog version of *War and Peace*. It lasted well over two hours and it was incessant. I'd not gone to sleep until half past 11, partly because I was writing yesterday's diary, but mainly because we were getting up an hour later today. After only about six hours' sleep, with less than an hour of deep sleep, I was really tired. We were on the top floor, I had ear plugs in and I had a bandana around my head and ears. It was like the princess and the pea. I could have been in a soundproofed recording studio and I reckon I'd have heard it. Even Anton heard it, and he sleeps like a log.

After yesterday's breakfast smorgasbord, I went Scottish with porridge, and it was lovely. Keith and Mark were already at breakfast, with Keith now operating at '90 per cent capacity' which was a real relief. Maybe it was sunstroke after all. We got ourselves changed ready for an acclimatisation day, a round trip via the Everest View Hotel (EVH). After missing out yesterday we hoped we could at least catch a glimpse of the mighty peak. The weather was decent, white clouds and blue skies, so we had a chance.

Expecting a relatively easy day, we started a straight walk up a few hundred steps to the very top of the village. With no warm-up and having finished breakfast only ten minutes earlier, I needed a rest after about five minutes. It was embarrassing.

After 15 minutes or so, we entered under an arch and the path flattened out. I had heard about the statue to Tenzing Norgay, alongside Sir Edmund Hillary, the first man to climb Everest, but I had forgotten all about it. I'm so glad Indra took

A beautiful morning, with the impressive tribute to Tenzing Norgay and the final view of the snowy mountain tops for a while.

us there. It was lovely. The real bonus though was seeing a few white-capped peaks in the skyline, including a brief glimpse of Lhotse, Everest's little brother, but still over 8,400m. It was an unexpected treat and my early lethargy soon dissipated.

The main point of the day was to get to the Everest View Hotel at 3,880m, about 440m higher than Namche. It seemed as though we were doing all the elevation at the beginning and the hard work returned. Indra was keen to get past a large group at the bottom of the path, so we had a quick short cut up a steep path and appeared 20m ahead of them. The next hour was tough. Another switchback route like yesterday, but instead of it being on a path, it was steps – much more energy intensive, and an indicator of its steepness. I channelled my inner Ben Nevis, and started a slow climb. I followed my training: 100 steps, then a rest. Only at this altitude, the rest stops were nearer to 30 seconds than ten seconds in the UK. Still quicker than most people on the path, but slower than Anton and Indra. They put no pressure on me to go faster; in fact they encourage me to go at my own pace, but I feel I need to go quicker for them. I was actually pleased when we got stuck behind another party for five minutes. I was sweating again and breathing heavily, but I was feeling it a lot more than yesterday. It was hard.

The cloud was drawing in. Namche had almost disappeared. Note the steepness of the path to the left of the picture.

I must have been doing better than I thought, as we got chatting to a guy from Singapore, about my age, who loved English football. He'd even heard of the Mighty Rams so I let him off being a Manchester United fan. All the way up to the hotel he kept pointing to me and saying to his guide, 'Here is the really fit one.' I didn't feel it but I took the compliment.

We weren't getting excited about seeing Everest even as we got towards the hotel. The mist had got up and was swirling constantly. We could make out Namche in places as it was below the clouds, but anything high was obscured. Even the great views at the Tenzing statue would have disappeared by now.

We passed a yoga retreat with some tourists taking coffee and a museum which we didn't enter. The terrain had flattened by now and the narrow path was close to the edge and a steep drop. It didn't bother me. My fear of heights was improving. Round the corner, the hotel appeared. We'd made it; 3,880m.

We still went for a drink on the terrace and kept hoping for a break in the clouds but it never happened. I introduced Anton to 'proper tea' rather than fruit tea which he'd only drunk so far. We all shared a pot for 750 rupees, about £5. There was still only one tea bag in, despite it being a medium pot, so it was never going to be strong enough for a first timer. I think I lost him when discussing the

We'd made it to the EVH, a hard journey for me, but not Anton and Indra. No chance of seeing Everest though.

concept of 'builders' tea'. Another British tradition he tried was the biscuit dunk. He'd never done it and was nearly 40. I had some Lidl oat biscuits in my bag and we shared them. I think he liked the dunking much more than the taste of the tea. Indra also enjoyed the dunking. They are good joiner inners.

It was getting busy in the hotel, as the other acclimatisers reached their destination. They seemed really disappointed that they couldn't see Everest, as if the hotel would magic the clouds away. I know it's a five-star, but even the Japanese owners didn't have the power to control the weather.

Indra had a round trip planned, back around the other side of the hill we'd just climbed, past the Yeti Museum, rather than coming back down the same way. I definitely wanted to see that. Turning right out of the hotel we started to descend and the mist cleared a little. We were approaching what would be my favourite part of the day.

As we passed down a dirt path, we saw our first yak, chilling on the grass. He then rolled over and started to scratch his back on the grass. It was comical as he was so massive. As the village of Khumjung approached, the plots of farmland were framed by dry-stone walls and resembled parts of the British countryside. The main crop was potato and the whole village seemed to be involved in it one way or other. It was

The village of Khumjung, probably the only place we saw on the trek that wasn't completely set up for the tourist industry.

a gentle walk, and the three of us strolled in quiet contemplation, rather than feeling that we had to make conversation. A comfortable silence had descended showing how easy we were feeling with each other.

Almost a suburb of Khumjung, we entered Solukhumbu, and passed the Samten Choling Monastery. Indra asked us if we wanted to go in, so we paid our 300 rupees and entered. Behind a curtain was the inner sanctum which meant removing our boots. The scene inside was extremely colourful. Statues of Hindu gods were plenty and the colours were vivid. The centrepiece was the Yeti scalp. It was 'genuine' of course. A well spent £2.50. Not sure it was the Yeti Museum I had read about as that was the only mention of the mythological creature. Maybe there's two yetis knocking about without their scalps. A bit careless if you ask me. Outside were some huge prayer wheels which I had to spin. They were taller than me and I am six feet.

We walked past the Sir Edmund Hillary school, out for the holidays so no one around, but obviously a big deal for the locals. His influence is everywhere – Lukla airport, bridges, schools, medical stations – he really didn't just rest on his achievement, he used his newfound fame and influence for good. What an incredible man he was.

Previous page and above: Samten Choling Monastery. Incredible colours and the famous Yeti Scalp as its centrepiece.

As we exited the village, there was a huge Buddha eyes stupa, looking down on a long line of Buddhist memorial tablets. A real example of how the Buddha eyes knit things together in harmony.

It was then a 20-minute climb up a reasonably steep section to the basin above the village before a 30-minute descent into Namche on less obvious paths. We were accompanied by a dog which had trailed us since Khumjung. Not sure how he'd have found his way home, it must have been three miles back to where he'd picked us up. We saw some building work going on down this route and porters were carrying large loads of wooden beams to aid the infrastructure. There was even a JCB in one of the locations. It had to have been helicoptered down – some more great logistics to aid development in those hard to reach places in the world.

As we entered Namche, Anton and I fancied lunch at a different place to the hostel, so we ended up in The Hungry Yak, the highest live music bar in the world, which had been promoted along the route from Phakding. First the dentist, then the live music. Namche has 'the highest' records for everything it seemed. We were the only customers but the food was good, the welcome was warm, and the music (for me, American blues) was great.

With the massive prayer wheel at the Choling Monastery.

Not much else to report for the day. I had a Coke craving so searched out a shop that sold Zero. It was 400 rupees. 'Only' about £3. I even splashed out on a packet of Lays crisps. What indulgence. I also managed to get a pair of reading glasses from the pharmacy. Not quite my prescription, but I'm visual again. I even found my original toothbrush. Happy days all round.

I returned back to the hostel in the light rain and mist. I hope the weather holds out for the rest of the trip. I'm not confident on my waterproof jacket and I don't

The view of Namche from above. Even with the cloud obscuring the hills beyond, it was a fabulous view.

want to be soggy for days. The chance of getting things dry will be slim from now. I tried to buy one, but their idea of XL didn't match the UK one so I left empty-handed. I do have a couple of 'festival' ponchos which should help if it got bad.

A pleasant evening with Mark and Keith again, and the customary dal bhat and it's an early night having written most of this in the afternoon. A five-or six-hour day to Tengboche (Teng-bow-shay, with bow as in bow and arrow) tomorrow. It should be mild ups and downs until the last couple of hours. A 600m climb to the village. Almost a repeat of the climb to Namche. At least I'll be warmed up by then so should avoid the repeat of this morning.

Stats for the day. A little skewed as Strava got confused in the fog adding about four miles to the log. Definitely 25,231 steps in the day, and 239 floors on Fitbit. A five-hour round trip which was longer than expected. Possibly 2,607ft total elevation in the day. Half a Diamox in both the morning and the evening, four and a half litres of water, 500ml of Coke and a few teas. CO_2 reading in the 90s – morning and at bedtime. Anton also showing no signs.

Going to be in bed by 9pm, so hopefully a much better night's sleep. Breakfast at 7am. Now it's getting into the serious part. I need to be on top form.

DAY 5: ACCLIMATISATION HIKE NAMCHE BAZAAR

STRAVA

Distance	Elev Gain	Time
10.7 mi	2,607 ft	3h 16m

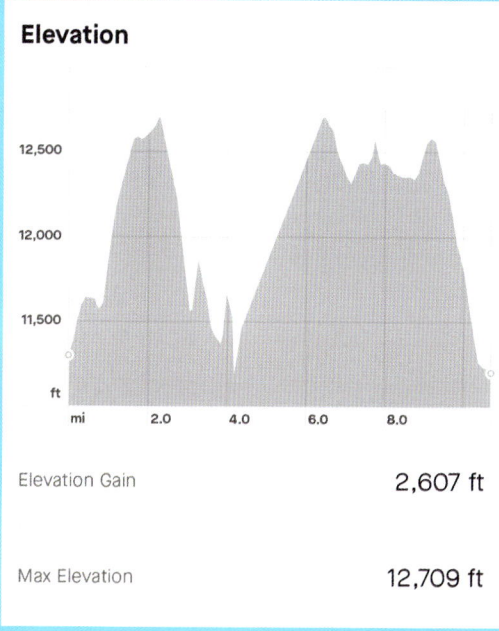

Elevation

Elevation Gain: 2,607 ft

Max Elevation: 12,709 ft

Pace

Avg Pace	18:19 /mi
Moving Time	3:16:03
Avg Elapsed Pace	28:58 /mi
Elapsed Time	5:10:00
Fastest Split	14s /mi

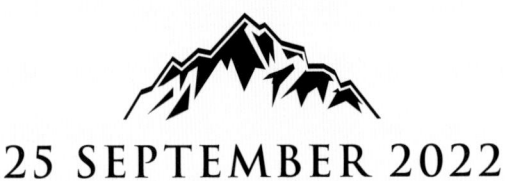

25 SEPTEMBER 2022

DAY 6: NAMCHE BAZAAR TO TENGBOCHE

First the good news. No Starlight Barking. Either the dog had been beaten to death for keeping the whole hostel awake the previous night or he was inside napping. I suspect it was the latter as the rain and mist that had started early evening intensified throughout the night and he wanted to stay warm and dry. As we were on the top floor (great for views), the rain banged against the tin roof (bad for sound). In theory the rhythmic sound of rain should be soothing. In reality, it was another contributor to my run of poor sleep. I sound like I'm banging on (a bit like the rain) and I suppose I am, but it isn't getting me down. As soon as I get up, my inner SAS kicks in and I get on with the day and I feel fine until bedtime again. Some of my long drives to the training walks (16-hour days) are really paying off.

We couldn't see Namche out the window. It was less than 50m away, but the fog had stayed, even if the rain had slowed down. Coming to Nepal at this time of year does leave you open to this as it is the back end of the monsoon season, so you do have to make do and not moan. Part of this adventure is the endurance and sense of achievement in a magical place. The mountain views are important and I would be gutted if we didn't see more of them but if that's the only reason to come, get a decent VR machine, buy a photo, surf some YouTube videos or watch the film *Everest*.

Part of my time awake was caused by worrying about my waterproof kit. If it was going to rain, I HAD to get something better. There was no rush to go out early due to the mist, so Anton and I went into Namche to buy a poncho and a day pack cover. The first shop owner we came to couldn't believe his luck as I bought both items there. It wasn't a day for shopping around. The day pack cover was 1,000

Collecting donations for the path upkeep, Pasang Sherpa is the third generation to continue this worthy cause.

rupees with little haggling (£6) and the poncho was the porter style – a large plastic bag cut down one edge. Wearing it like ET in his blanket it would cover you (and pack) almost head to toe. The shopkeeper even channelled his inner MacGyver and fashioned a tie system with a couple of bits of hessian. I was set; it cost me 200 rupees, about £1.30. Anton had modelled it, and looked very funny.

We could have hung around in the hope that the mist would clear, but we decided to just head off. Keith and Mark had already left while we were shopping so we decided to follow suit. Retracing our route up the steep steps to the top of the village, I felt much better than yesterday. With the shopping excursion and the mist delays, it was nearly an hour since I'd finished my porridge (with apple – strange combo, definitely going for banana tomorrow) so that must have been the reason behind the terrible performance on the same stretch yesterday. At least that's what I told myself.

At the point where we crossed through a Nepalese stile yesterday to go up more steep steps to see Tenzing's statue, we took a right turn instead. It was a slightly downhill stretch and the path was excellent. About 100m later, there was an old Nepalese man collecting money to maintain the path to EBC. He'd been doing it since 1984. He was asking for donations, and for a signature in his book, where you had to confess the size of your donation. People in front all donated but some were as low as 20 rupees, about 15p. I splashed out and gave him 500 rupees but still only £3. I donate that to the National Trust for maintaining the paths on my training walks, so why any different here.

The path was excellent, money very well spent. To make it even better the mist had lifted so although it was unlikely we'd see Everest or the other white-capped peaks today due to cloud, the lower hills above and below were all clear. If you were in a country other than Nepal, you would have been raving about the views. So I'm going to keep doing so.

We were making a really good pace, but once again without any feeling that we were rushing it. Whenever we wanted to take a photo opportunity we did. Anton and I even ventured into the subject of Brexit and the war in Ukraine and it was only day four. We disagreed on both but we survived and we're still talking to each other.

It probably helped that we'd caught up with Keith and Mark. Or rather a loo break had caught up with Keith. We had to stand upwind of the drop toilet, so heaven knows what it was like inside. He came out smiling, claiming he'd been in much worse. That's the Marines for you.

We came across a sign saying it was only 21 hours to EBC. What are we waiting for, we could be there in a couple of days of hard walking. Apart from near certain death if we don't acclimatise. Too dramatic maybe, but we wouldn't be very good if we didn't take it steady.

For the rest of the morning, we walked with the Scots and their guide to a natural stop by our first suspension bridge for two days, where a few tea shops had set up. The last 20 minutes were steeply downhill, but overall it had been a lovely walk, about five miles in two and a half hours with a few ups and downs on well-maintained paths. I could have been walking in the Derbyshire Peaks.

The first signpost to Everest. Without breaks, less than 24 hours to go.

After the bridge, we went to one tea shop, Mark and Keith another (the guide decides, I suppose depending on who they know, you just need to go with it). We could have had lunch but decided to wait for Tengboche at the top of the hill. There was some renovation going on at the tea shop, so they moved their tools and electrical parts off one table for us to sit down. Indra bought a packet of biscuits and shared them. We all started dunking them in our tea. From being a dunking virgin only yesterday, Anton was in full British tea-break mode. The tea shop had an outside loo which I ventured into. Like Keith's (I assume) this was another hole in the floor. Luckily for me it was just a wee; I'm not sure my knees could have taken the low squat.

I was psyching myself up for the last stretch. A 600m (in altitude) climb to Tengboche. At the bottom we saw a British lady smoking a cigarette wishing us good luck. She had pity in her eyes; eek, was it that bad? After the walk up to the EVH yesterday which was really tough,

The basic but practical loo.

THE TRIP

Opposite: Despite not seeing the mountain tops, the scenery below the clouds was still stunning – the milk river, rocks and plants all together to create wonderment.

would I be able to perform like Namche, or EVH. Indra said it would be about two hours to climb. It was 11.30am.

The path was constantly uphill, but it was wide and it was more Namche than EVH. I found it relatively easy. Anton took the racing line, straight up; I traversed across the path, reducing the incline of each step – something else my training had taught me, and also the porter approach I noticed. But I wasn't worn out and my heart never seemed to pound. In fact, we barely took any breaks at all. It wasn't especially quick, but we barely stopped – apart from yaks, donkeys and photo ops. I'm sure I was still red-faced and panting but as we now know this is just my ventilation system in full swing. I certainly didn't feel it as bad as on the previous two days.

We occasionally looked at the altitude on the app, and the metres of altitude gain flew by. I was considering decanting my spare water bottle into my water bladder, but Indra said we were only 15 minutes away. We got there in five, just as the rain was starting. Great timing. It had only taken us an hour. I felt really proud of myself. We were back at 3,880m.

The walk up to Tengboche, the valley stretching away into the distance.

Taking a breather on the way up to Tengboche.

Our hostel, the Hotel Himalayan, is our best one yet. It has a huge communal area and the fires are lit. It is really cosy. We chatted to Sindy and Brecht, the couple from the plane that we'd seen on the way to Namche (they're Belgian), and another friendly couple warming by the fire – Robert was from Ireland and his girlfriend Anna from Antigua, Guatemala. Jane and I had been there in September 1997. I remember exactly why I know the day as it had been the day Princess Diana died. We spent the day trying to find out news in this Spanish-speaking town after seeing a headline in a newspaper and ended up on cnn.com looking for news in a cyber cafe. It was the first time we'd ever used the internet for anything other than emails and we needed a friendly American to show us how to browse. How the world has changed in only 25 years.

In Tengboche, there is not much of a town, but there is a famous monastery which opened at three. We planned to go. In the meantime, we had some lunch, tested our O_2 levels (both in the 90s) and went on a mini-acclimatisation walk to a stupa above the town. It was steep but short and we were back in 15 minutes. Good job as it was raining. It was the most tired I had felt all day due to the rapid nature of the ascent, but we'd knocked up another 70m, stopping tantalisingly close to 4,000m at 3,927m. It has to help, especially as tomorrow we're going to

Dingboche at 4,410m, more than the 300m of ascent that is recommended per day at this level.

For lunch I had a plate of chips AND garlic soup. The chips were fabulous, really self-indulgent of me. In fact, I've had a real appetite since I've been back today and even opened my emergency pack of salted peanuts. I was tempted to have another Coke Zero but at 500 rupees and due to my shame at falling off the wagon yesterday I held firm. I spoke to three English lads, Alex, Ben and Robbie from Oxford University, trekking without a guide, and their room, between them, was only 500 rupees, so the hostel owners certainly make their money on the extras. I paid 600 rupees for a hot shower. It was lovely inside the cubicle itself, but the cubicle was outside in the rain. Not too bad, but if it was really cold outside rather than just ambient rain, I would have avoided it.

After my daily video call to Jane which I really look forward to, Indra, Anton and I went to the monastery. We'd timed it wrong (all right, *I* had) and we missed the very start of the ceremony. All the tourists sat around the wall while the monks chanted their incantations on raised platforms in the middle. They had the most fantastic, thick red robes on and a lot of them had ski socks on. It clearly gets chilly up here. One of the junior monks, who wasn't part of

We had made it to the Himalayan Hotel, my favourite place of them all.

Opposite: Tengboche Monastery, barely visable in the mist.

the prayers, was going round with a thermos topping up the monks' bowls with hot water. The lead monk was chanting really fast; I don't think he had a prompt, but I wouldn't have blamed him if he had. No photos or videos were allowed inside so everyone respected this. After about 15 minutes, all but one of the monks got up and left. A few of the tourists stood and started wandering around, looking at the artwork. Indra indicated we should stay seated until the final monk left, so we waited. The centrepiece was a huge statue of Buddha, with bold, colourful artwork throughout the temple. It was a lovely experience. In the entrance there was a donation box. I only had a few 50s and 20s, less than 300 rupees, so I put the lot in.

We've spent the rest of the day in the main room of the hostel, listening to the hubbub and enjoying the warmth. Anton treated me to one of his sachets of chai latte, a powder to add to hot water. It was sweet and a bit chocolatey. If he can dunk his biscuits, I can go for a hot milkshake.

I expect we'll be in bed by 8.30pm. I'm just charging my phone and iPad with my powerbank, then I'm going to leave it at reception overnight to charge fully.

The top of the mini-acclimatisation walk. Little visability, rainy and miserable, but vital to our wellbeing.

For 300 rupees of course. Apparently, it gets much more expensive from here on in and I want to be sure I have the juice for the money shots later.

It's been an expensive day, but a good one.

Maybe we'll see Keith and Mark again tomorrow, as they are next door. I think we're in the same place in Dingboche.

Stats. Both of us have O_2 readings of 90-plus at the end of the day which considering oxygen in the air is only 60 per cent of sea level, we're happy. We both have our appetites, and no headaches or nausea. We're in a good place. I drank four litres of water and lots of tea, so on schedule. Half a Diamox in the morning, half at night. I did 29,300 steps, Anton will have done about 20,000 due to taking the racing line uphill. We walked a five-to-six-hour walk in four and a quarter hours, even with a tea break. Strava says we walked 8.39 miles, but I'm not convinced it was that far as there is another little glitch after our stop for a cuppa. It also says we had 3,984ft of elevation. Again, not convinced, but we could easily have done 1,000m.

And the best bit of news for the day. We have hooks on the wall in the room for hanging coats and wet towels on. Such a simple thing to have, yet the first we have had in our four nights so far.

*****

Breaking news. It's 9.30pm and there's a bloke next door snoring for England. I promise I won't go on about him in the next diary entry. Not too much anyway.

DAY 6: NAMCHE BAZAAR TO TENGBOCHE

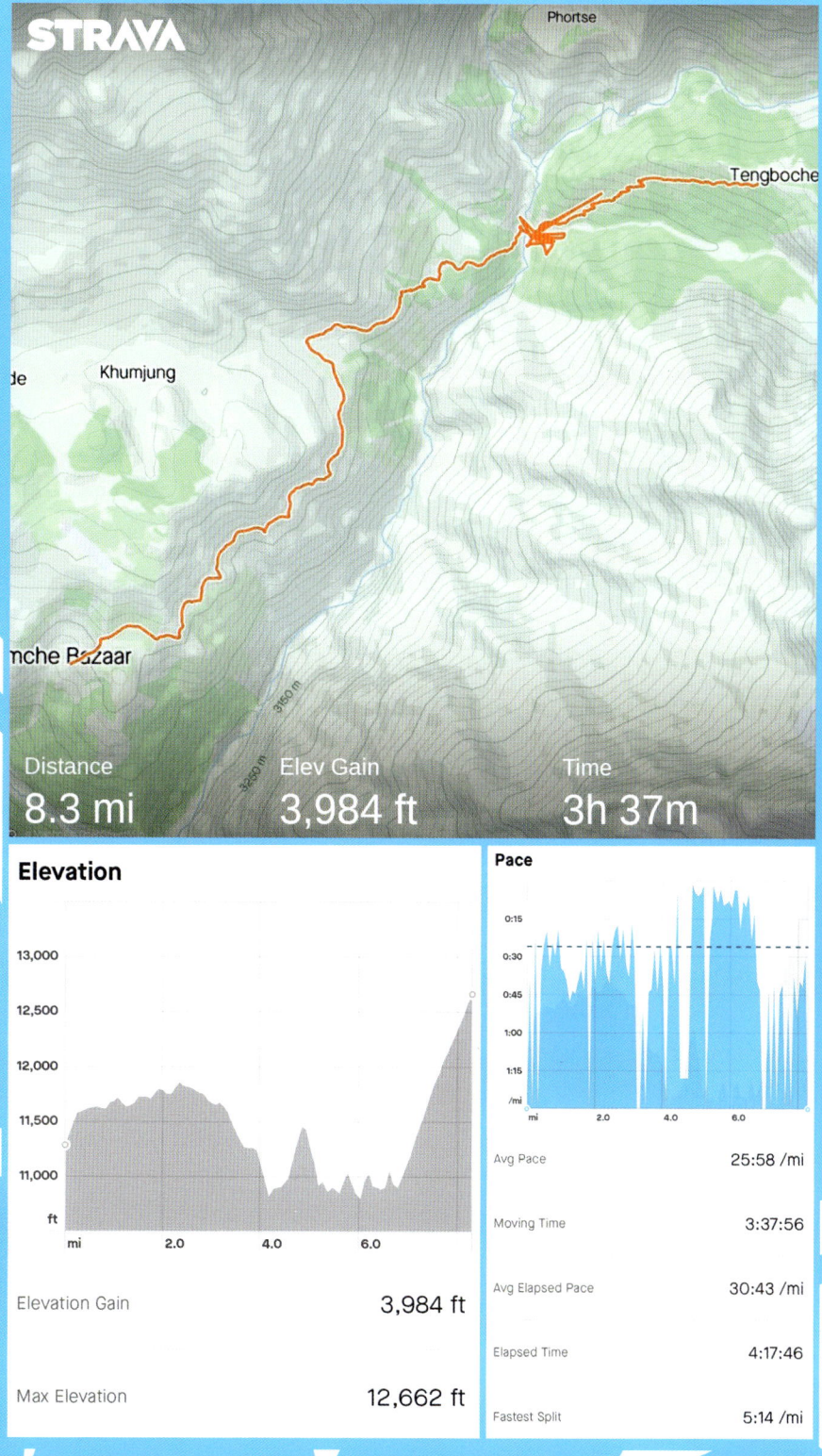

26 SEPTEMBER 2022

DAY 7: TENGBOCHE TO DINGBOCHE

I promised not to dwell on my sleeping, but I'm going to. Only because it is good news. Noisy snoring man next door didn't bother me, and I don't remember lying awake wanting to sleep. I did get up for the loo at 3am, so a good few hours there in the land of nod, followed by a rude awakening from Anton's alarm at 6.45am. More evidence of sleep. The irony is my Fitbit sleep analysis says it was worse than the night before. I don't believe it. I felt refreshed.

It was still misty sky higher up as we looked out the window, but instead of just seeing the monastery next door as last night, we could see the full extent of the village. Another four hostels about 100m away which we couldn't even see last night. Things were looking up. There were also several dwelling houses for the monks. They looked cosy.

It is my favourite hostel to date. We ventured down for breakfast, after another half a Diamox for me, and I retrieved my powerbank fully charged. The lady who ran the hostel was fabulous – helpful, friendly, smiley – and the food was great. The communal area was warm and inviting. It's a shame our two-night stop wasn't here. But it wasn't, so we settled the bill. Of the 1900 rupees that Anton and I had racked up, 1500 was mine alone, so I paid the lot. Anton bought the drinks at a tea stop later in the day to make up his share.

We finished packing and we were out the door at 7.40am for a five-to-six-hour walk to Dingboche (4,410m), 550m higher than Tengboche. If the weather was clear we were promised magnificent, panoramic views of the Himalayas. As it was we had magnificent views, they just stopped at the cloud atop the foothills surrounding the route.

A long line of Buddhist memorial messages to the dead.

The first 20 minutes or so was downhill through undergrowth. The birds were tweeting out of sight and the mist filtered through the trees. Anton said it reminded him of an Indiana Jones film, hacking through the Amazon with the jungle noises offering surround sound. Apart from the altitude and the heat, I knew exactly what he meant.

We passed a lot of people coming back the other way having completed their trip to EBC already. One lady was on a horse and had multiple layers on. It wasn't cold. She looked really ill. Her companions all had that concerned look on their faces which showed they could do nothing about it as they were completely beyond their expertise and were relying totally on their guide who led the horse. Yesterday, we'd briefly chatted to a lady of more advancing years from Oz, who had hired a horse to EBC and back from Gorak Shep. She looked in her late 60s so over ten years older than me but still another sign of how difficult some people find it (a great back-up option though if I crash and burn).

Another group heading our way were a couple of trekkers being led by an Outfitters Nepal guide, our company. We'd heard that it was originally a party of five and that three had been airlifted off the mountain after summiting Kala Patthar; a real ambition of mine – the summit not the airlift. The two trekkers confirmed this. The three had not even seen Everest as it was cloudy. Maybe they genuinely had altitude sickness, or maybe they just didn't fancy the three day walk back after such an anti-climax.

After walking through a really fascinating basin which looked like mangrove swamps to me (the one and only time I'd seen that vegetation so far), we started to ascend again. We hooked up once more with the milky river, a reassuring ever present on most of our journey to date. The weather was getting warm now. Although the mountains were obscured, the sun kept trying to break through, and blue sky threatened. It was definitely sun cream weather.

More metres of ascent, and we came across an Indian girl and her dad who we'd seen in our hostel the night before. She was on her hands and knees being sick against a rock. In the hostel, I'd seen sick in one of the basins as I went to brush my teeth, so it was probably her there too. It wasn't booze. Despite it being on sale everywhere, I have not seen one person even order one. They have all obviously 'read' the unwritten rules of the EBC trek. No alcohol! We actually saw her later as we stopped for a cuppa and she looked fine. She thinks it was food poisoning which sort of makes sense.

The next sad scene was a memorial to a French trekker who had taken a shortcut around a path, slipped and then fell into the roaring waters of the river. His body

Some really unusual vegetation, unlike anything else seen on the trek.

was never recovered. What a tragic loss, and yet another reminder to follow the rules of the hills, and not to be complacent, or too adventurous.

The path was a gentle rise, with the river to our right in the valley. We passed through Pangboche, which was much more vibrant than Tengboche, and I had to stop at one of the hostels to use the loo. Indra said the owner was his friend and

The milk river below with safeguarding for trekkers against the raging torrents. Another bridge crossed too.

one of our potential stops on the way home was here. Maybe he called in a favour as he told me I didn't need to pay.

We're starting to see the same people again and again. Our Irish/Guatemalan couple, the Belgians, three Irish men, the three students from Oxford etc. It is actually really nice to see them as we are all experiencing exactly the same thing.

Crossing the 4,000m barrier. Indra not quite getting what we were doing.

The wonder of the landscape yet the disappointment of the clouds. Even those trekking one day either side of us are not getting exactly what we are. It is an invisible bond in our memories for ever.

As the village of Somare approached we continued the gentle climb; 4,000m of ascent kept coming within grasping distance, then a small, natural descent would knock us back ten or 20 metres. But it was only a matter of time. As I kept an eye on the altitude app, it ticked to 3,996, 3,997, 3,998, then…A train of yaks passed us by.

We were stuck for a minute or so before we could continue to the magic marker. We had a selfie, holding up four fingers to indicate the milestone. Indra thought we were high-fiving, so over-egged our achievement, but once we explained what we were doing he burst into giggles and dropped his thumb. Only 1,500m to go.

We could have had lunch in Somare, but settled for a pot of mint tea. We'd only been going for two and a half hours, so too early to eat. We'd walked four miles and it had been easy. The proverbial walk in the park. Indra settled us in at a great restaurant with phenomenal views back down the valley. We had a pot (nearly three cups each) so we could savour it. I'm glad we did as Keith and Mark walked past, joining us for another 20 minutes or so. It had been our longest tea/lunch break yet, but we still had oodles of time.

Lunch in Somare. A long time to take in the views down the valley in the sun.

After Somare, the landscape had started to really change. The trees had virtually disappeared and it became a lot more barren. There was heather growing between the rocks and it became more easy to see the route ahead without the height of the flora. The paths were less prominent, best described as trails between the rocks, but it was impossible to go the wrong way, especially as there were fellow trekkers ahead leading the way. Mark commented that it was like the landscape on the walks in Scotland, and he was right. This trek has really brought back great memories of my training walks, using different walks in different locations to compare.

Indra suddenly got excited and started pointing to the hills above us. I thought it was going to be some strange animal, but just peeking through the clouds was a snow-capped mountain. It was fleeting, maybe 15 seconds, but left us wanting more. I hope we get it. Forecast tomorrow is okay, so fingers crossed it is blue sky with a spattering of cloud, in the direction of the peaks.

The floodplain of the river started to widen and you could see the confluence up ahead as two tributaries cascaded down their respective trajectories, either side of a hill, to join up with almighty force. The sound from under the bridge as they met was incredible. We all took in the moment. Anton even got quite close and pointed out sand on the edge. Some serious weathering had taken place there.

THE TRIP

Crossing the bridge. Very rocky terrain now.

The final stretch of the walk took us uphill for 20 minutes. It was reasonably steep but not a problem at this stage of the trip. Our group moved ahead of the Scots, but we all go at different paces. It didn't matter as Indra had been told that they would be in the same hotel as us.

Just around the corner Dingboche appeared. On a natural plain, it seemed to be thriving. Much larger than all the towns we had passed through other than Namche. The hostels all had their names on the roofs, advertising themselves to the passing traveller. As an acclimatisation stop-off, it needs to cater to two days' worth of trekkers not one, hence the size. We could make out ours, the Good Luck hostel. It looked huge. Let's hope it was good.

Today's walk had seen dramatic changes in landscape, a lovely walking temperature, great company and a pretty benign trail. If you could helicopter people into Tengboche in the morning and out of Dingboche at the end, anybody could have done it and been thrilled by it. If only it was that simple. The one thing missing was the mountain views. Nearly a perfect day's hike.

After a short climb to the left of the village, past two Buddha eyes stupas, we came to our digs for the next two nights. The clock was ticking over at four hours 59 minutes from start to finish. After more (pretty bland) garlic soup for me, we realised our friends hadn't arrived. Indra reassured us that they were staying in the same place but they would have been no more than ten minutes behind. Indra had been mugged off by the other guide. Not sure why. I'm sure Keith and Mark would have been as keen as us to hook up for a couple of days.

Anton and I were keen on another mini-acclimatisation hike, and Indra was only too happy to oblige again. The hill on the left of the village, Nangkar Tshang, was full of trails, snaking back and forth. Two stupas were lower down, with a prayer flag much higher up the hill. There were other hikers all coming down, having had the same idea. It was an easy ascent as the switchbacks took out the directness of the slope. The paths were covered with pipes, carrying water from the higher peaks to the village. At times you had to really pick your way through them; they were everywhere. A section of the slope had been fenced off. Indra explained that it was there to protect that area from yaks so they could see how high the vegetation could grow. At least I think that's what he said and didn't have the heart to ask him to explain it all again. It sounded plausible anyway.

As we approached the ridge, we'd ascended 70m, more than enough for the mission in hand, but it was still early so wanted to go higher. It was actually the route of tomorrow's acclimatisation hike, so once we got to 100m above the village and another Buddhist memorial, complete with intricate cairns, we called it a day and started to descend. It was still early, only three o'clock.

The Nepali SIM card didn't get reception here. I'd hoped at the top of the acclimatisation walk we'd get some notification dings on the phone but none came. It was 1000 rupees for 48 hours of wifi and 500 rupees for 12 at the hotel. After spending so much yesterday I decided to wait until tomorrow before signing up and getting in touch with Jane and my family and friends. I can also say goodbye to Jim on his last day in the UK before flying to Bangkok. I had warned Jane that signal could get sporadic, so she won't be worried.

The hot shower was 750 rupees, so I thought I'd try and put my cold-water training to full use and have a cold one instead. But where was it? The hot shower was obvious, but no sign of the cold one. I asked one of the staff members and he showed me to an outside barrel of cold water in full view of everyone and that was it. Seriously! Bad enough for blokes, impossible for women. I didn't bother. It was another bit of frustrating news after the soup and the fellow hostellers

With a south facing window in our room, and no electricity for charging our phones, we both got out the same gadget – the solar charger. Great minds and all

Looking down at Dingboche, the Good Luck Hotel behind. Still very cloudy.

that. More use of string, this time tied around a table leg, and mine was dangling out of the window catching the last of the sun's power. Anton's was inside. His phone indicator said it would be fully charged in five days! Not going to really work today, we can employ it tomorrow after our acclimatisation hike, when hopefully the sun will really work its midday magic.

We decided to go for a walk around the town; it looked at least as though this could be interesting, but the entrance to the hostel was on the left of the village, and the main drag was over to the right. There didn't seem an obvious path from one to the other. Indra saw us struggling so tried to find a route. We ended up having to go to the top of the village to get to the main road through the middle – about a half-mile round trip. It was so much more interesting in the village, some shops, cafes, even a medical centre. The trip so far has been excellently planned and the hostels great, but I think Outfitters called this one wrong. A captive audience for the hostel, which for one night is okay, but two?

I had a snack attack, not after sugar but carbs, so bought a tube of Pringles, the crisps of choice up here, from a shop on the main road. A reasonable 300 rupees (approximately £2). Back at the hostel, they were also for sale, at a ridiculous 800 rupees. Is it obvious I'm not impressed with our accommodation? I also bought a small bottle of Everest malt whiskey. I'd not seen it anywhere else, so didn't want to miss out. We have already decided to head over to the other part of town again

This shop has everything. Including Pringles, Cards and Everest Whisky.

tomorrow after the walk and make use of the board game cafe, and may even get a pack of cards for higher up on the trek.

The usual activity ensued. Back in the main communal area, we chatted, I wrote my diary and we waited for dinner. Anton hasn't brought anything to really amuse himself so looks at the map a lot while I am tapping away on my iPad. I need to write this while the memory is still fresh, but I do feel guilty. It was getting quite dark outside yet the lights were still not on. The fire had been lit and the room started to heat up. Dinner came and went and by 8.30pm a lot of the fellow trekkers were turning in for the night. We wouldn't be far behind.

I haven't been cold yet, and that includes this evening. We're going to 5,000m tomorrow; maybe I'll need an extra jumper.

Health: in the morning we were both 90 per cent on the O_2. After many ups and downs in the day, including me dropping to below 80 per cent very briefly, we have settled at 86 per cent for me. Anton is in the 90s. We're both showing no altitude sickness symptoms as we have no headaches or loss of appetite. I have a tickly throat, but it comes and goes. I don't think it's the start of the Khumbu cough yet.

Stats: 31,606 steps, five litres of water drunk and a maximum altitude of 4,436m. Kala Patthar is just over 5,500m. Tomorrow we could well be within 500m of our highest point.

DAY 7: TENGBOCHE TO DINGBOCHE

STRAVA

Distance: **6.8 mi**
Elev Gain: **2,181 ft**
Time: **3h 23m**

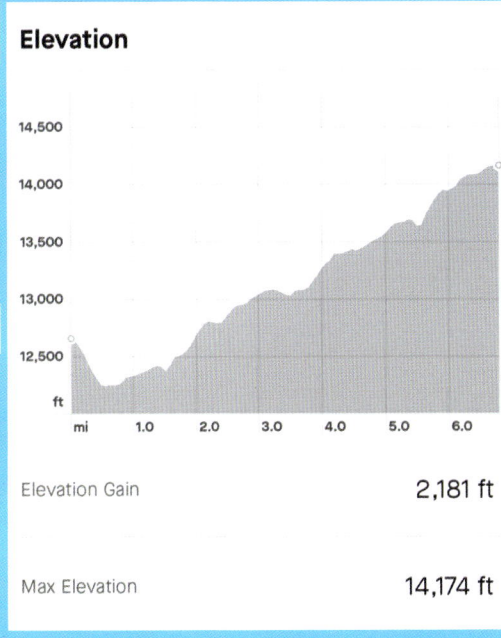

Elevation

Elevation Gain: 2,181 ft
Max Elevation: 14,174 ft

Pace

Avg Pace: 29:42 /mi
Moving Time: 3:23:04
Avg Elapsed Pace: 43:45 /mi
Elapsed Time: 4:59:12
Fastest Split: 26:51 /mi

Day 8: A beautiful, cloud free morning to wake up to. Our first clear day since the walk to Namche.

27 SEPTEMBER 2022
DAY 8: DINGBOCHE ACCLIMATISATION HIKE

On our mini-acclimatisation hike yesterday, we'd met an English fellow coming down from a bit higher up. We chatted about the cloud and he'd seen a forecast saying there would be five days of good weather. That would get us to EBC and back to Namche. Boy did we hope it was true. After a reasonable night's sleep, where I still haven't used my down sleeping bag apart from as a pillow, I looked out the window

'Anton, are you awake?' He grunted, sat up and we both stared in silence with jaws dropped at the beautiful clear blue skies, perfectly framing a whole landscape of snow-capped peaks. This is what we'd been waiting for. I got dressed quickly and rushed downstairs to make sure it was real. I have awoken in the Alps many times over the years and seen similar views of mountain tops, indicating perfect skiing conditions. Well these were similar, oh yes, apart from the fact that they were twice as high as the ones I'd been looking at all those years.

Back upstairs, we quickly packed so we could get out earlier than usual and make the most of the scenery. There wasn't a cloud in the sky but we are in the mountains and didn't want to miss a moment as the weather could change.

The purpose of the day was an acclimatisation walk, continuing our mini one from yesterday, further up Nangkar Tshang. There was no way we'd get to the top, it was over 5,600m and was for mountaineers not walkers, but there were natural stops all the way to going beyond 5,000m. We wanted to break that milestone and for the second day running crash through a thousand barrier.

We set off about 7.30am and we knew it would be a long trip, not just the walk but for the constant photo stops. After being starved of mountains for most of our first five days, we were filling our boots. The highest was Lhotse at 8,400m, the most scenic was Ama Dablam (translation – two mothers), still a mighty 6,856m,

The steep path up ahead, joined by some of the local wildlife. The milk river and Dingboche in the valley. Lhotse dominating the white capped mountains.

but seemingly larger due to its proximity. But they were only the highlights, there were mountains everywhere.

I had deliberately packed my Teenage Cancer Trust T-shirt, sent to me by my charity when I started raising money for them. If ever it was going to get an airing, today was the day, and my jumper was whipped off frequently to display it.

The first 100m of ascent was easy; after all we'd done it the previous evening, but the hill was steep and I knew we were going to be in for a tough climb. The last acclimatisation day, going to the Everest View Hotel from Namche had been my hardest so far, and this was going to come close, if not surpass it.

Every so often, there were prayer flags fluttering in the hills. We could see at least five of them, all higher than the next. They became mini targets and really helped focus on just taking it step by step.

We were pleased we'd set off as soon as we did as the cloud started to swirl. First one mountain, then the next became engulfed. Visibility on most of the vista was still fine, but we knew it could disappear in a flash. We continued upwards for an hour and I was blowing. Not fitness but oxygen. Every 100 steps I needed to stop and take 20 or so really deep breaths. We were higher than I'd ever been before and

Indra's favourite rock. Great for photo ops, with Ama Dablam behind.

my body just needed to get the precious gas in my lungs. Anton and Indra were their usual patient and superhuman selves. It was a three- or four-hour round trip, so the only rush was the weather.

Indra showed us his favourite rock on the walk, a slab that jutted out into the sky. We all took turns posing on it, then had a team shot after a couple of Americans (Don and Jerry) reached us and took our cameras. We returned the favour, so ended up being there for a few minutes. Instead of a forced stop, this became a fun one and it took my mind off my breathing. The rock was now also my favourite.

The clouds were getting thicker, but the views were still the dominant feature, only now individual peaks disappeared then reappeared as the wind blasted the clouds through the skies. Indra kept pointing out new mountains as we gained altitude; 4,600, 4,650, 4,700. We'd passed a younger, fit-looking guy who'd got to 4,800 and had to turn back due to feeling dizzy. I hoped I wouldn't be the same.

At one rest stop, where the Americans and their guide were also relaxing, Indra dropped his water bottle and it set off down the hill at pace. Indra chased after it, much to the amusement of the other guide. I wouldn't have dared. After a couple

We'd hit our next milestone. 5,000m above sea level. Above the clouds.

of failed attempts and an increasingly frantic descent, he came back grinning with bottle in hand. The guides are so nimble on their feet. Although I thought, 'Don't worry, it's only a bottle, no point falling and killing yourself over it,' Indra saw no issue. As Anton later commented, he had outrun gravity.

The clouds were getting thicker and the views of the mountains had disappeared. Anna and Robert passed us coming down. They'd set off an hour earlier and had had phenomenal views. Had we missed the boat?

We had a choice, keep going despite the weather, or return to Dingboche having achieved a healthy additional altitude for the day already. Of course, there was no choice, we had to continue. We wanted to break the 5,000m barrier, even if it was in the clouds. It was the best decision of the day.

I counted my 100 steps and each set added 20 to 30 metres to the altitude. The weather broke and the mountains appeared again just as we approached the milestone. The selfie of the three of us, in front of the mountains with the five-fingered salute (Indra knew what he was doing today) is my favourite photo of the three of us yet. The backdrop, the joy, the achievement and the camaraderie really shine through.

I was feeling emotional, it was time for my own thoughts. I didn't even realise Anton had taken this photo until I got back to the UK.

I was getting emotional. The significance of the day was hitting me hard. It was three years coming, with many false dawns and I was over 5,000m. The views were fantastic and I had my Teenage Cancer Trust T-shirt on. I reflected on why I was wearing it, and what our family had been through (and out the other end) and tears started rolling down my cheeks. I had my sunglasses on and sat facing away from the others pretending to need a rest. It was a deeply personal moment, and I didn't want to share it with relative strangers. I would have given anything in that moment to have Jane, Jim, Matt and Dan alongside me for the biggest family hug we'd ever had. The feeling hasn't really gone away all day. No doubt if I get to Base Camp it will return with a vengeance.

There was only about 100m left, and this was a scramble over rocks to the top, and we'd made it. An 800m ascent meaning we were even higher than Lobuche, our next stop tomorrow. There were a few groups there. Our American photography pals, and a lovely Canadian couple, Jonathan and Selina, who we'd met in Tengboche, as well as a couple of people we didn't know. The flag that marked the top was getting some serious photographic attention from everyone as we took it in turns to pose against it. We'd reached 5,065m. Kala Patthar is

5,550m. We were within 500m. If our bodies survive this day, we have a fantastic chance of achieving our goal.

We stayed at the top for about 30 minutes, as did everyone. There was no rush; the weather was decent and the more time we spent at the top the better for acclimatisation. The only surprise was that more people didn't arrive. The three lads from Oxford Uni rocked up, as did another solo English guy. Most of his group had got to 4,800m, seen the weather and descended. Apparently lots of people did that. I wish they'd had the courage to continue. The clouds were swirling and although the clouds outnumbered the peaks now, there were still great moments of clarity.

The descent was tricky at first. It is much easier to scramble up rocks than down them. Indra was concerned about me, but I never was. I'd been scrambling down mountains in the Lakes, the Peaks, the Yorkshire Dales and Scotland for weeks (years if you count all the National Three Peaks I've done). We did pass a few people coming up and we did encourage them to continue. Keith and Mark were two of them. Mark was struggling in the same way I was, just lack of oxygen in the lungs. We saw them later and they'd made it. We also saw the Indian girl from yesterday who'd been sick from food poisoning. She was bounding up the hill with a beaming smile. It was a really good feeling to see her fully recovered.

Made it. 5,065m, and a real sense that if we can do this without any signs of altitude sickness, Base Camp was within our grasp.

The path back down to Dingboche, steep and misty. The prayer flag markers showing the way.

We made it up and down in about five hours. We'd only covered three miles. But it wasn't flat of course. The Strava map was the perfect pyramid, unsurprisingly. I didn't ache, I had managed my breathing and I felt hugely satisfied with my day's work. Anton even patted me on the back and said well done. Blimey, I must have impressed him.

DAY 8: ACCLIMATISATION HIKE UP NANGKAR TSHANG AND BACK FROM DINGBOCHE

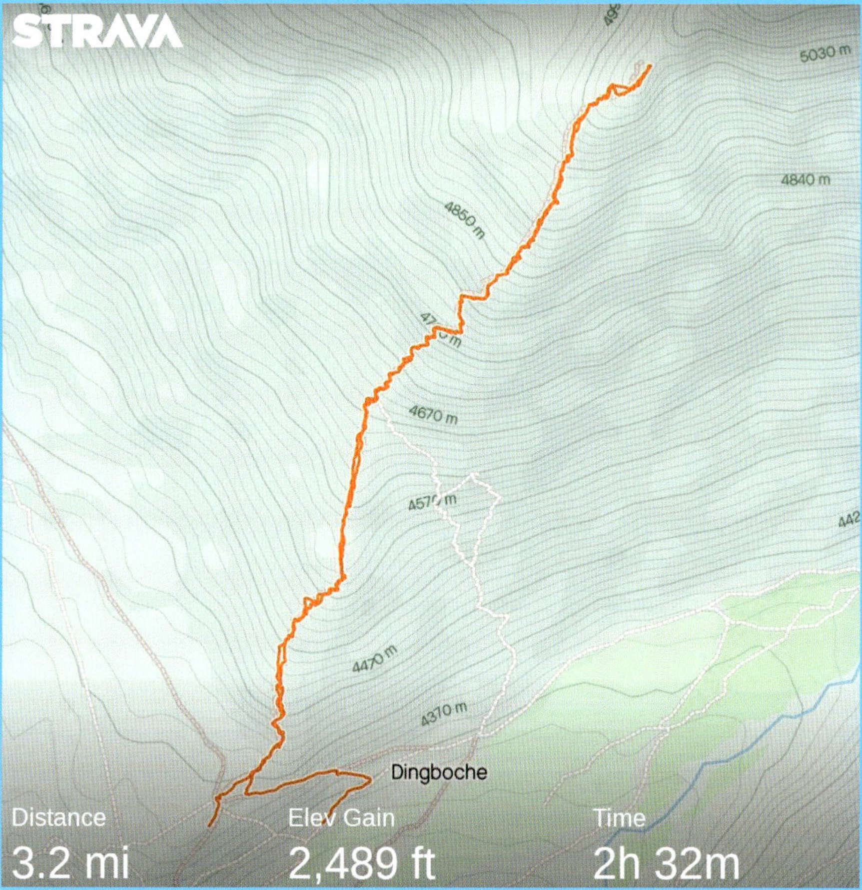

STRAVA

Distance: 3.2 mi
Elev Gain: 2,489 ft
Time: 2h 32m

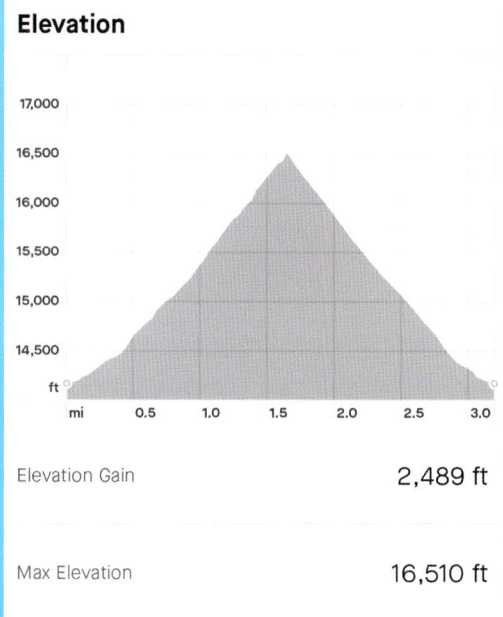

Elevation Gain: 2,489 ft
Max Elevation: 16,510 ft

Avg Pace: 46:58 /mi
Moving Time: 2:32:38
Avg Elapsed Pace: 1:26:59 /mi
Elapsed Time: 4:42:40
Fastest Split: 30:43 /mi

We had lunch (garlic soup; thank god only two more to go, I am ready for a change) and then got ready to go for a walk into the village. I splashed out on a 12-hour wifi card, made contact with the family on WhatsApp after two days, and then had a hot shower for 700 rupees. I may not see a shower for a couple of days, never mind a hot one, and after two days of trekking without one, I felt a duty to Anton. Saying that, I've not seen him have one since Namche. Maybe he goes when I am not looking. Maybe I have Covid and have lost my smell. Or maybe he doesn't have b.o. due to his lack of sweating. I think the Prince Andrew defence is the most likely.

We decided to go to the board game cafe on the main drag, and Anna and Rob were in there chatting to a couple of girls. They are so friendly, it is always a pleasure to see them. We ordered drinks and decided to play some games. As we'd bought drinks, the cafe owner charged our phones for us while we were there. Anton didn't know any of the games, so we had two games of Othello and then two of draughts. I'm pleased he won the last one; I don't think a 4-0 clean sweep would have helped Anglo-German relations even at this micro level. Don and Jerry also showed up. The cafe was a really nice place to spend a couple of hours and I would recommend it to anyone.

On the way back we bumped into Keith and Mark looking for a good coffee shop, so we pointed them to the board game cafe. We let them know our hostel name in Lobuche, so hopefully we'll see them there tomorrow.

Back at the hostel, I had a video chat with Jane which was lovely after a day of not sharing news. I also managed to catch Jim before his flight to Bangkok. After the emotions earlier, this family interaction was very welcome.

While I write this first part, Anton is playing cards with Indra with a new deck we bought near the cafe. It makes me feel so less guilty spending an hour on this. I'm on for egg and veggie noodles for the third night running. I have binned the dal bhat after three nights. Ironically, Anton has gone the other way and really embraced the Nepali staple.

After dinner we played cards. Anton didn't know any games. Othello, Draughts, now Rummy. What else can I teach him?

As the weather was so good first thing today, we're going to get up half an hour early. If the pattern continues, we'll see great scenery and be in Lobuche by about 1pm, ready for the next instalment of Anton's games education.

Stats. A whole Diamox this morning, but not half yesterday evening; 24,429 steps; CO_2 levels in the late 80s for us both this evening. No loss of appetite or headaches. Four litres of water drunk. Feeling good. Even my tickly cough has vanished.

28 SEPTEMBER 2022
DAY 9: DINGBOCHE TO LOBUCHE

We were nearly there. This was the day before Base Camp and we turned the lights off knowing that if we got a good night's sleep, we'd easily be able to cover the six miles to Lobuche. If the weather was going to be good, it could be an extremely memorable day.

The walls of the rooms were paper-thin, but once the French couple next door stopped yabbering, it fell silent. Then I was rudely awakened by the War and Peace message arriving from Namche a few days earlier. The Chinese Whispers cannot have been good as it only lasted 45 minutes rather than the two hours it had taken to send. Maybe even the Starlight Barking relay had got sick of it.

We'd planned to get up half an hour earlier than the rest of the trek as the weather had been brilliant at the start of the acclimatisation walk, so we set our alarms at 6.15am instead of 6.45am (in case you needed help on the maths). I awoke at about six and looked to see what the weather was going to be like. Yesterday, or the usual we had come to expect. It was a bit of both, but erring on the sunshine. By the time we'd finished breakfast it was really starting to improve. Could it be even better than yesterday?

We still had no signs of altitude sickness, so we started the climb from Dingboche for the third time after the acclimatisation hikes of the previous two days, only this time we dropped down into the valley opposite quickly. We had 500m to ascend, but over the whole day, and not in a couple of hours.

Indra taught us a couple of Nepali phrases, 'ramroardin' (phonetic) meaning good luck after our hotel, and 'jam jam' meaning let's go. So jam jam we did.

As we started to walk, it was noticeable how barren the landscape was. It stretched out desert-like ahead of us, with a smattering of greenery. Down to our left in the valley was the town of Pherice, somewhere we may stop on the way back

Looking back down the valley we'd walked up from Dingboche (to the left of the ridge, so hidden in the photo). Pherice, the base for so many helicopter journeys, is to the right near the river.

down, but now the hub of the helicopter taxi service. It was constant. Back and forth, like your neck at a tennis match. By the fifth or sixth time it passed us we almost stopped looking at it. It was very dramatic though, it seemed to be flying just a few metres above the rocks below. With the mist and cloud earlier in the walk, flying would have been dangerous, even with modern navigational devices, so I suspect there was a backlog.

Although the views ahead were really interesting, the money shots were behind us. Ama Dablam and a whole landscape of white peaks were visible among the swirling cloud. It lasted all day, and we kept turning round to record the view. We could well be seeing the same views on our return in two days' time (is it really only that long?), but if the weather drops we'd regret it.

We walked very steadily uphill for an hour, and the trails behind started to lengthen as we stretched the distance between ourselves and Dingboche. We passed dry-stone walls and the occasional dwelling and Indra explained that Dingboche (and probably Pherice) were evacuated for one month a year to appease the gods. It was considered good luck. So the whole population decamped to the hills, often in their tents. It was a very strange custom but who are we as westerners to judge others using our norms.

The views towards Ama Dablam. The paths are not steep and the stone huts abound. A really pleasant walk in the sun.

Yak dung being transported via the porter system.

It was obviously a route used by the locals, and not just those in the trekking business. The heavy lifting is done by the men but it isn't uncommon to see women carrying loads too. The load of choice today seemed to be yak dung. It was everywhere. Being carried, being collected, or being produced. It is used for burning. I've not noticed a very smelly ambience in any of our accommodation to date so it either hasn't been used, or it really is the perfect renewable fuel. Someone tell Extinction Rebellion.

As we started to approach a steeper part of the walk, Indra pointed out a mountain lake to our left; it must have been freezing. Feeding from the lake was our companion, the milk river. The floodplain was huge all the way to Pherice, but it was obviously past its highest point as different strands made their way down the hill to join up with fellow tributaries from other parts of the mountainous region.

It was such a beautiful morning. The walk was straightforward, the weather was great and the views were constant. Even though there were some clouds, the main view was not massively impeded. The huge mountain to our left kept coming in and out of view which added to the impact. We'd only had about an hour of great views yesterday. We were two hours in already and there was no sign of it fading.

The entrance to Thukla, a well-stocked shop and a lovely courtyard to have a cuppa.

After those couple of hours, we started to descend towards the river, ready for the crossing to Thukla. The way was unclear and there was no sign of a bridge. As we approached the water's edge I had the bad feeling that we'd be picking our way across the rocks jutting out of the raging surf. But the porters were crossing with sacks of yak dung or trekkers kits so there had to be something. There was but it looked very rickety. On closer inspection the wood facade was underpinned with something more substantial, i.e. metal bars. It wasn't a big span though, and we were soon across.

Heading up to the lunch stop of Thukla, there was a little courtyard surrounded by three or four restaurant/hotels. It was like a mini food court in an outside shopping mall. There was also a little shop which wouldn't have been out of place on the streets of Kathmandu. We ordered a pot of lemon tea and enjoyed basking in the sun. It had taken us two and a half hours to travel 3.32 miles, but I reckon at least an hour of that was staring in awe at the scenery. We were at 4,620m, another 300 to go for the day.

We got chatting to Bernard, a friendly Canadian who we'd bumped into a few times, and waved to a couple of Danish girls, Line and Liva, who we are seeing each day. The community of our 'friends' is growing.

After 40 minutes or so, we set off again for Lobuche. The sign said three hours, but these are always way over the actual. It was the toughest part of the day's hike though, a 45-minute ascent up a switchback path. Before going up, Anton and I made a slight detour to look back once more down the valley where we'd come from. The mountains were still visible amid some swirling cloud. Looking back at my photos, they do not do it justice. I have really tried to implant that picture into my memory, it was that good. We also waved to Mark and Keith just approaching the cafe. I thought we'd see them later but no.

The next ascent wouldn't just be the hardest part of the day, it was the only hard part. But it was short, and the usual method of traversing made it relatively simple. No one walks fast; imagine following a coffin at a funeral. okay, a bit faster than that, but not much. It gives you time to get air in the lungs. After the acclimatisation walk yesterday I found myself walking at that altitude so much easier. I didn't need to stop for 20 seconds every 100 steps today. On this incline we met Michael, a young Italian/Swedish combo who would later spend a lot of time with the Oxford lads and Danish girls. Articulate and funny, I liked him immediately.

Looking back down to Thukla after the steep climb to the memorial park. Ama Dablam still dominating, with the milk river to the right.

Just a small section of the memorial park, including the tribute to Scott Fischer.

The prize at the top was also the most poignant moment of the day. I'd read about the memorial park to people who died on Everest, but the scale of it surprised me. It is a seriously dangerous mountain. The entrance at the top of the incline was adorned with prayer flags, the colour a contrast to the bleakness of the conditions they'd have encountered. It was a fitting tribute to those who had taken on and not survived the ultimate challenge on earth. The memorials were commemorating a mix of foreign trekkers and Nepali sherpas, all side by side, as they had been on their expeditions. Indra pointed out the memorial of Rob Hall, the US expedition leader who had perished while trying to save his clients. You'd know him from the film *Everest*. There was also one to Scott Fischer, a name I knew but couldn't place. He had to be famous as a woman barged past me shouting to anyone who'd listen, 'I've got to have my picture with Scott Fischer.' It was in incredible bad taste. Think it, remember him, but don't make it about you.

After about 15 minutes of quiet reflection, we set off towards Lobuche. What had been a morning of turning round and looking back, became one of gaping in wonderment at a new landscape. If I thought the road to Thukla was barren, it hadn't a thing on this stretch. The river to our right was no more than a small babbling brook. You still didn't want to dip your toes in it, but you could put your

Looking forward to Lobuche now. Pumori to the front left and the Khumbu Glacier now to our right all the way to EBC. The prospect of arriving there tomorrow was becoming very real now.

hand in to test the temperature – something you wouldn't even dream of with the milky river. There were some flowering plants trying to get a foothold in the rocks, and some yaks looking for any vegetation they could find to munch on. The rest was rock and hills. Alongside us was a grey wall of rock which turned out to be the bottom of the Khumbu Glacier, the ice giant that is slowly sliding from Everest. Base Camp is on this glacier. It was a real sign that we were close.

Ahead of us was a wall of snowy tops, including the very recognisable Pumori, and to our right Everest's neighbour Nuptse. The mountain Lobuche, on our immediate left wasn't white capped at all, it was bleak rock. Indra showed us where it's base camp was and explained that climate change may be responsible for the lack of snow as it always used to have it. True or not, the blackness gave it a menacing scowl.

For the next hour or so we walked towards Pumori. It was my favourite part of the day. I don't just want to arrive and put my feet up, I like the walk as much as the sense of achievement at having completed something. By 1pm we saw a helicopter land just a few hundred feet away; it had to be the town. Sure enough, a final small incline and the town appeared. We were almost on top of it. It had taken us five and a half hours from start to finish.

EVEREST BASE CAMP

It was day seven, and although every day had been great – new experiences, new friendships formed, changing scenery and challenging ascents, this had been my favourite. The walk wasn't difficult and the weather had remained clear all day. It's like viewing a new house – if you see it in the rain and you still want to buy it then it's probably the right decision. Well I saw today with the sun shining, all the clutter cleared away, fresh bread smells wafting through the kitchen and newly decorated walls. There could have been damp, a leaky roof, terrible neighbours and planning permission for a 20-storey tower block next door – I would have looked past it all such was the majesty of the vista.

After checking in to our hotel, Hotel Peak VI, and being pleased to see Jonathan and Selena were also there, we had a quick lunch (no garlic soup, I hope I don't regret it), and headed to the Khumbu glacier for a mini acclimatisation hike. After climbing the 70m or so to the top, the sheer power of the glacier was evident. A huge gully had been gouged into the mountainside. Mini pools of water had formed intermittently. Rocks had fallen into the gully, dislodged from their perch by the slowly moving monster. If you kept quiet you could hear rocks crashing, but you could never see them.

On the ridge of the Khumbu Glacier, Pumori ahead, and the path up Kala Patthar visible. It didn't look too bad. By this time tomorrow, we'd be at Base Camp.

DAY 9: DINGBOCHE TO LOBUCHE

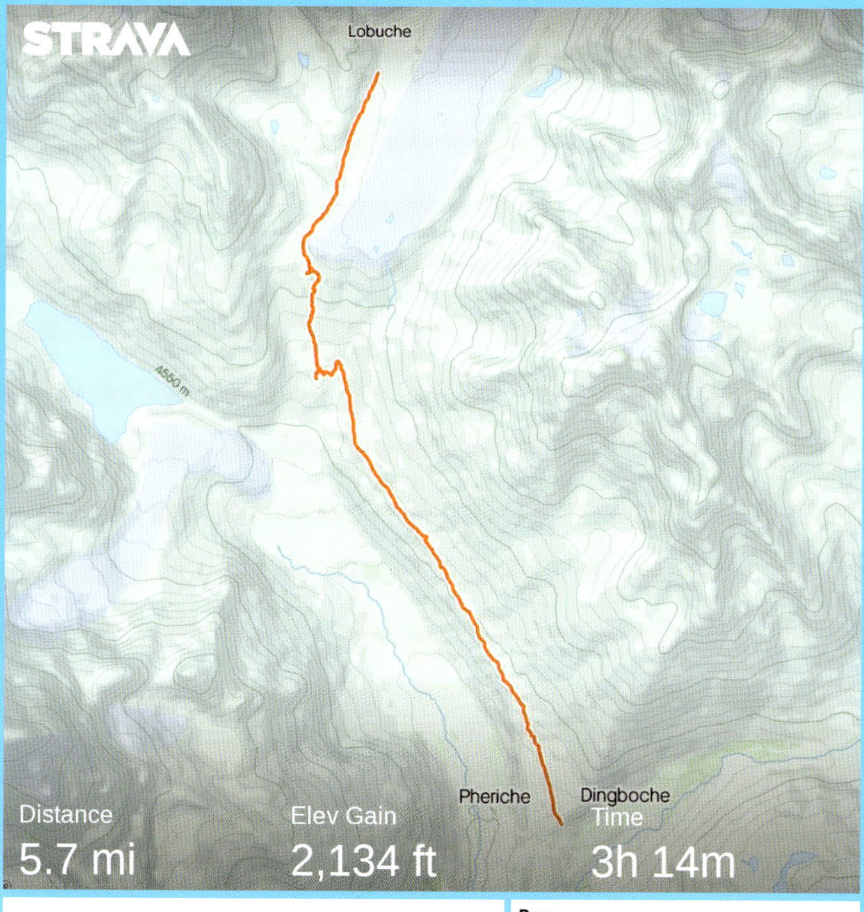

STRAVA

Lobuche · Pheriche · Dingboche

Distance: **5.7 mi**
Elev Gain: **2,134 ft**
Time: **3h 14m**

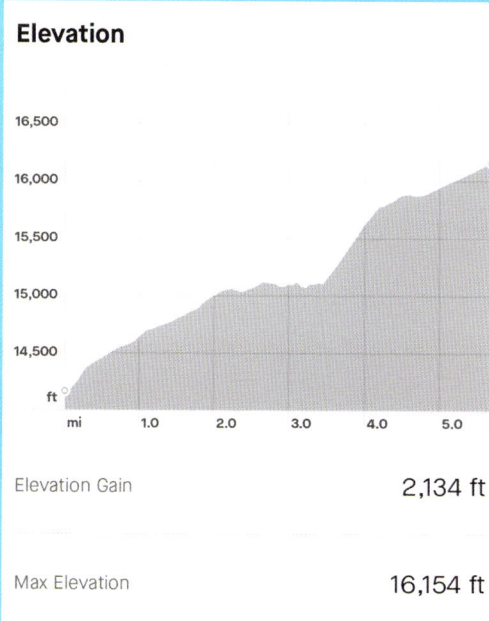

Elevation

Elevation Gain: 2,134 ft
Max Elevation: 16,154 ft

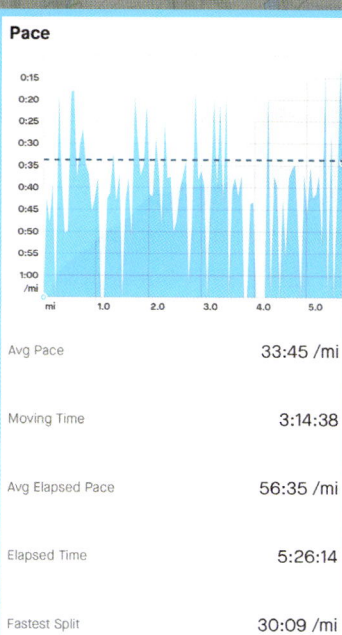

Pace

Avg Pace: 33:45 /mi
Moving Time: 3:14:38
Avg Elapsed Pace: 56:35 /mi
Elapsed Time: 5:26:14
Fastest Split: 30:09 /mi

We were joined by a Nepalese lady, Pritima, and her guide who we'd said hello to regularly along the way. She lives in the States and has come back to see more of her country. She was as awestruck as a couple of foreigners at the scene in front of us. You don't get much of this in Kathmandu.

At the far end of the gully, you could see visible ice, not just the greyness of the glacier. Indra told us that indicated Base Camp. We were going there tomorrow and now we could visualise the route. Unless I am struck down by very unexpected altitude sickness, I'm going to make it.

To the left was Kala Patthar, the Everest viewpoint climb only two mornings away. It didn't look especially tricky from here. Maybe it will be different at 4am with head torches on as we trek to 5,550m in the freezing cold for daybreak. We had passed some people coming down from there this morning. They raved about the view. It is the thing I have been waiting for, more so than Everest Base Camp really, and now I knew I had to do it.

Back into town, our hotel was deserted so we got changed and headed around the different hotels looking for people we knew. The Oxford lads were heading off with the Danish girls to do the acclimatisation walk, but we saw no one else we knew. In fact we hardly saw anyone. The bakery was empty and the few people we saw hadn't crossed our paths before. Where were they all?

Back at our hotel, I had started writing this when Jonathan and Selena came down for dinner. It turned out we were the only four guests. Initially disappointed that there wouldn't be a lively atmosphere, it was really good to have a much longer chat with them – jobs, travel, books we've all read. They have been on the fringes of our time so far, always around, always friendly, but we've never stopped and chatted with them much. Now they were firmly there. It was a bit of a three way conversation, with Anton seemingly happy to listen. Probably better than sitting around while I type. I did offer to show him some games of patience, one man card games, but he wasn't keen.

After a really pleasant evening, one of my favourites to date, and a very long story by their guide, we all made our excuses and headed off to bed. After all it is the big day tomorrow. Base Camp.

Stats: 29,751 steps. One Diamox in the morning, four litres of water. O_2 early 80s for me, higher for Anton. No sign of altitude sickness from either of us (or Jonathan and Selena either). No shortness of breath. Anton has a blister, he's not a cyborg after all. Now at 4,900m.

29 SEPTEMBER 2022
DAY 10: LOBUCHE TO GORAKSHEP TO EBC TO GORAKSHEP

Today was the day. After two years of Covid delays, 13 weeks of training, seven days of walking, and more garlic soup than I can ever eat again, it was Base Camp day. All the stories I had read about how difficult it was to get there, or about altitude sickness, or about the cold all seemed to disappear. I'd seen the route from Lobuche and it didn't look hard. I'd not got any altitude sickness symptoms, and it was relatively mild. I didn't even need my woolly hat or gloves. There was nothing to stop us getting there. It was a great feeling.

The day started off to a bit of a damp squib, literally. I'd asked Indra to fill up my water bladder the night before, after I'd put in the water purification tablets and electrolyte tablets. They fizzed up and the bladder had overflowed with the pressure. I kept it in a plastic bag in my day pack, but that was now wet. My rucksack was actually leaking. I emptied the plastic bag of excess water and put it back in my rucksack. It would have consequences later. We also saw Keith for the first time in ages, but there was no sign of Mark. Keith wasn't feeling great but Mark was worse and had decided to descend from Lobuche, possibly a side effect of the Diamox. We weren't sure if Keith would even make it. He was going to give it a couple of hours to see if he improved.

The weather was beautiful. We had been so lucky. Since Dingboche, we'd had sun for most of the day. The views were great and the mood was good.

We set off along the edge of the glacier for a three-hour walk to Gorakshep, where we'd dump our bags and then walk the last two hours to Base Camp. It was slightly uphill, but barely noticeable. The path followed a small stream alongside the glacier, and for about an hour we followed it. A few people came in the opposite direction, raving about the views from Kala Patthar. All the while Pumori on the

Waking up in Lobuche to perfect weather for such an iconic day. The walk to Base Camp.

Heading to Gorakshep. The glacier to the right with Nuptse majestic in the skyline, but obscuring Everest. The terrain is barren and rocky.

A fantastic view down the valley. See how small the people are at the foot of the photo, indicating the sheer scale of the landscape.

left, and Nuptse on the right dominated the eyeline. Despite the good weather for two days or so, we'd still not seen Everest. Even at EBC you couldn't see the top. Could today be the day?

The terrain then became distinctly different. Rather than walking on a simple path, it became steeper and a bit more of a scramble. You could tell roughly where you were going, but it was a case of picking your own route through the rocks. We also skirted the edge of a hill and the path became more recognisable again, but the rock was loose underfoot and with the steep drop-off to our right, you needed to concentrate. Anton and I were still taking lots of photos, until Indra told us to hurry on a particular stretch. Only about 20m long, there was evidence to our right of rocks tumbling down the hill into the water of the glacier below. Clearly Indra thought there was a risk of rocks dropping down from above and either knocking us off the path, or at least giving us a smack on the head.

As soon as we rounded the corner past this stretch, Indra got very excitable again. Was this it, the big moment? It was. After many chances of seeing Everest scuppered because of the cloud, there was nothing getting in the way this time as the highest peak in the world poked its head from behind Nuptse. It was brilliant and anti-climatic at the same time. It was much smaller than Nuptse, it just shows what perspective does for you, but it was still visible. You had to look carefully to make sure you'd not mixed it up with another mountain but the main giveaway was the plume of snow being blown constantly from the top. I had a real sense of being somewhere special, but I yearned for a better view. Kala Patthar still featured very strongly in my mind. But that's for tomorrow.

But we had seen the top of Everest, even though it was tiny. I was going to be able to tell my friends after all. Of my targets today, it was one down, one to go. Now Base Camp was the only goal left for the day. Only…

The rest of the walk to Gorakshep was more of the same. Shale and rock paths, ups and downs, and views to die for. I couldn't wait to get there and move on. After a small incline, the first of the hostels came into view. We were to be in the first one, and unlike the previous day, it would be busy with our pals. Was it going to be the perfect day? It had only taken a couple of hours rather than the three that the route had said. Time for lunch and then drop most of our kit and head off to EBC. I had my final garlic soup (Kala Patthar tomorrow after all) and we psyched ourselves up for the destination we'd been dreaming of.

After eight days of walking, there it was, the highest place on earth. Poking out from behind Nuptse to the left, it has wisps of snow blowing from its peak.

Our porter, Sontos, had arrived with our main kit and the bags were in our room. We unloaded what we didn't need, and set off. It was to be such a good three hours; I'll remember it forever.

The walk took us once again along the edge of the Khumbu Glacier. Dramatic evidence of the power of the ice mass was all around. Great scars had been ripped

Barren yet mesmerising. The white glacier in the distance was EBC. In less than two hours we'd be there.

Approaching Gorakshep, the path up Kala Patthar very obvious ahead.

into the surrounding mountains. Rocks and stones had been tossed on to the top of the ice giving it a grey veneer but underneath you just knew what its constitution was. Small pools had formed, and the crashing of more rock on to its top was more prevalent. All the while, the white giants, blue sky and wispy clouds formed a film set backdrop. It was a remarkable contrast of imagery.

DAY 10: LOBUCHE TO GORAKSHEP

STRAVA

Gorak Shep

Lobuche

Distance	Elev Gain	Time
3.0 mi	992 ft	1h 49m

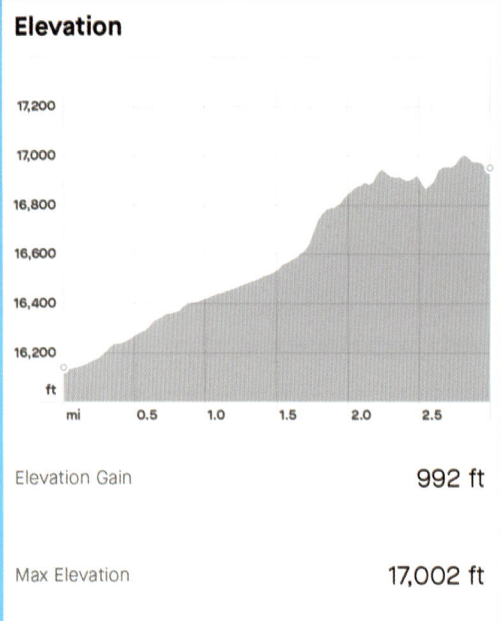

Elevation

Elevation Gain: 992 ft
Max Elevation: 17,002 ft

Pace

Avg Pace	35:15 /mi
Moving Time	1:49:00
Avg Elapsed Pace	49:45 /mi
Elapsed Time	2:33:49
Fastest Split	28:26 /mi

Heading down towards EBC, some people in my books didn't go down as it looked too hard to get back. Nothing was stopping us, we were almost there.

As we got closer we could make out some tents on the edge of the ice. I was convinced this was Base Camp. It looked to be about an hour away. Indra though told us that the original Base Camp (where we were going) was actually a lot closer, and we could now make out the famous rock marking the location and we could see people gathering there. We were going to be there in about 20 minutes. As we walked along a ridge, we started to pass a few of our friends coming back from EBC already. I started handing out my business card to them, explained I was writing a book, and asked each of them for ONE good photo so that I could include it within. You will see them in the book.

The path descended towards EBC from the ridge. One book I'd read described how some people stayed at the ridge as it would be too tiring to get back. If that is true, then they must have been really suffering as it was barely any descent at all. We passed by a large pool of water with very steep sides, and then Jonathan and Selina came towards us beaming. They'd completed their journey; we were minutes away.

One more small incline and we rounded the corner and there it was. Everest Base Camp. The famous rock with the altitude – 5,364m – written on it. What an

At Base Camp with Ben, Robbie and Alex and the custom flag.

achievement for everyone who had made it. My Everest Base Camp cap was now validated. I'd made it. I didn't have to throw it in the bin after all.

The atmosphere was great. It was a mild temperature, sunny and windless. No one was in a hurry to leave and everyone got as long as they wanted with the marker. I pulled my flag out of my bag, a George Cross with logos in three of the quadrants – Teenage Cancer Trust, the Derby County Ram and Boots Hockey Club. I had starting having this made in 2020, but the fourth quadrant had been blank for over two years. Now it displayed the year 2022. Two years after the flag had first been started. I took off my jacket to display my TCT T-shirt and held the flag aloft in front of the milestone.

A lot of our friends were also there. Ben, Alex and Robbie joined me for an English photoshoot. Michael and Anton understandably didn't join in as they weren't English. Michael did take the photos. Lots of them. I felt very proud of myself, very proud to be English and with the lads, and very privileged to be representing such a great cause at such an iconic location.

Others took their turn at the rock after me and I joined Anton a few metres away just staring at the panorama. A lot of people would have described this as surreal, but it was very real and I didn't want it to disappear. Not yet anyway.

THE TRIP

A little crowd was now building by the rock, but it was very good-natured. Anton had a few pics on his own there and then Indra and I joined him for the photo of our own little gang. It had been a good eight days, and I then became proud once more, this time of my travelling companions. We'd all done it.

We hung around, watching people have their own turn on or in front of the rock. Some Argentinians pulled their country's flag out and felt their own national pride at reaching their goal. One girl was doing handstands in front, trying to get a unique Instagram shot. It was lovely to see. Everyone was full of joy. And we were part of it, both our own experience but theirs too.

We stared up at the hills surrounding Base Camp that were towering above us – Everest hiding behind Nuptse which seemed close enough to touch. We looked at the glacier, now white rather than grey, and a sense of how insignificant we really were against this natural power hit me. I could have stayed for a couple of hours, but inevitably it had to come to an end. We had one last look at the glacier up close, then the view, then the rock, then we started on the path home. We passed a few more of our pals coming the other way – Anna and Rob, Pritima, and then finally Keith, resplendent in his kilt. He'd made it and I couldn't be more pleased for him. He later showed us a photo of him on top

A solo photo in front of the iconic rock. With few crowds, there was no rush. It was a great feeling.

With Anton at Base Camp, the glacier behind.

of the rock, kilt on, shirt off. Very *Highlander*. I'm glad we'd gone by then. He looked scary.

I even enjoyed the walk back, but Anton started to feel dizzy. Maybe the altitude had finally caught up with him. He was safely back on the path after the small climb back to the ridge, so wouldn't be doing any scrambling, but the closer we got back to Gorakshep, the worse he seemed to get. He'd not had any Diamox, so he had one when we got back. He was desperate not to miss Kala Patthar in the morning, but would he risk it feeling like this. He went for a lie down, so I chatted to an Irish couple, Eilish and Daniel, until dinner time. Anton reappeared. He felt a little better, but it was touch and go whether he'd be fit enough to wake up in the middle of the night and shift his bones up another 300m of ascent. His oxygen levels were okay so hopefully just a blip.

I felt fine, a very minor headache at the most. The Oxford lads and Michael, Keith, Jonathan and Selina and a few others were definitely going up in the morning. I was too. I hoped Anton would make it.

I was gutted to find that my iPad had water damage from the earlier leak. The screen was red. I'd used up a full powerbank charging it and it was useless. Luckily

DAY 10: GORAKSHEP TO EBC AND BACK

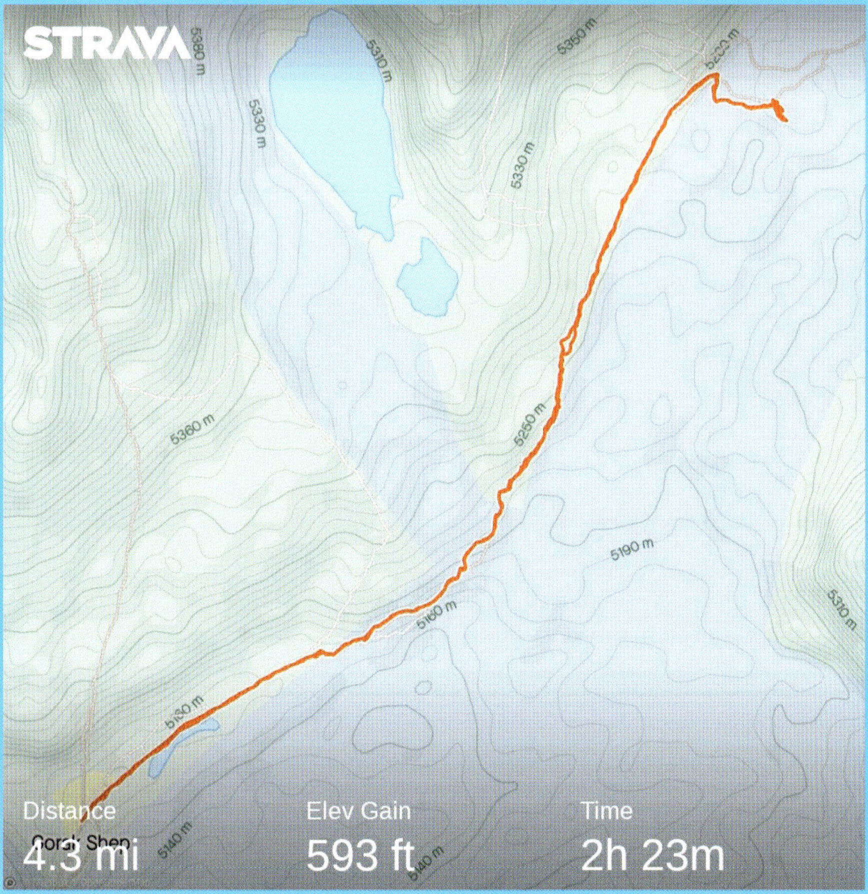

STRAVA
5380 m
5310 m
5330 m
5350 m
5200 m
5330 m
5360 m
5250 m
5190 m
5160 m
5310 m
5130 m
Gorak Shep
5140 m
5140 m
Distance
4.3 mi
Elev Gain
593 ft
Time
2h 23m

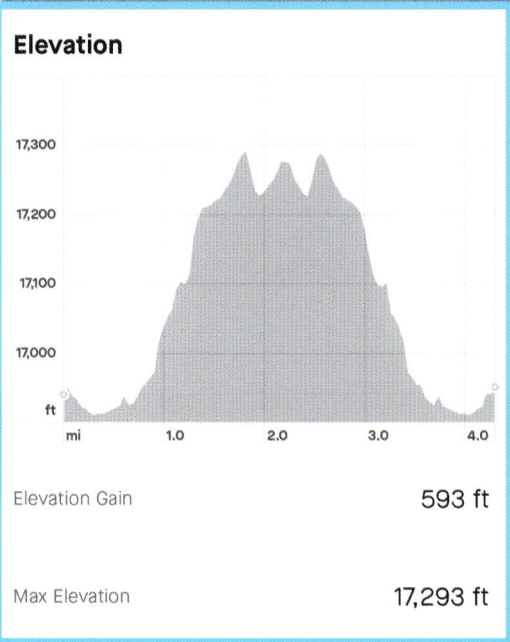

Elevation
17,300
17,200
17,100
17,000
ft
mi
1.0
2.0
3.0
4.0
Elevation Gain 593 ft
Max Elevation 17,293 ft

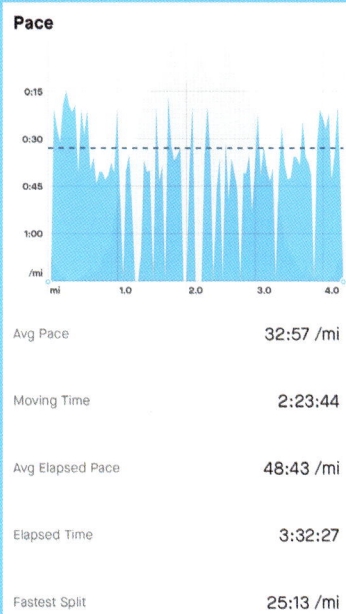

Pace
0:15
0:30
0:45
1:00
/mi
mi
1.0
2.0
3.0
4.0
Avg Pace 32:57 /mi
Moving Time 2:23:44
Avg Elapsed Pace 48:43 /mi
Elapsed Time 3:32:27
Fastest Split 25:13 /mi

Heading back to Gorakshep after making EBC. There was a spring in my step.

I had my backup phone, but what about the day nine diary. I had written it on the iPad and not sent it home. If I'd lost it all I'd be very despondent as I'd have to recreate it. Spontaneity is so much better in this form of writing. I didn't want to have to think about it all again.

It threatened to be cold that night. It was our highest overnight stop and temperatures can get below -10 degrees, even at this time of year. I prepared my bed and for the first time got inside my down sleeping bag. In the end I didn't need it, but I was glad I had it.

I needed a good night's sleep. It was Kala Patthar tomorrow for daybreak. A really early start, but with the best views in the world potentially. I didn't want to miss it.

Stats: four litres of water, O_2 in the low 80s, one Diamox in the morning. Lobuche to Gorakshep was 3.09 miles, with about 300m of ascent. To Base Camp and back was 4.36 miles. A further elevation gain of around 200m, and only two and a half hours of actual walking time. In the day I'd walked 33,453 steps.

30 SEPTEMBER 2022
DAY 11: KALA PATTHAR, THEN GORAKSHEP TO PANGBOCHE

After the excitement of reaching Base Camp yesterday, today would be one of exhilaration but also the most physically and mentally demanding days of the whole adventure.

I thought back to the picture I saw in the Nepalese restaurant in Beeston before my trip – Everest and the Himalayan region from the top of Kala Patthar. It was truly mesmerising. And now I was on the cusp of seeing it for myself, assuming the weather held out. We'd had two really good days, surely it would last another. None of the authors in the books I'd read had made it to the top; only one had even reached halfway, but I'd seen the trail we'd be going up the night before, and although it looked as though it would be hard, we'd been through worse this week. The difference this time is that I'd be going up in the dark, freezing cold, at over 5,500m. Actually, it does sound tricky.

None of my 'gang' were thinking of backing out or feeling the side effects of altitude sickness. Even Anton, who had been feeling dizzy last night, was going. If I was last man standing then who knows, but with such a positive atmosphere around the lodge there was no way was I missing out. There was a debate about what time to leave. Set off too early and you'd be waiting at the top too long in the freezing cold, too late and you miss the sunrise. Indra was insistent that a 4am start would be correct, so most went along with that. He is the expert, and guess what, he got it spot on.

Anton set the alarm for 3.40am. I don't think I slept particularly well anyway, a mixture of sleeping above 5,000m and the hope that the weather would be good enough. I must have dropped off as the alarm jolted me awake.

We'd prepared our kit the night before. Lots of warm clothes and hats and gloves. I even had the Outfitters down coat in my bag in case I needed it at the

The path we'd come up, steep and steady. What views though.

top. There was no way I'd need it on the walk up. With an ascent of 600m, I would generate enough heat to keep me warm on the climb, but spending half an hour at the top in sub-zero temperatures would definitely test my physical resilience. If I got there.

There were a few all setting off at the same time but we were waiting for Keith. He came down at 4.08am for the 4am meet time. He'd actually been up earlier but was told that the weather wasn't good so went back to bed, then changed his mind. I bet he's glad he changed his mind.

As we walked from the hotel towards Kala Patthar with our head torches on, you could see a string of lights ahead. They were stretched at least 400m from front to back, so we followed. My head torch was okay but Anton's was like a full-beam headlight making mine redundant so I just took it off after about five minutes. I didn't notice any difference.

The hill started steeply, but soon settled into a steady incline. I wasn't struggling as we passed the 5,200m mark. Keith was though and told us to carry on without him. He would just follow the path. It was true, there was no way you could get lost. After we tried to wait for him he insisted, so we carried on at our own speed.

We passed a few groups as we started to get to the halfway point. Some books have said that the views are as good from here. No chance were we taking that risk, it had to be the top. The views would have been good halfway, but not comparable.

Everest got bigger and bigger the higher we climbed as it started to emerge from behind Nuptse. Thinking we'd seen it yesterday, this was on a different level. As the night started turning into day, in that period before sunrise, you just knew you were doing something special that you'd be able to implant in your memory (and your photo album) for ever. There was the odd moment that the clouds came across and you crossed your fingers that it wouldn't be permanent, but we got lucky. The weather was great for most of the time.

It was getting tougher. We were approaching the point where the air had only 50 per cent of the oxygen at sea level and I had to keep stopping to take some deep breaths. Most of the time on the trip I needed to just have a break, now I needed to sit down too. I got into the 100-steps-then-find-a-nice-rock-to-perch-on pattern. Then I'd suck in the precious air. At the start it was 20 deep breaths, then 30, then 40. The lyrics to Survivor's 'Burning Heart' from *Rocky IV* kept running through my head. 'When the body says no, the spirit cries never.' Really cheesy but it was genuine. I wasn't going to be beaten. Not this close.

But we were getting near the top. Head lamps were no longer needed as the first hint of the sunrise appeared. A glow of orange below the skyline. Anton kept

The clouds swirling. Indra and Anton in front of Everest (on the left).

At the top of Kala Patthar just before daybreak. It was what I had come for and I had made it.

his on which affected the night vision a little. It was only when Indra asked him to turn it off that he did.

There was a congregation of people at the top, some we knew (Jonathan and Selina, Robbie, Alex and Ben, Michael) but surprisingly quite a few I had never seen before. How had we travelled the same route for eight days and not bumped into them? It didn't matter, I felt among friends and turned to enjoy the view.

To say that Base Camp was the ultimate destination is true. That's what everyone knows and the congratulations on social media indicated that I needed to do no more in their eyes to have achieved my goals. But this was my personal ambition. More than Base Camp this was the view I had dreamed of. The first 'wow' moment was when the sun hit Ama Dablam. The pyramid shape was perfect for the light and the orange reflection has probably given me my finest photograph of the whole trip. My favourite mountain, now it was my favourite memory. But don't think that it was all downhill from there, either figuratively or literally.

Turning behind slightly to the left, you started with Pumori, its classic cartoon mountain shape so close you felt you could reach out and touch it (like Nuptse yesterday). Then slowly panning round clockwise you passed peak after peak.

Everest was as magnificent as anytime we'd seen it so far, then Nuptse, then Ama Dablam in the distance, then, then … it just kept going on. All bathed in the early morning light, there was a vista of about 270 degrees. All with the true scale of the Khumbu glacier below. It really was a jaw-dropping view. Is there a finer one on earth? I'd loved my walks in the UK, and I do believe that some of the views there were among the most spectacular I'd see, but this was another level altogether. We were standing close to the top of the world. It was 5,600m above sea level, freezing cold but I didn't feel it. The adrenalin must have kicked in big time. I just wanted to stay. So we did for a few more minutes. I thought I'd be emotional after the other day, but I wasn't, just completely exhilarated.

But all good things must come to an end. Anton's hands were freezing. They were cold at the best of times, but he could barely feel them. I'd lent him my over-mittens from skiing but it may have gone beyond the point of doing any good. My rucksack was sparkling with little ice crystals indicating that it was sub-zero. He wasn't the only one, others were also descending to get warm. Selina later told us that she'd had to run down to try and get warm again. I wasn't too bad, I didn't feel the need for the down jacket even, but I was glad I'd packed my ski gloves.

We could still see people coming to the top, including Keith who'd made it. But we were now on our way down.

Ama Dablam at dawn. Breathtaking.

EVEREST BASE CAMP

Part of the panoramic view. Everest and Nuptse in the middle, then Ama Dablam in the distance. The Khumbu glacier at the bottom. EBC is down there somewhere.

As we started to descend, it wasn't the end. Climbing, we'd had our back to the view, but going down it was all in front of us. Before we'd been stopping to catch our physical breath, now we were stopping to catch our breath at the view. It was almost dawn now and although we'd not seen Everest glowing like Ama Dablam I felt I'd seen everything I could have hoped for after days of missing the 'big one'. I kept looking at it all the way down. No other peak got a look in. It was the biggest mountain in the world and it deserved my full attention. Truly an unforgettable experience.

We arrived back at the hostel at about 7am, three hours after leaving. We'd packed a bit but had that job to complete. I had porridge again for breakfast; it is a daily occurrence now but the heat was needed more than ever. Anton seemed to be warming up. It was tricky to tell. Keith eventually made it back down and Jonathan and Selina joined us too. It was great to share our experiences with each other.

Opposite: Gorakshep from halfway up Kala Patthar.

DAY 11: GORAKSHEP TO KALA PATTHAR

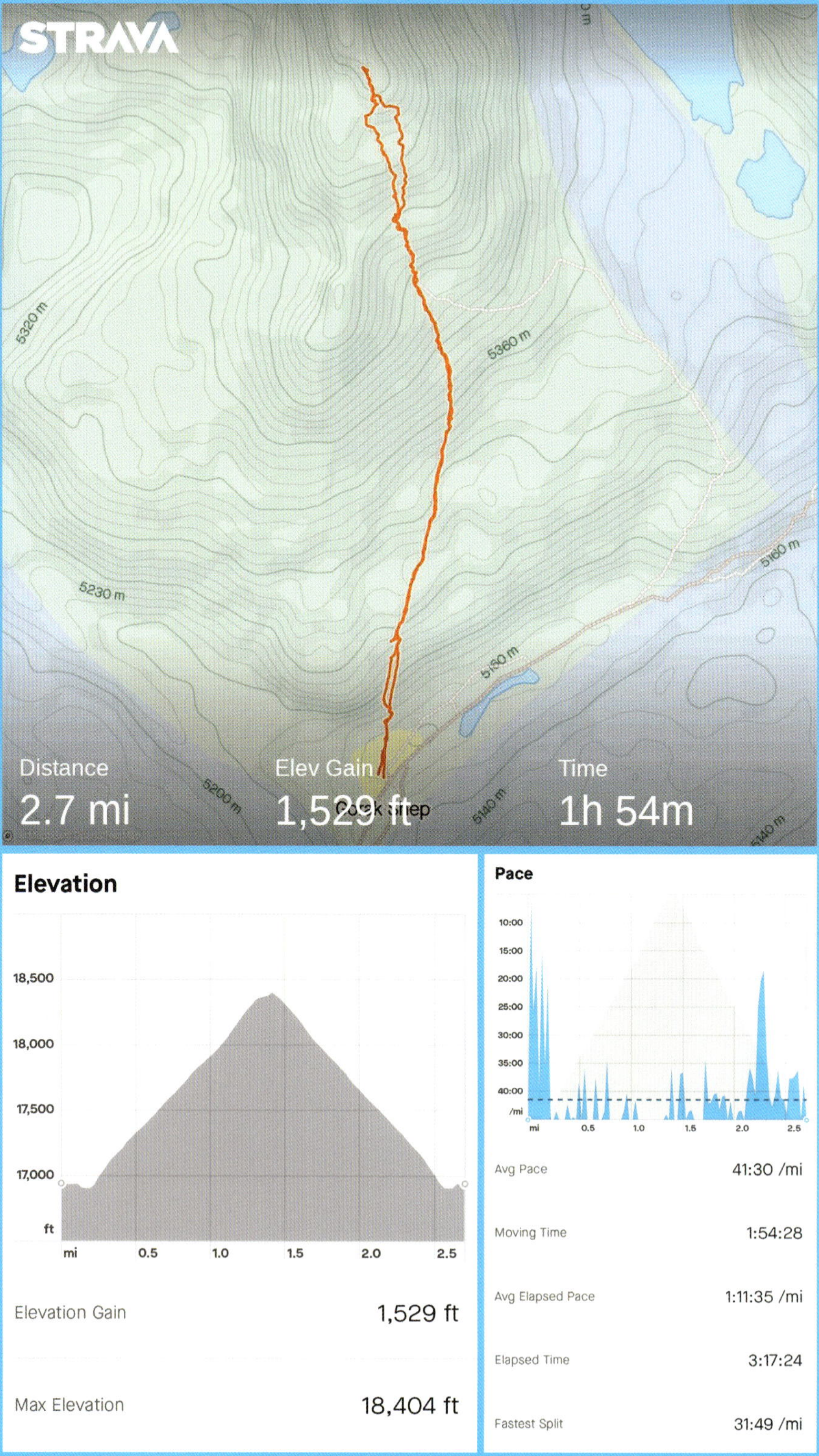

STRAVA

Distance	Elev Gain	Time
2.7 mi	1,529 ft	1h 54m

Elevation

Elevation Gain — 1,529 ft
Max Elevation — 18,404 ft

Pace

Avg Pace — 41:30 /mi
Moving Time — 1:54:28
Avg Elapsed Pace — 1:11:35 /mi
Elapsed Time — 3:17:24
Fastest Split — 31:49 /mi

THE TRIP

The reason I was here. Everest in all her glory.

Then the day took a turn for the worse. I am not sure why but it was to become my hardest day, both physically and mentally, of the whole experience.

Someone commented that Anton rarely spoke. It was true. He didn't. I'd tried to make lots of conversation with him over the last eight days, but I don't think he asked me one question about me. He knew about my jobs, kids, travel etc, primarily through conversations I'd had with others. You know the general getting-to-know-you chit-chat that people go through when they meet. But there was nothing. I decided to experiment. It was not one of my best decisions. That's an understatement. It was one of my worst ever decisions.

After packing our bags, we were ready to go. It was about 8am and we knew we had a tough day ahead. The minimum was to get back to Pherice, about the same distance as Dingboche but the other side of the acclimatisation hill from a few days earlier. The general consensus from everyone else was to go to Pangboche, a further hour and a half down the hill. I'm glad we did it in hindsight but it nearly cost me my health and my sanity.

Keith had already set off to catch up with Mark who had turned back yesterday, so after saying goodbye to Jonathan and Selina who were going a different route, we headed off to retrace our steps back to Lobuche, then Pherice. This was where I started my experiment. I decided not to make conversation. I'd done it for eight

Approaching Lobuche for the last time.

days and I wanted to see if Anton would be able to stand the silence and strike up conversation.

For the next five hours, the experiment proved that he could. Not a word to me on the walk. Not even about the walk itself, you know the usual 'oh look at that' or 'what part of the trip to Base Camp did you like the best'. Nothing. He only asked Indra two questions about the walk in that time too. I got deeper and deeper in a mood. I love talking to people and I wondered if I'd mainly been talking to myself for days. I had more interaction with the trekkers passing us on the way to Gorak Shep in 30 seconds than I'd had with Anton in the previous 30 minutes.

After about an hour of walking in silence, Jonathan and Selina caught us up. Their alternate route was via Lobouche, so for 20 glorious minutes I had a lively chat with them. Why is it so easy for most people yet I was spending 11 days, virtually 24/7 with someone who clearly didn't want to, or know how to develop that personal bond? It is something I have never come across with anyone before and I started to wish I'd come on my own.

Despite the silence, the weather was great and the scenery was still spectacular. It had been less than 24 hours since we had been coming the other way but I couldn't remember some of the route. In the excitement of heading on the final leg

THE TRIP

to Base Camp, I must have been walking on auto, with my head firmly fixed on the skyline and not the terrain. There was a familiar part, where Indra had jumped around when spotting Everest for the first time on our trip. You know, the one with smoke on. This was closely followed by the quick dash through the avalanche hazard which I remembered and a curve in the path with a steep drop on to the glacier. But that was it. I had to take photos on the way back just to make sure I remembered what it was like getting there.

We arrived In Lobuche after a long, slightly downhill path. Funny how I noticed it going downhill, more than I noticed it going uphill yesterday. We crossed below the 5,000m mark for the final time. I lay back on a rock and shut my eyes, basking in the sun but really wanted to see whether there was any attempt at conversation. There wasn't.

Indra asked us if we wanted to stop in Lobuche or head straight for Pherice. We pushed on. I bought a bottle of water as I'd packed my bladder away in my kitbag. After dutifully carrying four litres a day, I was relieved to not have it with me. Sontos would also have been happy as I transferred over four kilograms from my duffel bag to my backpack. A feeble attempt at trying to give him something in return for all the carrying he'd done for us over the last eight days.

Looking towards Ama Dablam and the memorial garden

The entrance to the Memorial Garden, with Ama Dablam and hundreds of prayers flags. One of my favourite images of the whole trip. It sums up everything about Nepal.

DAY 11: GORAKSHEP TO THUKLA

STRAVA

Gorak Shep
Lobuche

Distance: **4.9 mi**
Elev Gain: **181 ft**
Time: **2h 27m**

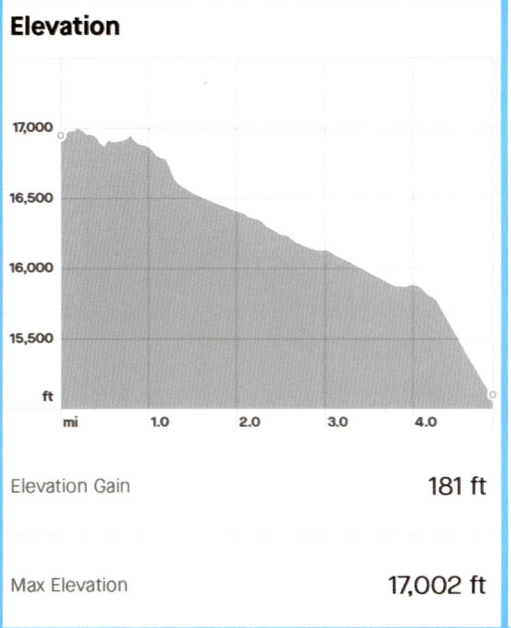

Elevation

Elevation Gain: **181 ft**
Max Elevation: **17,002 ft**

Pace

Avg Pace: **29:48 /mi**
Moving Time: **2:27:33**
Avg Elapsed Pace: **35:25 /mi**
Elapsed Time: **2:55:19**
Fastest Split: **22:20 /mi**

THE TRIP

The trip from Lobuche to Pherice would drop us another few hundred metres but it was mainly steady. I was in a real hump by now, so led the way. I haven't put my headphones on at all, preferring to listen to Nepal. Whether it was the silence of the hills, the crashing of the river or the shouts of the Yak herders, I didn't want to obscure any of the senses with artificial interference. But I was tempted now. Anything to distract me from the silence.

The landscape started to change as we headed back to Thukla for a drinks stop. We passed through the memorial garden again but barely paused for further reflection.

Then it was the staircase down once more, passing red-faced and distressed trekkers coming in the opposite side. Had we been like that?

At the cafe I deliberately sought out company. There was a fellow on his own, who I'd seen knocking about and asked if we could join him. We introduced ourselves. Kenneth was travelling with four Thai guys but I'd only ever seen him on his own. He was only too pleased to have company. We chatted about travel mainly and I found out he was Canadian and had been to Machu Piccu and Mount Fuji. His Thai companions were very slow and had suffered from altitude sickness. I knew more about him in ten minutes than I knew about Anton in eight days.

After a cuppa, we descended for about 50m (as the crow flies) and then back over the wooden/metal river crossing which had been so hard to see until the last minute two days previously. I had my hands in my pockets but Indra insisted I take them out. Was it for balance? Probably. Was the bridge riskier than I imagined?

We crossed without incident of course and headed slightly uphill to the fork in the path. Instead of turning left back to Dingboche, we took a right down a steep hill to Pherice. I couldn't take it any longer. I lay the groundwork by asking Indra about his wife, then asked Anton about his. It was an open-ended question, 'Tell me about your wife.' I only knew her name, her job and how they met. He could have made anything up, or told me all the good things, or expanded on the basics of their life, but nothing. I asked if she was younger or older and a one word answer followed. I then asked him if he wanted to talk about her. He said 'not really' and that was the conversation over.

It took me to the edge. I stormed to the front once more and just walked in silence. Down the rocky section, then the path we'd seen from above, I was desperate to find someone to talk to. What looked like it should take 30 minutes

EVEREST BASE CAMP

The path to Pheriche. It seemed so long to get there.

DAY 11: THUKLA TO PANGBOCHE

STRAVA

Distance: **6.4 mi**
Elev Gain: **315 ft**
Time: **2h 53m**

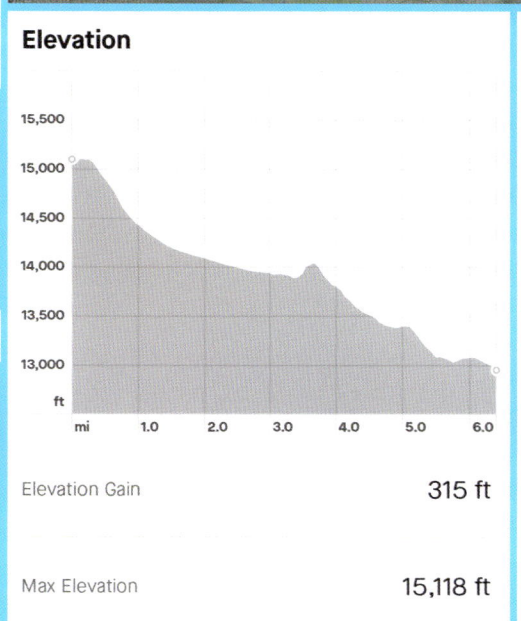

Elevation

Elevation Gain: 315 ft
Max Elevation: 15,118 ft

Pace

Avg Pace: 27:04 /mi
Moving Time: 2:53:49
Avg Elapsed Pace: 34:26 /mi
Elapsed Time: 3:41:05
Fastest Split: 23:27 /mi

was actually double the time, but we eventually made it to Pheriche, a place I knew they'd be a few people I could enjoy their company with.

The downside of going with a guide is that you are pot luck on the venue, whether lunch or overnighters. We passed a lodge with people sat around, but Indra took us right past that to a lodge with no other guests. In the mood I was in, this was the last thing I needed. We ordered and then ate in silence. I'm not sure if Anton noticed the tension but Indra certainly did. When Anton went to the loo, I asked Indra to get me a separate room for the night. After eight straight days and nights with a stranger I just needed some privacy.

We headed off to Pangboche after we'd agreed to carry on. My legs had started to hurt and my sense of self-pity had heightened. It was an hour and a half and it seemed longer. The trees and plants were back. I'd barely even noticed.

The weather dropped too and it was getting cold. I had my bandana round my ears, Indra style, and this really helped keep the chill away. The scenery started to mist over. One saving grace in my otherwise tough day was seeing the mountains, still gracing the sky. Now with even that gone, I couldn't wait to get back.

Eventually we made it to my free toilet stop on the way up, the Amadablam View Hotel. I had a feeling we'd stop here on the way down – favour for a favour and all that. I immediately carted everything off to my private room. It was lovely to have somewhere to go without Anton. I even paid for a hot shower, 600 rupees, but it went cold after only a few minutes and I had not warmed up.

I was pleased to see people in the main room I knew, the Danish girls and the Irish couple Daniel and Eilish who'd I'd met only yesterday. But I didn't feel like socialising. I was cold, tired, miserable and was shivering. Was I coming down with something? I felt awful. I had a quick nap under both of the duvets in the room and managed to get downstairs for dinner. The English lads had turned up. Three of my favourite people on the trip; my mood improved slightly. Anton and I even played a few games of cards while I chatted to the others in the room.

Was this the start of the thaw in my icy veneer?

At 8pm, after getting up at 3.45am and walking for six hours straight AFTER Kala Patthar I was so tired I went to bed. I put *Quadrophenia* by The Who on my spare phone and I don't even remember getting past 'The Real Me'. It was track two. After struggling to get to sleep for most of the nights I was gone. I hoped I'd be feeling a lot better tomorrow. Both physically and mentally.

1 OCTOBER 2022
DAY 12: PANGBOCHE TO NAMCHE BAZAAR

The privacy and long rest made a massive difference both to my health and my mental state. With a later start planned I'd had nearly 12 hours alone in my room. I'd had my best night's sleep and the aches and pains of the previous day's long walk had disappeared. The shivering had long stopped and I felt full of beans.

I also reflected on my attitude yesterday and realised I'd been a complete idiot. I teach students that behaviour can be changed but not personality. I'd expected Anton to be different to how he was to bend to what I wanted. It wasn't fair. You are who you are, and although unlike anyone I'd met before, Anton was who he was and it was not up to him to entertain me. I went back to normal and guess what, it was a much better day. The trip for me is not life-changing as some say; I have done some pretty special things over the years, but how to deal with this relationship was a huge learning for me. If he didn't want to get too close by talking about personal things that's his decision. Everything else about him was great – patient, determined, friendly and completely trustworthy. I was really pleased I was with him.

My iPad had also kicked back into life, probably as it dried off. Maybe that had been part of the reason for my mood yesterday, combined with the 'comedown' from my adrenalin high of Kala Patthar. I sent home my day nine diary before anything else happened.

At breakfast, I had a long chat with Ben, one of the Oxford lads, about life, careers and travel. I have really enjoyed being around the three of them. The same age as my youngest, I get them, and it made me realise that despite the outward confidence and travel experience, an experienced word often gives young adults food for thought. My NTU mentoring also kicked in. I think Ben really appreciated the chat. If not, he was too polite to mention it. Either way, I hope I offered some

Showing off our new scarves in front of the aptly named Ama Dablam View hotel – complete with the view.

ideas and experience for him to mull over. I try not to offer advice, just options. Advice can be seen as 'telling' others what to do, something I hate when done to me. Whether he takes on board any of those ideas is irrelevant; options just need to be offered. Twenty-year-olds are perfectly capable of making great decisions, given the chance. Ben looked like he'd be one of those who would make great decisions and I look forward to seeing them play out, even if it was just via LinkedIn.

As we left the hotel, the landlady gave Anton and I a Buddhist scarf each. It was a lovely gesture and we dutifully wore them all day. She didn't need to, but what customer service.

We had a five-hour walk to Namche on the agenda for today. It had taken one and a half days to get to Pangboche on the way up, so this was going to be easy. Or so we thought. Considering we descended from approximately 13,000ft to 11,250ft in the whole day, we also climbed nearly 1,900ft. It was tough.

The upside was the weather. We had really struck lucky. Since the first day in Dingboche, we had had some great views of the mountains and today was no different. The standout mountain, as usual, was Ama Dablam. I'd read that it was most people's favourite mountain and I can see why. It is so visually attractive, a

Ama Dablam, forests, a stupa and gorgeous weather. A decent start to the day.

little twin peak but stand alone and dominant. Everest is the big draw but it is often obscured by other nearer mountains so never quite gets the dominance its size deserves (Kala Patthar excluded).

After my gloom of yesterday, I was my usual irreverent self. I also noticed a real change in Anton. He must have noticed how different I was yesterday and was probably baffled why. I wanted him to enjoy the last two days as much as I wanted to. It seemed like we were both making a real effort.

As we headed for Tengboche, we didn't talk about anything personal as usual, but we did talk about the scenery, the vegetation, the animals and our memories of going the other way. If you remember, it had been poor weather, with little upward visibility. Now we had the full panorama and it lightened not just our mood but our fellow travellers. Cheery hellos were abound, especially with the trekkers coming the other way – they were closer to EBC, we were closer to the relative metropolis of Namche.

Then we hit the first hill. I remembered coming down it, but had forgotten how steep it was. Only about 150m of ascent we climbed to Tengboche, but it was tough. Surely after nailing Kala Patthar only yesterday, and with a few hundred metres of altitude descent under our belts it would be easy, but this was probably the hardest ascent of my whole return to Lukla.

Finally we reached Tengboche and the weather was glorious. Looking back we saw Everest for the last time, standing majestic and determined in the distance among the other lesser peaks. Last time we'd been in Tengboche we'd barely seen the other side of the monastery, such was the cloud cover. Anton and I decided to

Tengboche memorial stones framing the mountains beautifully.

THE TRIP

stop for a cuppa at the hostel we'd stayed at on the way. It was the least we could do. It was my favourite stopover on my whole trip and they deserved our custom. It was lovely to see the hostess again. Despite it being a few days and with many travellers passing through, she recognised us. It doesn't take much to make me feel appreciated, and she had the magic formula.

The next hour was equally tough, even though the first 20 minutes were downhill. One of the harder climbs on the ascent, it was tricky going downhill. I was reasonably okay going up, but downhill I jolted the knees. I don't walk with poles, but this was probably the only time on the trip I would have liked them. We passed trekkers coming in the opposite direction, mostly blowing out of their nether regions and wished them well. All the while in the back of our minds knowing we had a steep incline once we hit the bottom. I think they did too, only for them their day ended at Tengboche. We had another couple of hours to Namche.

Over the next 30 minutes, once we'd hit the river at the bottom, we climbed. I had vowed to count to 200 steps before stopping but I rarely reached it. Either a yak train appeared or a photo op presented itself. I must have warmed up, as I managed the 300m ascent without much trouble. I am much fitter than I was, I was certainly better than I was 30 minutes previously, and it showed.

The rest of the walk took us around the edge of the mountain. Indra pointed out the Everest View Hotel on the peak of one of the foothills and Khumjung to the right. I was convinced it was Namche; it was weird seeing something from a distance I'd been to on the acclimatisation walk, and still not recognising it. Namche was a bit further on, but out of sight.

For the next hour we just walked, either in friendly silence or general chit-chat. We passed Buddha eye stupas, and marvelled at the changing scenery. Deep valleys, lush vegetation and the ever-present milk river dominated the eyeline. Not knowing what views we'd had on the way, we both stopped and made many photo breaks. I suspect when we compare photos from day four of the hike they'll be similar. The cloud cover now obscured the big ones as it did on the outward leg. But it didn't matter, It was a stunning view.

I hear lots of trekkers constantly asking their guides how far it is to the destination – desperate to get to there, like kids in the back of a car on the way to a family holiday. I make it a personal thing never to ask Indra 'how far'. It smacks of desperation and I also love walking so I just keep going until we arrive where

On the way up to Tengboche it had been foggy and miserable. Now gorgeous sunshine. Not so good for those coming up, but Anton stared in wonder at the views.

we're going. Without even realising how close we were, we turned a corner and the first buildings of Namche appeared. We passed the now unoccupied table which had been fundraising for the paths, and headed down to our hotel, the 8848m that we'd stayed in for two nights on the way. On the way, we saw our first cat of the whole trip. Loads of dogs, but no cats. I wonder why they're so rare.

Back into Namche, it really felt like coming home.

I asked for another private room as I'd enjoyed it so much the night before, but it came at a cost. No ensuite (not an issue) but no charging point in the room, or more importantly, no free hot shower. I'd really let Anton down here. He'd lost out on the better facilities through no fault of his own. We both had hot showers (500 rupees) in the communal shower and met downstairs. Mark and Keith were there. It was great to see Mark had fully recovered. We'd not seen him since Dingboche.

I mentioned to Anton that I was going shopping and then to find a bar showing the English football (it was Spurs v Arsenal) and he wanted to come. Despite not opening up about his life, he really wanted to spend time together and this compounded my guilt from the day before. He'd even agreed to set our mealtime for 7.30pm rather than the usual 7pm to make sure I could see the end of the match (remember he doesn't like football).

We went shopping, or rather I did, Anton just browsed. Three T-shirts, a shot glass and a bandana later, I'd spent enough for the day. I'd get the rest in Lukla or Kathmandu. We saw Keith and Mark on the streets of Namche and agreed to meet Keith in the Irish bar for a beer while watching the match. Mark didn't like footy so would just read his book in the hostel. It would be my first beer since Kathmandu. I figured 'what the hell'. I didn't need to worry about altitude

The first beer for 10 days. It was lovely.

sickness now, just hangovers and they were easily avoided. Weren't they? We also bumped into Don and Jerry, our American friends, and invited them to watch the match. At least one of them had heard of Arsenal! They didn't show. Can't think why?

The bar was pretty busy for the match, with most supporting Spurs. The bar only had one brand of beer, Barasinghe, a local craft beer. It was 800 rupees for a can, about a fiver. On the menu was Everest at 500 rupees, but no sign of it. With a captive audience I don't blame them for going for the more expensive option; an extra 300 rupees was never going to put many off. I bought Keith a beer, Anton had a tea. Then Indra and Keith's guide came in. Indra was just after a

In the Irish bar enjoying a pint with Keith watching the match. It could have been any bar, in any town, in any part of the world.

DAY 12: PANGBOCHE TO NAMCHE

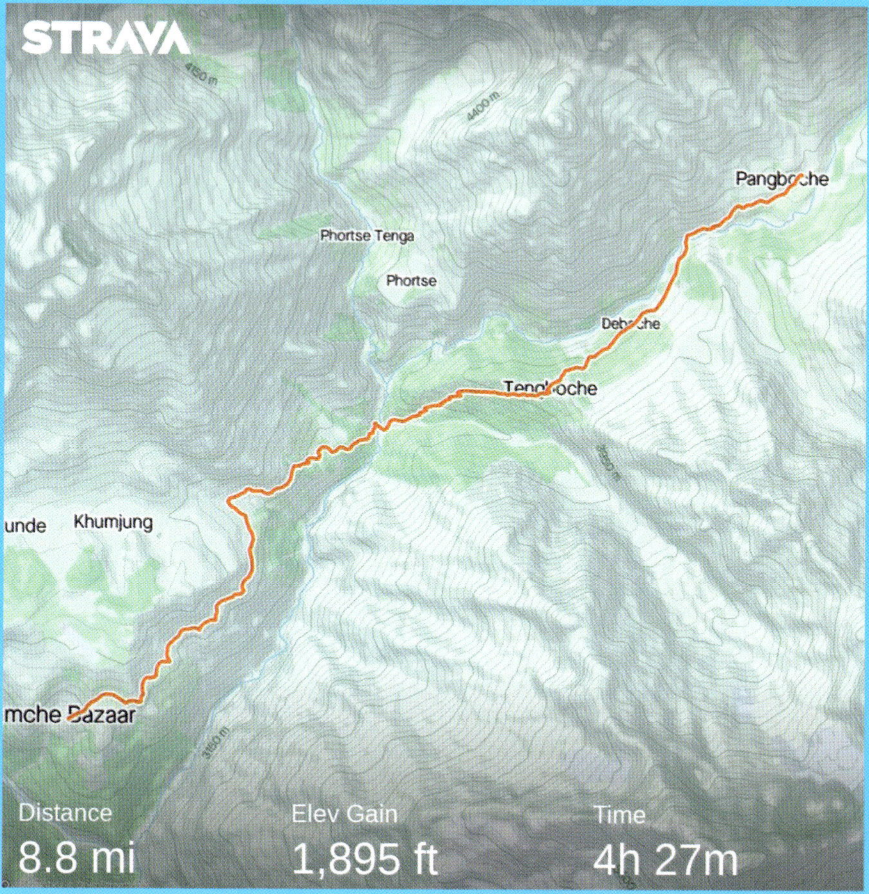

STRAVA

Distance: **8.8 mi**
Elev Gain: **1,895 ft**
Time: **4h 27m**

Elevation
Elevation Gain: 1,895 ft
Max Elevation: 12,954 ft

Pace
Avg Pace: 30:11 /mi
Moving Time: 4:27:36
Avg Elapsed Pace: 40:59 /mi
Elapsed Time: 6:03:21
Fastest Split: 24:11 /mi

rum so went and found a bar that served it, but Keith's guide stayed and watched the match and had a couple of beers. Or rather he spent the whole game talking an inch from Keith's ear (in front of me) about Son Heung-min, Tottenham's South Korean forward, and how the English media don't rate him because they love Harry Kane so much. Absolute nonsense of course, everyone loves Son (apart from Arsenal fans). It shows what happens when you get all your knowledge and stats from the *FIFA* computer game. He knew all the nationalities but nothing about the actual game. It was comical as he was drunk on two cans but after an hour highly irritating.

After the match, it was back to the hostel for dinner, and then back to the pub for Liverpool v Brighton. You really can get the English Premier League anywhere. Full of Liverpool fans, I laughed my socks off when Brighton scored the equaliser in the last five minutes to make it a 3-3 draw (growing up in the 1980s gave me an irrational dislike of the Reds). Anton and Keith were there as were the Oxford boys and Danish girls. It was nice to be surrounded by people I knew and liked.

So what had started in the hills at Pangboche had ended in a pub in Namche and a very home-like experience. I only had a couple of beers all night as we still had walking to do tomorrow, but it was a lovely end to the day. Indra was even tiddly when we got back; he'd obviously found the rum.

2 OCTOBER 2022
DAY 13: NAMCHE BAZAAR TO LUKLA

I wondered what affect the beer would have on me, and the rum on Indra. Neither of us seemed to be suffering any side effects. Despite the relatively late night, we had agreed to set off 8am, so up at seven. It was the last day of an incredible journey and we didn't want to rush it. Sure it would be nice to be in Kathmandu, relaxing in the sun with a beer on a rooftop cafe, but that would also mean my time in this part of the Himalaya would be over, probably for ever. At 52, and with lots more of the world still unexplored, it is unlikely I'd be back, so with bag packed and phone battery full, we stepped out into Namche for the last time.

I love this little town, full of surprises on the curved alleys that wind around the hills and with a smile from everyone you meet. It was sunny as we started the walk, giving us our first glimpse of the size of the mountains behind the foothills. It had been cloudy on all three days we'd been there earlier in the journey, now the weather gave us one final hurrah for our last chapter in the hills. It seemed a perfect way to exit my new favourite place in Nepal.

The first part of the journey was downhill, for a long way. I remembered that I didn't find it too difficult going up, and it was the same going down. Paths rather than steps, there wasn't the pressure on the knees I'd felt coming down from Tengboche yesterday. At the Everest viewpoint, there still wasn't a view. It was a good job we'd not relied on it as this would have been our last chance to see the highest spot on the planet. I hoped that those coming in the opposite direction weren't disappointed either, there are plenty of chances on the trip, just a little patience is needed. We also met Don and Jerry again. They asked about the match. I told them about the very entertaining 3-3 in the Liverpool game which baffled them. In US sport there always has to be a winner. I tried to explain that in football, not losing is sometimes as good as winning. Don said he wasn't expecting a philosophy lesson at 3,200m. I told him I was just explaining football.

Over the next section of the walk to the Hillary Bridge, we kept passing each other as we either rested or stopped for photos. Mark and Keith also joined in this little game of tag. As we arrived at the bridge, memories of the walk up came flooding back. Was it really only nine days since we'd crossed it on the way to Namche? So much had happened. Friendships forged, challenges overcome, new experiences encountered – and we'd stood at 5,600m looking at the most amazing panorama I am ever likely to see. It was a time of quiet reflection for all of us.

After crossing the bridge for the final time we started to notice the sheer volume of people ascending towards Namche. The main trekking season starts in October, and with some bad weather in Kathmandu for a few days, grounding flights to Lukla, it seemed that the tourist doors had well and truly opened. I estimated that we must have passed 1,000 people coming towards us – with a mix of excitement at the prospect of getting to EBC, and also trepidation at the thought of the climb to Namche. Base Camp wasn't busy when we were there. Everyone was patient, got as long as they wanted for the photos, and were generally in a congratulatory

A spectacular cloud formation to start our last day of walking.

Above the Hillary Bridge.

mood with each other. But I reckon only about 200 reached it on 'my day'. What would it be like if five times that number descended in six days' time? Would there be queues like at the top of Snowdon on my training walk? I silently thanked my job as a lecturer for having to go slightly earlier than recommended so I could get back for the start of term, even with the weather risk involved. With fewer people, relationships are broader as you recognise people en route and chat away in the hostels. Would today's cohort build them the same with such large numbers of fellow trekkers? I hope so, but I'm not convinced.

From the Hillary Bridge to Phakding, our stopover on day one, we walked for a couple of hours in the sunshine. There was a lot of local activity, seemingly stocking up on supplies for the busy period ahead. Porters and beasts carted heavy loads along the paths. The restaurants which had been quiet on the way up were now filling up almost everywhere along the way. Our first cafe stop, where just Indra, Anton and I were customers, now had a dozen people all enjoying the great views we'd had in our formative trekking days.

The volume of people really hit home at the entrance to the National Park. Following a steep but short climb to the entrance, the permit area was packed. There must have been 150 people there, all waiting patiently while their guides queued at the window issuing them. It wasn't bedlam, but it was very busy.

Almost immediately we hit Monjo, and we settled in at a great cafe for a cuppa. It was a small village which had few people stopping at it on the way, but again it was busy. Great for the locals, I was really pleased for them.

The whole journey since the bridge had been generally downhill, but with some uphill parts which we now barely noticed. On earlier parts of the walk, I'd

The crowds at the entrance to the Khumbu Region. Contrast the numbers here to only nine days earlier.

Heading to Phakding (over the bridge and up the hill). We knew Indra was hungry.

remember my training walks and think, 'If I can do Scafell Pike, or Ben Lomond or…, then I can do this.' Now it was, 'If I can do Kala Patthar, or Tengboche, or the Everest View Hotel, then I can do this.' My terms of reference had completely changed. At the prospect of any hill, even one that was about 50 steps, tiny really, my mountain experience kicked in. Really drop the pace, traverse across the hill, breathe deeply. It didn't matter that I was now below 3,000m, it just happened naturally. I wonder if I'll do the same back in England.

We passed familiar landmarks, villages, waterfalls, viewpoints and realised we were nearly at the end of our adventure. It was reassuringly familiar, but also desperately sad. We passed a very overweight man, who was struggling up a minor hill. He asked if we thought he'd make Kala Patthar. If he made Gorakshep and still wasn't affected by altitude sickness, he had a chance, he'd just had to set off earlier than 4am. He gave us details of his Instagram account which featured a cartoon elephant. He was blogging about his trip and how he hoped to get a lot fitter. I admired his ambition and determination, as well as his humour and attitude. He was also the first Syrian I think I've ever met. So different to the caricature Syrian you get from the press. We wished him well.

This place has everything!

Indra, who usually walked about two metres behind the last person, suddenly shot to the front and picked up the pace. We know what this meant – he was hungry and the lunch stop was close.

Sure enough, around the next corner we saw Phakding, and a few minutes later we were settled into the restaurant we'd stopped at after day one. It was really busy with excited trekkers, staying over after day one of their journey. We chatted to a few of them, and they asked some questions but I didn't want to give too much away. I remembered listening across the room to a couple in the same place ten days earlier giving Keith and Mark 'their' experience of EBC and I didn't want to listen to a second-hand account then. I was sure the newbies would have felt the same now. Let them enjoy the surprises that the trip would deliver first-hand themselves. It was also weird to think that this was an EBC cut-off point. All those we'd passed from Namche to Phakding would be arriving one day earlier than these trekkers and as a result would have a different experience to those only a few hundred metres behind.

At that point we saw three of the 'gang', Pritima, Mark and Keith. It was a classic mix of experience and novice in the cafe, and I reflected on how these three, and the others we'd met, had really added to my experience. I'll miss them.

A couple of myth-busters here too. I had heard stories of how terrible the loos were on the trip, and how you needed to keep constant supplies of loo roll and a cigarette lighter for burning the loo paper on the mountain if in desperate need to go. In all of the 11 days trekking, I only saw one person caught short without a toilet (male), and I personally only had to use one squat loo for a number two, and it was here in Phakding, only three hours from Lukla, not 5,000m-plus at the top of the mountains. On the walks there are loads of opportunities to use facilities in the many cafes and restaurants along the way. They may be basic, and often you will need your own loo roll, but they were usually western style. So ladies, don't panic. Unless you have some serious bladder control issues, a she-wee is not needed.

The second myth-buster is about begging children. I mention it here because I had started to reflect that I'd not seen one. The books were full of stories about how you shouldn't encourage them, but I just didn't see them. Loads were playing with their mates, having a great time by the look of it, or trying to fly homemade kites. But no hands out asking for cash. Then just one kid tried his luck after Phakding. I was tempted – he looked very scruffy and in need – but I reluctantly followed the advice and kept my money in my pocket.

The walk from Phakding was one I was dreading. Tales in the books about the horrendous climb to the top should have been the thing that occupied my mind, but it wasn't that for me. It was the very final leg of the trip. In less than three hours it would be over. We decided not to rush. It was only 1pm, we had loads of time and we wanted to drink in every last sight and sound. More people passed us in the opposite direction, obviously coming from different planes at

The last spectacular view of the trek. On the way up to Lukla. A sad part of the day for me as it marked the end of the experience.

Lukla, and the clouds had obscured some of the higher peaks. The clouds didn't matter. What had started as a trip of new experience and wonder now became a walk of trying to capture in our memories the views unfolding in front of us. Sontos had even managed to subcontract the portering on this last leg. Easy work if you can get it.

The last hill was not difficult. On the way down, I'd thought it had been over-exaggerated in the books and so it proved. It was uphill, true, but not especially steep, and after everything we'd done in the last 11 days, it was a mere inconvenience, not a challenge. Lukla appeared on the horizon and within minutes the archway to the town was 30m away. I started running, shouting 'race' like a five-year-old. Anton raised an eyebrow and Indra shrugged so I stopped. It was a trick, they started sprinting to the line and in all things 'good team spirit' we crossed the line together. It was a fitting end. We'd started together, we ended together. It was perfect.

After last night's lack of free hot showers, and feeling terrible that Anton had missed out, we shared again for the last night. The room was superb, loads of space, a big bathroom, a hot shower and lots of hooks and shelves to sort our stuff for the flight back to Lukla in the morning. We dumped our stuff, and headed into town to get some more cash for the tips and to buy some more stuff, another T-shirt for me as well as some socks and pants (I'd run out of clean underclothes).

The last stretch up the relatively modest incline up to Lukla.

We saw Mark and Keith and agreed to meet them in the Lukla Irish pub for the Manchester derby later. Then it was back to the hotel for a shower before dinner.

Sontos joined us for the only time on the trip, and Indra sat with us. It was tip time, so they waited patiently for dinner to finish before Anton handed over the envelopes to each of them. They fought the urge to open them in front of us and after a few photos in front of the 'Go Hard or Go Everest' sign we all shook

We'd made it. 11 days after we'd set off on a trekking adventure, we were back to Lukla for the last time.

hands and thanked Indra and Sontos for everything they'd done to make our trip so memorable. It would be the last time we saw Sontos.

After dinner we headed for the pub. By the end of the match Mark and Keith and Ben, Alex and Robbie were also there, as well some other walkers. Another couple of beers only and it was back to the hotel for a 4.45am alarm, ready for the mountain flight from Lukla. I couldn't believe how much I was really looking forward to it.

Stats: walked 11.02 miles, of which 6.58 miles from Namche to Phakding. We descended from 11,300 feet to 9,300ft over the whole day, but with all the ups and downs, we'd actually ascended 2,611ft uphill during it. The whole day took seven hours 20 minutes. We'd walked 38,476 steps.

And it was over.

Final stats

According to Fitbit, I walked 344,291 steps in the 11 days from leaving Kathmandu and then arriving back in Lukla – an average of 31,300 per day. I am so glad I did all that training. The biggest day was the Kala Patthar day, with 47,699.

DAY 13: NAMCHE TO LUKLA

STRAVA

Namche Bazaar — Jorsale — Benkar — Phakding — Chaurikharka — Lukla

Distance 11.0 mi
Elev Gain 2,611 ft
Time 5h 42m

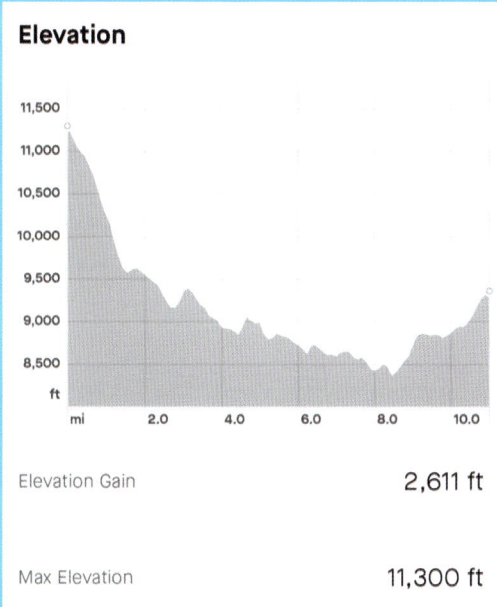

Elevation

Elevation Gain — 2,611 ft
Max Elevation — 11,300 ft

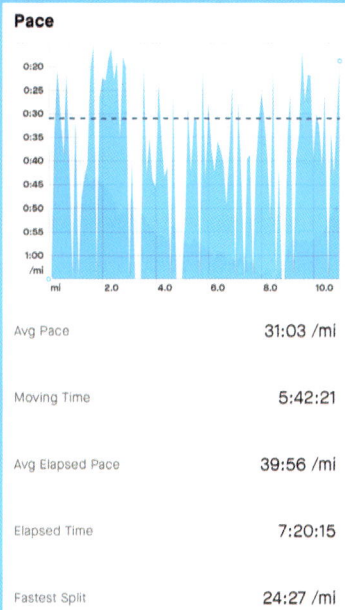

Pace

Avg Pace — 31:03 /mi
Moving Time — 5:42:21
Avg Elapsed Pace — 39:56 /mi
Elapsed Time — 7:20:15
Fastest Split — 24:27 /mi

3 OCTOBER 2022
DAY 14: LUKLA TO KATHMANDU

The alarm jolted us both awake at 4.45am; we'd obviously had a decent night's sleep – two beers and a good dinner certainly helped. We'd mainly packed but I was keen to avoid the weight issue at the airport again. I'd only offloaded some weight on the way (all the snacks had gone) but I'd bought a bottle of Everest whisky and some T-shirts, so I needed to be canny. With four layers on my body and two on my legs, including my heavier trousers, I was very warm, but as soon as the bag had been weighed I could remove some layers at least. I also had my guide book, three power banks and spare phone on my body. I felt like a walking *Crackerjack* contestant. I just needed some cabbages. (Anyone born in the UK before 1980 will get this). I left my cigarette lighter, hand sanitiser and binoculars behind. I'd never used the binoculars before the trip. Here I had tried to look at one of the mountains, and didn't like them. I'd also got them free on a balloon flight years ago. I figured if I wasn't going to use them in this location I never would. Indra gladly took them. The bags were much lighter and I was confident that I'd hit the target.

We waited at 5.15am for Indra and Sontos. Indra rocked up at 20 past, the first time he'd ever been late (it didn't matter), and Sontos didn't show at all. He'd probably been out spending his tip money and 'overslept'. Another guide helped us with our bags on the five-minute walk to the airport. It was to be unlike any other airport experience I'd ever had.

There were four flights early that morning and it almost seemed to be first come, first served. Mark and Keith were there and we just assumed they were on the same flight as they had been on the way out. The Oxford lads and Michael were there too as was Kenneth. Check-in was organised chaos, and with no X-ray machines for the bags, the security were doing spot checks, searching the bags by hand. Apparently they were looking for lighters and gas canisters, but that news came from a passenger so could be an urban myth. I walked through the passenger X-ray with all the 'stuff' on me. It beeped but he just waved me through. I was in without the surcharge from the outward journey.

After stripping off two layers, and putting all my electrical things back in the bag, I felt much more comfortable and joined the fellow travellers in the packed, but not excessively so, departure lounge. Every time a plane landed, people moved to the windows to get a better view of the landing. Then it emptied slightly as the passengers for that flight left to take their place for the outward journey.

I thought I'd be nervous, but the only nerves were which plane I'd be on. All my pals had gone on the first three planes. Would our five-minute delay mean we'd have to wait for the next batch of planes? Another one arrived and our flight number was called. I'd only been worried for a few minutes, it was irrational. Then one of the most remarkable things I've seen at an airport happened. After being called, we queued outside. Luggage was being unloaded from the plane while our stuff was being simultaneously loaded. The passengers were ushered off quickly, and we started embarking. I got a great seat on the right-hand side by the window. An older Japanese man sat next to me. He was still doing up his seatbelt when the

Looking down the runway at Lukla airport.

plane started taxiing to the start position. I'd been sat down less than five minutes and after a 30-second safety briefing that no one listened to, the plane was ready to go. From landing to taking off again, only about ten minutes had passed. It was incredibly efficient.

The engines revved and the noise intensified. Landing was uphill, taking off was downhill. If you've ever been parascending, where you run off the hill and hope that the parachute catches the wind, then you know the sensation. The plane accelerated down the runway and within seconds we could see the green fields below us as we effortlessly lifted into our final journey. It was good weather and I said goodbye to Lukla, the mountains, and the Khumbu region for the last time.

I was under the wing, so the view of the main mountains was restricted slightly, but it was still there. I silently wished the current trekkers well on their quest to EBC and just enjoyed the scenery.

As before we were flying below 3,000m and we could see the activity on the ground below us. Before I knew it the plane started juddering a bit and I could see in the cockpit as the pilot and co-pilot quickly moved levers, pressing buttons and generally just engaging in activity. Something was happening. There was no sign of Kathmandu, and we'd only been in the air for about 15 minutes. We were

Our last look at the Khumbu region from the plane window.

THE TRIP

Inside the plane. Not much elbow room.

descending quickly, and then I saw a runway ahead. I'd completely forgotten that flights to and from Lukla now went via Ramechap airport, a five-hour drive from Kathmandu. The deadline for flights to and from Kathmandu was 1 October, when apparently the airport gets busy with international flights, so the smaller flights are shifted during the busy period. What I thought was mild panic in the cockpit was just preparation to land. I was never really worried, I trusted the pilot, but as we landed the Japanese man next to me started clapping and some others joined in. It seemed he'd been having similar thoughts.

Ramechap airport was rammed with those trying to get taxis back to Kathmandu and those waiting to fly to Lukla. The Oxford lads and Michael asked if we had any room in our taxi and Indra said he'd see. We had the same minibus driver as before, and there was space for ten. There were only three of us so we could accommodate them. We even had another couple and the guide who'd helped us with our bags in Lukla on the bus. They'd been quoted $20 a head for a taxi. Our taxi would only cost them $10. A win all round. I bought a bottle of water. It was 30 rupees, about 20p. I gave the vendor 50 rupees and told her to keep the change. After paying upwards of 250 rupees at the top of the mountain it seemed ridiculously cheap.

We'd heard horror stories about this road journey from the trekkers in Phakding. I remembered back 25 years when we caught a bus from Pokhara to Kathmandu and how it seemed hit or miss whether we'd make it in one piece. I think we'd even sat on the roof at one point back then so we could jump off easily if it tipped off the road. But I never felt in danger once on the journey home this time. The driver was patient, only a little heavy on the horn, and managed to negotiate the trickier ways through the potholes, traffic bottlenecks and even a funeral procession.

I had planned to spend some of the journey writing my diary, but I ended up next to Alex which was a much preferable option. Like Ben a few days earlier we had a long chat about life, careers, experiences and plans. Also like Ben, I knew whatever he chose, Alex would be a success. A really switched on, dynamic and interesting person. I only wish I'd had time to get to know Robbie this well, but if his two travelling companions were anything to go by, he'd be similar.

The landscape took us around the hills, over bridges and through towns and villages. Some of the roads were really good and we could pick up some speed. Some of the roads were terrible. I suspect that this route will improve dramatically over the next ten years as the roads are repaired and improved. Even if I'd been sat alone, I wouldn't have had my head down writing, I'd have been looking out the window. It was another insight into real Nepal and I liked what I saw. I would even go so far as to say it was a better option than flying straight to Kathmandu. Of course, doing the reverse trip at 2am in the dark wouldn't be great but we'd avoided that.

We stopped at a services for some food and a loo break. Michael was moaning about the driving as it was stop-start and he wanted to sleep. Sitting at the back he couldn't see the obstacles the driver had faced. All eyes turned to Anton who was asked what he thought as he was a semi-professional racing driver. In true Anton style he was brief but insightful, 'We're still alive.' There was another group in the services, and one lad had a University of Nottingham sweatshirt on. I surprised him by introducing myself, saying I lived only three miles from his uni and lectured at their rivals. He laughed. A story for him to tell when he gets back to England.

We arrived back in Kathmandu and Anton was dropped off at his hotel; all the others were dropped at a central point and I was taken to the door of my hotel. It was our taxi after all, so we did deserve the special treatment. It was sad saying goodbye to everyone. I'd enjoyed their company and wasn't planning on going

THE TRIP

On the road back to Kathmandu.

to the 51st best nightclub in the world later that day with them. I'm sure they were pleased too. I hope I bump into them again one day, but if not I'm sure I'll probably hear about them somehow.

Back at the Moonlight Hotel, I was disappointed not to be in the same room as before. The new one was on the sixth floor, a bit smaller but still comfy. I ordered some food and a beer from room service and fell asleep after finishing them. It was the end of a hectic time, now I could relax, and I intended to.

The only reason to get up was to meet with Anton and Raj, one of the directors of Outfitters Nepal, for a post-trip meal. The meal was on the company, and we went to a great little steakhouse called, the Black Olive. In the heart of Thamel, it was quiet when we arrived at 6pm, but by the time we left it was packed. The 'Trekkers Steak' was delicious and less than 1,000 rupees (£6.50). We both talked about how great Indra had been, and how well organised the trip had been. I had a little moan about the accommodation in Dingboche, but my initial feeling towards it had dissipated over the two days we were there so it wasn't a vehement protest. Raj also gave a really good explanation for choosing set places to stay and eat – guaranteed access in the busy times – it made perfect sense. The only improvements we could think of was to use every trip as a promo opportunity.

Photos each day, comments from customers, Outfitters flag at EBC etc. I didn't feel they did enough to promote themselves, and they had a lot to shout about. He certainly liked that.

It was a good effort coming out with us. I cannot imagine margins being high, and it was a lovely way of keeping the contact with the company. It was specially appreciated as it was during one of the important festivals in Nepal. Raj should really have been with his family, but as a director of the company he knew this was important too. The only person missing was Indra. He was with his family and I didn't blame him one bit. I suspect I'll never see him again, but whoever gets him as their guide in the future will have hit the jackpot.

As Raj left, Anton had another pudding, and I another beer. It had started hammering it down. Mark and Keith had sent me an email to say where they were, but I missed it, and by 8.30pm, Anton had gone back to his hotel, and I was asleep in mine. The nap had staved off some of the tiredness, but the steak and beers put it back on.

My new friends from the trip

Just a photo gallery now of some of the people I met on the trip. You made the whole experience so much more complete. Thanks for being good friends, even if it was for a fleeting time. We share an experience that was unique to us.

Indra and Anton.

THE TRIP

Keith and Mark.

Alex, Ben and Robbie at the top of Kala Patthar

Jonathan and Selina at EBC.

EVEREST BASE CAMP

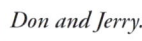

Michael at EBC.

Don and Jerry.

Pritima (right).

Line and Liva.

Cindy and Brecht.   *Bernard.*

REFLECTIONS ON THE TRIP TO BASE CAMP

A LIFE-CHANGING EXPERIENCE?

It wasn't life-changing for me, my original 17-month trip around the world in 1996 and '97 with Jane certainly took that crown, but I can see how it might be for others. EBC is a very serious challenge, testing stamina, humour, physiological changes, relationship building, organisation, preparation, patience, and sheer bloody-mindedness at times. As a way of building up key skills for life back home, whether it is in your personal life or your career, it is invaluable. I still learned a lot from the trip, despite being 52 and having travelled to the region before. Every day can bring you a new experience – you're never too old to keep learning.

If you've never been to this part of the world before, you will see the organised chaos of Kathmandu, encounter the friendliness of the people, witness some incredible sights and thoroughly enjoy your time there. If you've been before, you will still stand in awe at the scenery, it is never boring. I would recommend it to anyone – life-changing or not.

CAN ANYONE DO IT?

There are some categories I would definitely rule out, and it is a catch-all. If you have trouble walking for long periods of time, whether that is due to a disability or you have dodgy knees, ankles or hips, then steer clear. There isn't any wheelchair access in the mountains. You are walking upwards of five hours most days, and the terrain is up and down. There are some relatively flat parts, but they are not in isolation. To get to them involves steep inclines and descents. If you can walk up and down hills consistently without pain, then you should be okay. Walking poles will help but I never used them. Many did.

I saw people there of all shapes and sizes. Don't let weight put you off. Obviously the heavier you are the more you have to carry up the hills. I was about 105kg when I went – over 16st – but felt fine. I wasn't as quick as some of the leaner walkers, but I more than held my own. You do need to be reasonably fit though. See the section on training.

TRAINING

I read lots of books about training for EBC, and some talked about lifting weights, running etc. Mark was a national judo champion in his past and still took his fitness very seriously; Keith was doing a half-ironman only a week after EBC, but I was on a par with them in my ability to walk at a decent rate despite being considerably heavier.

I found that there is no substitute for training for the event you're undertaking. Going to EBC involves walking for 11 consecutive days, over different terrains and different elevations. You also have the downhill bits too, something you cannot replicate in a gym. So my advice would be to train by doing that. As part of my training you have seen that I walked for long days on some of Britain's highest and varied hills. It is time consuming, and if you work full time, with a family, it could be tricky getting away for a full day's walking, but you will get it back in spades on the EBC trek. When you're on certain hills, maybe the uphill to Namche on day two, you can compare it to training days you've done. If you did it then, you can do it on the way to EBC.

Don't think half an hour with the dog in the park every day, or an hour on the treadmill in the gym once a week, is enough. I suggest you really plan some long trips. And take a heavy pack with you. You will be carrying upwards of five kilograms on a daily basis with you in Nepal, so why wait until you get there before seeing whether you can take the load. It also builds up your shoulder muscles so they don't ache after a few days.

PREPARATION
(including having the right kit)

Linked to training, make sure you try and replicate conditions as much as possible. Wear your intended Nepal kit on your training walks to see what niggles appear.

Your boots should be comfy and not give you blisters, no matter how expensive they are. I had a pair of £120 traditional leather boots and they never felt 100 per cent comfortable, so I bought a pair of £50 own-brand synthetic boots from Decathlon. They fit perfectly and I only had one blister on my toe in over 500 miles of training (walking down a very steep descent, so not surprised; most boots would have been unable to deal with that terrain). If you don't love your boots you will dread putting them on. They need to be your best friend. I had no blisters in Nepal at all.

How are you going to hydrate during the walk? It is recommended that you need to drink more than three litres a day on the trek. Maybe you need a bladder with a drinking tube. I love mine. I filled it up (it carried three litres) and took it on every training walk, even if it was just a five-miler around the local area. It gets you used to sipping, as well as carrying a weighty load. If you're going for a bottle, practise with that.

Try the things you are going to be eating/consuming on the walk. If you have some electrolyte tablets, or water purification pills, or Diamox, or energy gels, practise with them on your training walks. If you have a physical reaction to any of them, or as importantly, any combination of them, it is better off having that reaction at home, rather than at 4,000m.

What clothes are you planning on wearing? Do they rub, irritate or annoy? They could be the most expensive kit on the market but if they bother you, like your boots, get rid. This includes the day pack. I found I couldn't wear a T-shirt while carrying it as it chafed my upper arm, so I always had a long-sleeved wicking top as a base layer. Only through practise did I spot this. Think about your underwear. I can chafe badly around the groin, especially when it is a longer walk. I used tight lycra running shorts from Sports Direct as underwear and never had any issues. What will you be wearing? Top brand, most expensive, doesn't always equate to the thing that's best for you. I had unbranded ski socks, Mountain Warehouse wicking tops, Lidl skins, a Go Outdoors bag and own-brand Decathlon boots. No top brands, so much less expensive, and they worked for me.

SELF-GUIDED V TOUR GUIDE.

There were a few people on our trip who were self-guided but the majority had a guide with them, often one to one. It is possible to do it without one. You cannot get lost, it is a very defined route and there are many people doing the same thing (with guides). However, if you want a hassle-free trek, then a guide will smooth the way. They book hostels, organise permits, hire porters, have training for spotting illness (especially altitude sickness), point out things of interest, identify mountains and they speak Nepali. The universal language on the hills is English, most people speak it, whether fellow trekkers or the hostel staff, but if you want to make a point that is not understood then the guide can help with it.

There may even be a seasonal issue. It was relatively quiet when I was there and there was rarely an issue with full hotels, but if you're going at peak season, you may be spending some time finding a spare bunk for the night, when it is the last thing you want to be doing after a full day's walking. A guide will phone up and arrange in advance, and if they're regulars they'll get priority.

Our guide, Indra, was great. So I am biased. I would have a guide if I did another challenge. If he'd been rubbish I'd probably be dancing to a very different tune. The Nepal Government have since declared that guides are compulsory, but it hadn't been ratified at time of writing. Please check before going on a solo trek.

LARGE GROUP v SMALL GROUP.

In a large group, you may have a wide variety of capability, so some will go a lot faster than others. This can cause frustration for the quickest – and the slowest. In my experience, in a smaller group you tend to stick together more. A large group will though give you a wider variety of people to chat to, so making it potentially more interesting from a human perspective. It could make the group more insular, not needing to mingle with other trekkers. I was always reluctant to engage with the one or two larger groups I encountered on my trip as they had closed body language, unlike those travelling in ones, twos or threes, who want to build outside relationships.

TIMINGS

The season starts in October in earnest, and it was obvious on our way back that traffic had massively increased. I went late September, and I was pleased as it was less crowded and relatively warm. I didn't use my down jacket once, and used my down sleeping bag only once. But we did get lucky with the weather. After four days of relative cloud cover we had five great days, just when we needed them. The later you go into October, the more chance of avoiding the end of the monsoon and 'guaranteeing' cloudless skies, but it will be colder. Saying that, it rained consistently for the seven days I was in Kathmandu after the trek.

I think it was the crowds that made me prefer the early start the most. With fewer people you really got to know others on the same route as you, and at EBC, the atmosphere was relaxed and patient. If five times the number of people were all wanting their five minutes, I can imagine it being fractious. No evidence of course, I wasn't there when it was busy, just a feeling.

THE HOTELS/HOSTELS.

I read a lot of books about the trip and the impression that came through consistently was one of hardship. I didn't go when it was very cold so there was never the physical aspect of trying to keep warm. But I found the hostels fine. They were like ski lodges, a huge communal area, with loads of seating for mingling. It was decent spec too, not shabby. Usually a fire was on in the middle of the room, especially at higher elevations. Guides, porters and trekkers all used the communal area. There was usually a counter manned by the hostel owner, and at every place you could buy drinks, snacks, loo roll or get wifi passwords or charge your phones. More on this later.

The rooms were basic. Often just a pair of beds in a box room. The walls were often plywood, so not very soundproofed and I can imagine them getting cold in the winter. But although basic they were fine. The duvets and sheets seemed clean,

Left: The room at 8848 in Namche Bazaar. Basic but comfy. This room was ensuite with hot water on the way out. On the way back we were in our own rooms (see text) with communal loos, but the rooms themselves were similar. Right: The Himalayan Hotel in Tengboche, a good example of the shared rooms on the trek. Comfortable and clean.

The Himalayan Hotel in Tengboche, this is the typical communal area in the hotels - spacious, warm and inviting. A great place to unwind after a day's walk.

The communal space at the Trekkers Lodge in Phakding.

and they were warm. With my own sleeping bag inner and a couple of layers, I was never cold at night. Some of the rooms had ensuite, some had communal facilities, but again these always seemed clean. In the really cold winter nights I can imagine it would be tough going to the loo in the night, whether ensuite or communal. But not an issue for us. The height of luxury was getting hooks on the wall to hang clothes. Some didn't have them. So basic, yet so necessary.

The price of the hostels was cheap. I heard 500 rupees for a triple room in one place, only about £3. But there is an expectation that you eat there. One place was really explicit: eat off the premises and your accommodation costs double. I was always happy to follow this basic rule, especially in the evening. Our rooms were included in the cost of the package from Outfitters.

If you like a hot shower you can get them at most places, but they cost. The most I paid was 700 rupees, still less than a fiver. They were also outside or in a place that could be cold to get to. Nice when you're in, but not great for either side of the shower. I didn't see any cold showers anywhere. I know some who didn't shower for days. You couldn't tell; everyone smelt the same.

You won't get five stars, but what do you expect? It is somewhere to eat, sleep and move on. And every place we stayed fit the bill.

See later for food.

WI-FI/INTERNET

I bought an NCell SIM card in Kathmandu before heading off to the trek. It cost about £30 for oodles of 4G. Most of the time it was available, especially lower down and ironically at the top. Apparently there is a mast near EBC. In Dingboche and Lobuche we had the worst signal, but I bought a wifi code from the hostel owner. In both cases it was 500 rupees, only about £3, for 12 hours of connectivity. Not a big deal and explicit. No haggling over terms, the price was even printed on the unique ticket you bought with the password on. With the wifi and internet connections, I didn't make one traditional phone call, instead video calling Jane via WhatsApp. There is no reason not to have internet access in the hills.

ELECTRICITY AND CHARGING

This was trickier. In Phakding and Namche we had sockets in our room which fit English plugs. I think they'd have fit European ones too as they were a clever design. I needed some insulation tape to keep the plugs in the sockets at times, but it was free and we could keep our devices topped up. By Tengboche, we were in paying territory: 300 rupees for a full charge of any device. Higher up, they distinguished between powerbanks and phones, with the powerbanks sometimes costing 1500 rupees (about £11) for a full charge. One place was priced on time in the socket, so if you have a quick charging plug you should get it cheaper. It was expensive, but I didn't want to miss out on any photos, so kept everything topped up. I probably ended up paying about £30 for this in total. Looking at the photos now, it was worth every penny.

One tip worth sharing is to keep your phone in airplane mode until you actually needed the internet. It really reduced the amount of juice needed. Another tip is to keep your devices warm. Near the top I had them in bed with me. Not quite a teddy bear, but they kept warm and didn't discharge too much overnight.

FOOD

Every hostel has an extensive menu, from Nepali fare, to pizza and chips. There was always the basics of rice, noodles, pasta and enough variety not to be bored of the meals. The dal bhat had unlimited top-ups so if you were hungry then that would be the meal for you. It wasn't bland either, vegetables to go with the rice and lentil soup as well as poppadoms and a spicy pickle side dish which always helped give it a kick if you wanted it. I settled into porridge for breakfast, usually garlic soup for lunch and a mix of dal bhat, fried potatoes or noodles for tea.

On a couple of days I craved crisps and bought a box of Pringles and scoffed them in one sitting. I tried to avoid fizzy drinks (Coke, Fanta and Sprite at every location), bottled water and alcohol. On the way down, I relented a bit and became much more decadent. I was though trying to reduce my plastic waste as much as possible. I always used the local water for my drinks bladder and used water purification tabs combined with the cola flavoured electrolyte tablets to hide the taste and prevent illness. Bottled water (in one-litre bottles) was as low as 50 rupees at Namche to a high of 250 rupees near the top.

There was lots of chocolate available, mostly Dairy Milk, so usually right up my street. However I only had one chocolate on the whole trip, one given by the restaurant on the way to Namche on day ten of the trek!

The food was nearly always surprisingly good. The garlic soup got a bit more ropey nearer the top, but the portions were plentiful and it was presented well.

A typical Dal Bhat, this one from the Hotel 8848 in Namche, with unlimited second helpings.

Prices increased significantly nearer the top, but it was all included in our package costs so we just ordered what we wanted. If you were on a budget you'd probably think more about it. Unless you're a really fussy eater, there is nothing to fear from the food.

It was for me a purely vegetarian diet. Apparently the meat is prepared in Kathmandu and carted to the hills without refrigeration. It was widely advised not to eat it, and there was enough choice not to have to.

There were many different choice of drinks. Fruit teas, hot orange/lemon, instant coffee and hot water were always high on my list. They came in different sizes – cup, small pot (three or four cups), medium pot and big pot with the associated price rise. We only ever needed a small pot which Anton and I usually shared.

I took my own snacks: Lidl muesli bars and Peperami. I took two per day to Nepal which was a bit excessive, so I shared them with Anton and Indra.

COSTS

You can do this really cheaply. Book your own flights to Lukla, no guide, hire your own porter or even carry your own bags, use the local water and purify it, eat dal bhat every day, not worry about wifi and restrict your battery usage on your phone and powerbank just for photos. I reckon I was spending £15 a day nearer the top. Not much in the scheme of things but it could add up.

I went direct to a Nepalese company for the holiday. I didn't book through a British company, some of whom wanted £2,500 for the trek. I went direct to Outfitters Nepal, checked they were legit, and paid $1,550, excluding international flights. This included a really nice hotel in Kathmandu, flights to and from Lukla, guide and porter, permit fees, transfers to all airports, guided tour of Kathmandu, all meals and hotels on the trek and free use of a duffle bag, sleeping bag and coat. Reflecting now, it was well worth it.

My flights with Qatar Airlines to and from Nepal (Manchester, via Doha) were originally £600, but after Covid, they went up 50 per cent to about £900.

Insurance was around £250, which included helicopter rescue.

I also spent a fair bit on kit and things in Nepal (T-shirts), some of which I didn't explicitly need but I like browsing walking kit. I reckon that was about £500 to £1,000.

In all I think I spent about £4,000 in total, but some of that was kit which I can reuse. On a budget, you could probably do it for £2,500, but that would be cutting back on the nice things.

Was it value for money? For me it was.

PORTERS

The porters are the workhorses of the mountains. They don't just carry bags for the trekkers, they carry produce, drinks, building materials – even yak dung – all of which keeps the trekking industry going. Some of the loads are incredibly bulky and awkward, from door frames to long wooden staves, but all of them are weighty.

The porter's carry virtually anything, regardless of size.

The method of carrying them is over the top of the back or shoulders with a strap round the forehead. Their neck muscles must be phenomenal. They often walk with a stick in one hand, and a pulley string in the other. This allows them to shift the load slightly, releasing pressure on one part of the back as and when it gets too onerous.

They come in all ages, and both men and women carry, although young males is the predominant demographic. I did see younger kids, probably early teens, carrying loads, as well as older men who looked like they should have retired years ago.

The porter community did seem close-knit. There were often large numbers of porters all having their 'pit stop' at the same time, chatting away ready for the next stage of their journey. For a lot of them, this is the apprenticeship for their career in guiding. Indra started off this way too. Once they have enough experience of the hills, they get a registration to guide. I don't know if there is an exam for this, or just gut feel from the commissioning agents.

What I do know though is that you should be trying to make their job as simple as possible. If they are coming past you, from either direction, give way. I saw too many people completely wrapped up in themselves, not taking a small step aside to allow the workers to do their jobs.

TOWNS

On the mountain, the towns are set up for the trekker. Nearly every part of them has businesses – shops, lodges, cafes, bars – that specifically relate to the tourism industry in one way or another. There was even a snooker club in nearly every place. We did walk past a couple of places on our first acclimatisation walk near Namche that had more of a local feel about it. Not on the well-worn route, it seemed a much more 'normal' depiction of life in the mountains. Locals working the fields or working on building new facilities such as a school extension in Khumjung. But by far the biggest industry was trekking.

Namche is the biggest town and you could get anything you wanted for your trip. It could be walking kit if you were going up, or souvenirs if coming down. There are chemists, grocery shops, bars and restaurants aplenty. The second biggest town was Dingboche, primarily because it was a two-day acclimatisation stopover. Not as big as Namche, there were still some independent shops, but less emphasis on the kit and souvenirs, more on snacks and the odd little extra (I bought playing cards there).

But even the small places tended to have an independent cafe or bakery if you didn't want to stay in your hostel. It is a well catered for industry.

ALTITUDE SICKNESS / HEALTH

Altitude sickness was always my biggest fear. Would my body be able to cope with the limited oxygen at the higher stops? Not much to do with physical fitness, it was a physiological thing. I took the following precautions:

Drink plenty of water. Some guidelines suggest three litres a day, others as high as five. I went closer to the upper end each day.

Keep out of the sun (wear a hat and apply plenty of suncream). You don't want to get sunstroke and altitude sickness mixed up. They had similar symptoms.

Monitor your blood oxygen level. I had a finger monitor which loads of people used. If it was in the

Relative Oxygen Rate at different altitudes:

Altitude in mtrs.	Altitude in feet	Oxygen rate
8,848	29,028	33%
8,000	26,247	36%
7,000	22,966	41%
6,000	19,865	47%
5,500	18,045	50%
5,200	17,061	52%
5,000	16,404	53%
4,500	14,764	57%
4,000	13,123	60%
3,500	11,483	64%
3,000	9,843	68%
2,500	8,202	73%
1,000	3,281	88%
Sea Level		100%

From the Top of Mt. Everest to Sea Level

80s or 90s then you would probably be okay. If someone felt ill, yet their O$_2$ measure was decent, then it made them think that maybe they weren't too bad.

Garlic soup. Placebo or effective traditional precaution, it doesn't matter if it works. I had it on six of the first eight days and didn't suffer.

Front-of-the-head headaches are more likely to be altitude sickness (according to the guides).

Diamox. Be led by your doctor, but I took half a tablet a day for three days, then half morning and night for two, then one a day for four days.

If you take the precautions and you still get it, then it's just bad luck, but if you haven't taken them you will kick yourself.

OTHER MEDICAL THINGS

I went completely over the top. I took loads of painkillers and anti-inflammatory tablets, cold and flu remedies, plasters, bandages, Deep Heat and Deep Freeze, Savlon etc. I reckon my first aid kit was a kilogram in itself.

The things I would definitely take are:

- Compeed Blister plasters (or magic plasters as I call them; Anton used some on his blister)
- Some paracetamol and ibuprofen
- Cough sweets in case you get the Khumbu cough
- Water purification tablets
- Diamox altitude sickness pills
- Electrolyte tablets – to give you energy and take away the taste of the purification tablets

Just because I didn't use a lot of what I took doesn't mean I would say not to take it. Maybe the security of knowing it was there meant I didn't suffer. The lodges though would be well-stocked and there were mini medical places at Namche and Dingboche for certain. I had read some bad things about the effects people were having and went overboard.

EVEREST BASE CAMP

Always stand uphill from the animals!

RULES OF THE MOUNTAINS

The first thing is to be safe. Follow the instructions from the guide. There are distinctive paths all the way to EBC, so you cannot get lost, but stick to them. Going off-piste could have some consequences that you don't want to encounter. There are some hazards along the way.

The milky river is incredibly powerful. Beautiful but deadly. Tempting though it is to dip your toe in, best steer clear.

The animals transporting produce/stuff just walk. They don't know that it is a 400ft drop to certain death, they just follow the path. When you encounter them, stay uphill. It would be ironic (and stupid) to be pushed off the mountain by a massive yak.

Don't go too quick. You've got all day. If you're setting off at 8am, five hours only takes you to 1pm. What's the rush? Enjoy the view, take loads of photos and take it slowly on the uphill parts. Try traversing across the path, and definitely follow the lead of the guide. They walk very slowly.

In the lodges, make sure you eat in the place you stay. It is expected and polite to do so. Some of the places have negotiable rates for things like charging your phone. One place even had some Pringles for sale at 800 rupees, but wouldn't sell them as they were out of date. I said I didn't mind, bought them for 300 rupees, and they were still crunchy.

Apparently, don't throw stuff on the fire. It is considered rude. I never saw anyone even try, so I don't know if this is true.

Listen to your body. If you're in a small group and you feel a bit rough, see if you can set off a bit later. There's always plenty of time after the walk, so make sure you can do the day before you start. That extra couple of hours could make all the difference. Drinking lots of water also helps. Alternatively, if you really think you're suffering, the only real cure for altitude sickness is 'descend, descend, descend'.

Do the acclimatisation walks, and go as high as you can. These were the toughest walks of my whole trip (Everest View Hotel from Namche, and Nangkar Tshang from Dingboche) but I am convinced they really helped stave off altitude sickness. Some of my fellow trekkers didn't go all the way up Nangkar Tshang (5,000m-plus) because the views weren't good after the clouds came down. Remember what the walk is for, acclimatisation not views. Don't lose sight of the prize, EBC or Kala Patthar on days eight and nine. Are you really not going to prepare as well as you should for the best two experiences of your whole trip because of the lack of views on day three or day six?

KIT –

I'm not going to give you a comprehensive kit list, many other books and online sites can give you that, but I can give you my top tips.
The kit that I would definitely recommend (in no particular order):

Spare shoe laces – I used both my spare laces, one for each boot.

Long johns – made my nights warm and cosy.

Trainers – I didn't take any, just my sliders, and I ended up walking everywhere in my boots when my feet needed a break from them.

Take some ear plugs, and possibly even an eye mask. The walls are thin. Get as good a night's sleep as you can. But practise with them at home too. They can be uncomfortable so the more you're used to them the better.

Insulation tape – I used it for the electricity sockets, but would have been useful for repairs.

Penknife – used for cutting up string to make a washing line.

Snacks – Biscuits and Peperami came in handy to stave off hunger pangs and add carbs and protein. I took too many so shared, but I was glad I had them.

Flag – I loved having mine at EBC, and other nationalities liked theirs too.

Sleeping bag liner – I had a fleece one. Warm and homely.

Pillow case – a top tip. You can keep all your bedtime clothes in it during the day so they're together when you need them, and they also do their day job – cover the pillow at night – just in case you worry whose head has been on the pillow before you.

Bin liner – to keep your dirty clothes separate to your clean ones.

Basic first aid – as described earlier.

Ziplock bags – different bags for different bits of kit, complete with labels. Underwear, socks, wicking tops etc. I found it really easy to find things, even after a long day's walk.

Things I wouldn't take:

The solar charger – the weather wasn't good enough and the charging was really slow. It just added weight. Would be good for festivals, but not for the hills. I didn't see anyone else have one on the walks.

Guide book – I thought I would read it every day but didn't open it once, and it just added weight.

Binoculars – tried to use them once, but didn't add a lot to the zoom on the camera.

Cigarette lighter – lots of loos around, and also easy for blokes to have a wee (although I didn't see many behind rocks as there were lots of toilets). May be different for women.

Knife, fork and spoon – didn't need them.

REFLECTIONS ON KATHMANDU AND PATAN

For seven nights I stayed in Kathmandu after my trek. I had grand plans, rafting, Pokhara, Bhaktapur, golf, sunrise at Nagarkhot. Most of these fell by the wayside, partly due to the ten-day cultural/religious festival that really reduced the amount of the tourist trade, but mainly due to the weather. It rained nearly every day, sometimes torrential. So I just hung around Kathmandu, did some sightseeing, bought some things to take home, and basically relaxed. So instead of a blow-by-blow account, just some observations about the city and people, and some on the things to see and do.

GEOGRAPHY

Kathmandu sits in a bowl of foothills. From the sixth floor of my hotel, on a clear day I could see some snow-capped peaks above those foothills. The dominant feature is the Swayambhu Mahachaitya (commonly known as the Monkey Temple) which sits on top of a hill, proud and dominant looking down on to the city. There is a separate section about things I did in Kathmandu where I talk about my visit there.

The main tourist focal point is Durbar Square, a collection of temples, museums and statues. It was badly damaged in the earthquake and is still being rebuilt. It is less than a mile from Thamel.

There is a lot of urban sprawl, with houses, hotels and businesses standing next to each other. The only really defined area (for me) is Thamel, the tourist section. Having done some walking through the outskirts there are also some really poor areas. Apparently you do need planning permission to build something, but the uniqueness of a lot of the properties shows that it may be more about structural safety than aesthetics. I liked it. It is also a lot bigger than I remember. I recall an

Khatmandu from the top of the Monkey Temple, stretching out as far as the eye can see.

entry in my diary from 25 years ago that I could see the outskirts of town from the top of the Monkey Temple. Now I couldn't. Inevitably cities grow, and there lies the challenge for the local government, especially in the post-earthquake rebuild stage.

Patan is the next town on from Kathmandu, but as it is only about two and a half miles away, I am making my observations of both towns together as they have very similar characteristics. Patan has its own Durbar Square, but not a Thamel. It is still touristy, especially around the Durbar Square area.

WEATHER AND SEASONS

According to our city tour guide, there are six seasons. I assume the traditional four but also the festival and monsoon seasons added on. Back in Kathmandu, I was in the festival season, where it should have stopped raining. It hadn't. When it was dry it was very warm, well into the 30s, but unfortunately I didn't get too much of it, especially in my first few days after returning from Lukla.

THE LOCALS

The people are very friendly. It is true that in Thamel and beyond a lot of them work in the tourist industry, either shops, bars or restaurants, and they're trying to take your tourist dollar from you. However, I managed to pass several different shops each day where I stopped and chatted to the proprietor. They didn't seem to mind. The 'guards' at the hotel saluted and beamed whenever I went past. The taxi drivers all wanted to chat. I cannot remember an unfriendly interaction. By the time I left, I'd been in Kathmandu for a week and all the trekkers I had met had gone home, so my 'mates' were the locals. Especially those I'd bought from or the guards at the hotel. No pressure to buy again, just happy to talk.

PICTURE SHOPS/ART GALLERIES

There are lots of picture shops all selling the same type of pictures – mandalas, the six steps to nirvana, trekking scenes (nearly all featuring a bridge, a stupa and a yak), or just street scenes. I came with every intention of buying two or three so was happy to chat to the owners. Although they kept bringing out more and more different styles if you didn't like the ones on display, I never found them pushy. I paid 8000 rupees for a mandala which I love. Could I have got it for 7000 rupees? Possibly but 1000 rupees is only about £6.50. I never really haggled strongly; the basic price was reasonable I thought.

My mandala, bought in Thamel.

One thing that could become annoying is people attaching themselves to you and walking alongside you wanting to talk. There was always an ulterior motive, usually to get you to one of the galleries, but it never bothered me. I was on my own so was happy to chat and always promised to visit their gallery another time. They're only doing their job and you can get into some interesting discussions – England v Oz in the Ashes was a particular favourite of mine. Once I'd bought my pictures, and mentioned it as soon as someone latched on to me, they stopped wanting to chat.

TRAFFIC

Apparently it is regulated, although evidence for it is thin on the ground. In Thamel, the trekker section of town, it is mainly taxis cruising around looking for business, or locals on motorbikes weaving in and out of the narrow streets.

A typical street scene in Thamel.

There is the odd cycle rickshaw calling out for passengers and a police presence is common. But it seems to work. There is a constant sound of horns, but they are never tooted in anger, more as a warning that they are there. I've not seen any road rage at all. With shops spilling on to the streets, fruit sellers taking up valuable space and tourists walking around oblivious to the traffic, it could be crazy but it seems to work.

Outside of Thamel it is more free flowing, mainly because it was so free for all. Nominally driving on the left, traffic cuts in front of each other on both sides of the road and it is just accepted. There are very few traffic lights and the occasional policeman directing traffic at a busy junction, but people just get on with it. I love it. The traffic is slower than in the UK, mainly because you never know what the person next to you is going to do (until they blow the horn), but it seems safe. If there are few rules no one gets angry about them being broken.

TAXIS

In Thamel, I tried to get a cab for the six-mile trip out of town to play golf. I was quoted 2000 rupees, which soon dropped to 1300 rupees when I walked away, but the taxi driver wouldn't go even to the 1000 rupees I was prepared to pay. A kindly shopkeeper, Ram, showed me an app called Pathao, a Nepali version of Uber, only this one included motorbike taxis too. After downloading it, and completing registration in English, I was quoted 250 rupees for a motorbike and 750 rupees for a car. I chose the bike and had a thrilling but safe trip across town. There was no spare crash helmet for me though so I clung on tight. He never went fast and I would do it again. I gave him a 100-rupee tip – 70p.

On the way back it was raining, so I opted for the car taxi instead. The driver called me after accepting the fare to confirm pick up. I'd forgotten about that part of the service; Ram had helped me on the outward journey. I couldn't converse with him. Luckily the gatekeeper at the golf course helped me out and spoke to the taxi driver about where I was (the taxi driver was at the hotel reception, not the gates where I was). Unlike Uber you can also pay in cash. I would recommend using the app for longer journeys, if you have a friendly, English-speaking local nearby to help you out when the complimentary phone call is made.

All of my other taxis/transfers were organised by Outfitters, and it was the same driver in a minibus.

TREKKING SHOPS

They're everywhere. And they're cheap. The kit may not be genuine but they looked decent. If you've not bought kit you can get anything you want in Thamel. The only downside is not being able to practise with your kit (see training). I would certainly advise against buying boots here to trek in. Maybe to take back

My T-shirt collection on the line back home

with you, but don't risk it on a four-, eight- or 11-day trek. I heard of one girl who did that and had daily blisters, really harming her enjoyment of her time in Nepal.

PASHMINAS/YAK WOOL BLANKETS/T-SHIRTS/CLOTHES AND BAGS SHOPS

These are also everywhere and you take your chance on them. I paid on average 500 rupees for a printed T-shirt, about £3.50. I bought 11. With designs approaching treble figures, in a multitude of colours, you just need to see what you fancy. There are also embroidered T-shirts which are a little pricier, but I didn't buy these as I thought they would irritate my skin on the inside.

The shops also sell many type of bag. Document bags, purses, hand bags, rucksacks etc – all material, all good value. I had a shoulder document style bag with four different compartments for 400 rupees which I used all holiday. The zips were a bit dodgy by the end, so don't expect any lifetime guarantees on them, but they are interesting, practical and cheap.

There are many shops selling 'genuine' pashminas, scarves, yak wool blankets etc. The going rate seemed to be about 2000 rupees for a pashmina. I've no idea if they were real or whether that was the tourist price, I suspect you could get at least 25 per cent off that if you tried. There are so many to choose from, it can be overwhelming. If you know the colour you want, probably best start there or you'll be shown everything under the sun. The yak wool blankets seemed to be about 1500 rupees each.

The shops also sold Nepali clothes. Bright colours, often stripy, and in many different designs.

TOURISTS TRYING TO FIT THE LOCAL CULTURE

I'm not sure where I stand on this, but you get most tourists in their walking gear, or their Nepal T-shirts which they've bought. Some people though go full sari or highly embroidered Nepalese wear. Even most of the Nepalese don't wear this latter outfit most of the time. Is it attention-seeking or genuine cultural sensitivity? I can't make my mind up.

During the festival here, on one day, all the locals had a bindi (red spot) on their head, some even had wheat behind their ear. It is a cultural thing, so even though it is mainly a Hindu festival, everybody is involved including the Buddhists. There were also tourists doing the same thing, and again I was in two minds. I didn't have it done, I felt I'd be gatecrashing their festival rather than celebrating with them.

RESTAURANTS

So many to choose from, you probably need to follow your nose. One of my favourite meals was a fried egg baguette at a little fast food-style place. I don't know what sauce is in it, but I've been back a few times. It's only 250 rupees for the biggest size and it is so good. There are also any style of cuisine you could fancy. I liked the steak restaurants or the pizza ones. So western! The most expensive dishes

My favourite fast food cafe in Thamel. Great egg sandwiches.

The litter along the banks of the river.

are less than 1000 rupees, which is great considering the beers in the restaurants are over 600 rupees each. I've been in steak heaven a few times. My favourite is the Black Olive Cafe. Their Trekkers Steak is fabulous and they pour a spirit over the whole meal and set it alight. Fiery theatre – they had me hooked.

LITTER

It isn't clean, especially the rivers for some reason. Piles of rubbish accumulate and there are few bins. Apparently the politicians try and get elected on cleaning things up, but with education, roads and other infrastructure also a priority it seems to be overlooked. When I asked one of my art shop guides why rubbish was everywhere, his simple reply was, 'It's Nepal,' as if nothing can be done about it. It is a real shame, and I hope the locals change their attitude. Please don't rely on the regulators to deal with it.

ELECTRICS

My father was an electrical engineer before he retired, and we have had some work done at the house where we spent some time with the electrician. Most electricity cabling in the UK is hidden from view via underground cabling. Here is wasn't. Great clumps of wiring were everywhere. One malevolent individual could knock out the whole of Thamel with a set of well-honed electrical pliers. I took some photos for my father to see. Here is one example.

ENTERTAINMENT

In the bars and restaurants you could get live music, sports bars, or just hang-out places. I'm sure there are places to go if you want more of a younger nightlife, but being in my 50s, I didn't seek it out. The live music was mainly British/American. My Oxford friends were going to a club voted the 51st greatest club in the world. Sounds good – for them. I watched the football one night – in an Irish bar. It was all right, and the beer was cheap, but there was the resident bore there, bragging about living in Asia for 20 years and hating the UK, even though he was English. I was glad when he read my body language and bored off. I did go to a couple of bars with local bands which was fun.

THINGS TO DO IN KATHMANDU AND PATAN

This isn't a tourist guide, but more a catalogue of things I did, in the order I did them.

DURBAR SQUARE – KHATMANDU

I went three of four times in total, including my first day pre-trekking and then on a tour on my penultimate day. On none of the occasions did I pay the 1000-rupee entrance fee for tourists. On the first few occasions, I knew I was going with the guide later so I was saving my entrance fee for then. However, when I was with the guide, the museum was shut, and the Living Goddess wasn't there, so he just told

Durbar Square, Kathmandu.

me some history as we looked at the buildings from the other side of the chain link fence. Having been to Kathmandu before, and having walked around Patan's Durbar Square, I didn't feel the need to do the tour, but others experiencing Durbar Square for the first time loved it. It is grand, architecturally interesting and busy.

DURBAR SQUARE – PATAN

I walked to Patan through some very non-touristy areas. Google Maps takes you the direct route, so sometimes you're walking down areas not on the beaten track. It was fascinating. One street along the river was like a shanty town, with accommodation seemingly thrown together using whatever materials they could find. I never felt unsafe though even as I got the understandable stares from the locals. A balloon seller led the way. He was only about 12. I bought a few balloons from him, but let him keep them to sell again. I like entrepreneurial spirit in the young.

It was also during the festival, so as I approached Durbar Square it was noticeable that it was not as busy as would have been normal. Like in Thamel, shops that would normally have been open were shut. Trays of food were outside many houses as offerings to the gods.

View of Durbar Square Patan from the restaurant. Glad to be out of the rain.

Very similar in style to the Kathmandu equivalent, it also showed earthquake damage, with scaffold on some buildings as repair works were undertaken. They were doing a good job. There were a lot of beggars there, and the usual tourist fare, but just one street away was a very busy outdoor market. I walked up and down it, probably 300m each way. It was really vibrant with few tourists.

It started to really rain, so I ducked into a cafe which had six floors, settled in at the top and people watched for an hour. It was great, even listening to the Americans on the table next to me pretending they knew all about eastern culture and getting picked up on it by their guide. Police were trying to direct traffic and taxis were trying to ignore them. Locals were sheltering from the rain, often in the Durbar Square buildings themselves. I even had a beer while doing this. A lovely way to spend an afternoon.

I really liked Patan in 1996 and it was no different here. I was glad I went.

A CLOSE SHAVE IN THAMEL

I'd never been shaved before. After a couple of weeks not having a manual one, I was about to buy a razor, when I walked past a small barbershop with no customers. There are many of them around Thamel. With the 'why not' mantra coming to the forefront, I spent the next 20 minutes being lathered up, shaved twice and then moisturised. It cost me 200 rupees so I gave him a 100-rupee tip, just over £2 for shave and tip. It was such a close shave, I barely needed one a week later. I'm a convert.

SWAYAMBHU MAHACHAITYA
(commonly known as the Monkey Temple)

This is the dominant sight if you look out across Khatmandu. About a mile from Durbar Square, I had another interesting walk there courtesy of Google Maps and the festival. It seemed to be a destination for tourists but mainly locals. I reckon western tourists were 20 per cent of the visitors when I was there, and that's a very generous estimate. It must have been one of the main festival days. The women were resplendent in their very colourful saris and the men all sported the red bindi forehead mark.

It is a Buddhist stupa, sitting at the top of a steep hill. I remember it being hard work to climb but offering great views of the city. At the bottom were stalls selling fruit and beads, henna tattooists and little temple-like structures. But the biggest sights were the monkeys. They were everywhere. Darting around effortlessly in

Monkeys abound at the bottom of 'their' temple.

their quest for food, often with a baby monkey running behind or even clinging on for dear life, they were very entertaining. I got lucky. One local lady had brought some food and they swarmed towards her, like pigeons when someone gets the seed out. There was a brief stand-off between some dogs and the monkeys; the dogs really were top here. But the lady shooed the dogs away – she was a monkey feeder through and through.

Consequently, the walk up to the top was not swarming with monkeys, they were busy getting their share of the spoils lower down. It was steep, but after Kala Patthar it was easy. After paying the 200-rupee tourist fee, I stepped on to the flat base of the stupa. It was rammed. Temples, shops, prayer wheels and food sellers all competed for the attention of the visitor. All the while the four directions of the all-seeing Buddha eyes at the top of the stupa were keeping watch over proceedings. It was busy but fun. A lot of the locals were stood on the walls, trying to get the perfect Instagram pic of Kathmandu behind them. I thought it looked really dangerous until I looked over the edge. It only dropped about two metres to the hill side.

At the top of the Monkey Temple, so representative of Nepal.
Opposite: The steep climb to the top. During the festival, it was a very colourful and glamorous day.

I just took it in, did a couple of laps, took some pics, spun some prayer wheels and felt very content with life. It was also not raining. A double win.

SEEING HANDS MASSAGE

I'd been recommended this place by Anton and Keith, both of whom had been. It is run and staffed entirely by the blind. Hence the 'Seeing Hands'. I'd never really had a professional massage before, just a touristy Turkish one on holiday a few years earlier. I expected it to be relaxing and soothing. I didn't have any aches from trekking, so an hour of general rubbing and kneading was expected.

I suppose the point of the blind massage is that the sense of touch is very acute and their hands can really identify issues with the body. I had a lady called Laxmi. Her blind husband signed me in, and her ten-year-old daughter was knocking around too. Her daughter was the only sighted person I saw all the time I was there and she spoke great English. I suppose she did help her parents out in some way but they were both extremely capable of dealing with their disability.

Seeing Hands Blind Massage Clinic.

I stripped down to my boxers and lay face down. She asked me if I had any issues I needed sorting out, and I said no. After about five minutes she asked me my age, and when I said 52, she told me she thought I was in my 40s. Great customer flattery.

She found issues I didn't even know I had. With a mixture of hands, forearms and even elbows at one point, she found more knots in my muscles than I knew I had muscles. Every time I cried out in pain, she asked if I wanted her to be more gentle. I did, but I also wanted her to deal with the issues, so of course I said no. Not forgetting the British stiff upper lip that I had to maintain. After an hour, and with my back, shoulders and legs thoroughly manipulated, time was up. Keith had had an hour and a half. I think I'd have been crying out for mercy if it was any longer than my allotted time.

I did feel better for it though. I really liked the principle of the blind masseuse and, in a masochistic way, I enjoyed the massage. So that's what really happens. Never again will I snigger as one of my friends tells me about going to a massage parlour in Bangkok! It was 2000 rupees (about £13) for the hour so I tipped her 500 rupees and her daughter 100 and left aching and tender, but really pleased for the recommendation.

At the first tee at the Gokarno.

GOKARNO FOREST RESORT

I am a hack amateur golfer. I play maybe ten to 15 times a year and I can play some holes like Tiger Woods and some like a dog with a stick. Inconsistency is my watchword hence no handicap but I do enjoy it.

I'd booked a round of golf months ago. It wasn't cheap, at 6000 rupees plus club hire, plus caddy, plus taxi, but it was a one-off. None of my mates had ever played in Kathmandu and bragging rights were assured. I'd even changed my date and tee time twice due to changes in my itinerary, and they always fitted me in. Maybe I should have known it wasn't busy from that.

I arrived on my motorbike taxi (see previous) met my caddy and bought some lake balls. These are always cheaper. I had no idea how many I needed, but the man behind the counter sold me eight, saying I could sell them back at the end if I still had any left.

I was so excited to be playing, but a little nervous playing with a completely fresh set of clubs. In Nottingham, I'd packed my glove, some tees and my golf shirt, so I was ready.

The first tee shot went into the trees, but the caddy found the ball and I shot a five on a par four, not too shabby after a drop shot. I had already noticed that the ground was very wet. By the end, the terrain got me down and parts of my game suffered badly. I couldn't wait to finish.

A few things left me feeling very underwhelmed with the experience.

Playing alone wasn't fun. I'd never done it before and I didn't like it. The caddy was pleasant and tried his best but it wasn't the same as playing with your mates.

The ground was so wet that the fairways barely existed. I was driving and putting okay but every other approach shot was like a marsh shot. Not their fault due to the rain, but a reduced price could have been offered.

I caught up with a couple of fourballs ahead. They were obviously pals and at one point played a par three as an eight. They did let me play through, but – at the next hole was another fourball. When one of them took a full two minutes to play a shot, I just missed that hole, ducked in front and played 17 in total.

In all, I didn't enjoy it. Partly my fault for not playing well, partly the course. I had five balls left, 750 rupees and the manager in charge refused to pay back as I'd paid by credit card and she'd cashed up. I refused to budge, saying it was all going to be the caddy's tip, and she eventually got some cash out which I did give to the caddy. Whether the bloke who sold them to me got a tongue-lashing I'll never know, but it was only right.

It then started to rain heavily, further dampening (literally) my mood. I paid about 10,000 rupees in all, nearly £70. It was a nice resort, but not a great golf course, and I'm glad I did it, but it wasn't the really fulfilling experience I was hoping for.

SHREE BOUDHANATH STUPA

I'd never been here before, despite my previous visit to Kathmandu. I was on a tour of the city, provided by my trekking company Outfitters. Meet time was 9.30am so I turned up in reception exactly then and felt I was late from the stares of my companions to be. The guide, Birodh, was there, as were four

Lithuanian men, three friends about my age and the son of one of the men. They were friendly enough, but I'm not convinced they really wanted to be on the tour and that I was slowing them down.

In the same minibus and with the same driver as usual, we crossed the city. When we stopped, I realised my motor bike taxi driver (on the way to play golf) had pointed this place out, but as we were whizzing past on a motorbike (me without a helmet and clinging on for dear life) I'd not really been paying attention. It turned out to be the biggest stupa in Kathmandu. How had I missed it?

It was huge, far bigger in size than the stupa of the monkey temple. Costing 400 rupees to get in, it was set in a courtyard, and the whole perimeter was like a mini Thamel – restaurants, cafes, shops for paintings, kit, T-shirts etc. It was a strange 40 minutes. While the guide was really keen to give the history, maybe go for a coffee, certainly visit an art gallery (inevitably) we seemed to be in a hurry.

There were a couple of monasteries to visit, one of which we took our shoes off so we could go inside. Monks were chanting as they had in Tengboche, but it seemed more calculated, designed for the tourists rather than a proper

Looking out over the complex from the monastery.

observance of their beliefs. I hope I'm wrong. We didn't bother going inside with the second as the views from outside on the balcony were so good (we'd gone up a couple of flights of stairs). Candles were being lit, smoke was coming from a street food stall below and the general hubbub of the square was evident.

Then it was on to the art shop. I'd already bought three paintings, but I was interested in the process. Only me and one of my party, Valentin, went into the studio. The others stayed downstairs, not in the least bit bothered. It was interesting to see how the paintings were done, apparently taking months to complete using several different artists who had different specialties. Then we got the sell, but it wasn't pushy and I preferred my mandala to any choices he showed us (a heavy dose of confirmation bias thrown in there). When he asked me how much I'd paid for my mandala and I told him 8000 rupees, he sniggered and said his were 5000 rupees. Yet they took months to paint! Was I missing something? Did I pay over the odds? Possibly, but if so, it was only £20. Not a big deal for something that I will treasure for years.

The rest of this part of the tour was a relatively slow walk around the stupa. Once you'd seen its size, there was not much extra wonderment. You couldn't go inside it, just skirt the perimeter, so we did and moved on.

PASHUPATINATH

This was another place I'd heard of but never been to. This was apparently one of the holiest places in the whole of the Hindu world. It also had a very macabre USP: it was a place for open-air cremations. I know it is a Hindu tradition to burn the bodies of anyone over ten (or unless you were pregnant) within 24 hours, but as a tourist attraction? I'd been to Varanasi in India which had a similar reputation. Three of the Lithuanians didn't want to go. I thought for a bit I'd be completely outvoted and not be able to go, but Valentin sided with me again and just the three of us went. It was strangely uplifting. There were dead bodies, but they were completely covered in head to toe with linen, and there was a whole activity around preparing them for their final journey. The family had come together at incredible short notice to carry out the ritual.

There were about ten places for the pyres to be lit. Some were almost at ember stage, some being prepared. Luckily we never saw one being lit. I wouldn't have wanted to see that. But the process was explained. The sloping shelf down to the river pointed straight to the temple, the final journey of the spirits to the gods.

A very solemn place.

Kids were trying to make a living selling water. People were throwing money on to a temple roof for good luck (apparently the kids go and get it when the police aren't looking). And families were gathering.

The site itself was quite ornate. There was a really interesting set of temples, all identical, in honour of Shiva. When looking down them, through the hole either side, it was a classic mirror effect illusion. Think Pink Floyd's *Ummagumma* album cover. There were holy men, charging for photos and people cleaning up after a funeral. I even saw an on-site cornea donation clinic – almost like a Hindu donor card.

THINGS TO DO IN KATHMANDU AND PATAN

Overlooking the river and the temple for monetary offerings.

I didn't feel like a gawper, and I don't think the families would have been too upset that it was so public. It was a sacred ritual to them. Having a few respectful tourists was not going to stop them celebrating the life, and mourning the death of their loved one.

We probably stayed about 30 minutes, and it was enough.

Meeting up with the minibus and the other three, they didn't want to go to Durbar Square, but did want to go to the tea and spice shop. They spent a lot of time and money making multiple purchases. As I say, it was a really odd day.

Opposite: Not an illusion, no mirrors involved.

10 OCTOBER 2022
DAY 20: THE FLIGHT HOME

I had planned to leave during the evening of the 9th, but the flight was bumped to 3.30am the following morning. The 9th October was 26 years to the day that Jane and I had tried to leave Kathmandu in 1996 when we got hit by a bird strike. We ultimately left on the 10th then, now the exact same day that I was leaving in 2022. Was it an omen? Am I destined never to leave Nepal until the 10th, even if I go again!

It meant a whole day kicking my heels in Kathmandu as I had to check out at noon. After a week in Kathmandu I didn't need to see anything else, so after a very lazy morning where I sat about writing about my reflections and activities in the capital, I had a last, long nostalgic look around Thamel. This included a bun and a coffee in the Pumpernickel Bakery for a bit of people-watching.

It was a good way to end my holiday and made me realise that although I loved the city, it was time to leave.

I returned to my hotel, where I'd left my bags, and spent a few hours chilling. A couple of bottles of beer, a bit of food and two football matches on the telly passed the time. I was the last one in the bar, but the staff didn't seem to mind, even though I was no longer staying there.

I waited for the taxi at 11.30pm, but it never came so it was back to my Pathao app and within minutes (and some help from the security guard at the hotel) it

10 OCTOBER 2022   DAY 20: THE FLIGHT HOME

was there. Less than 20 minutes later, through the deserted streets of Kathmandu, I entered the airport and that was the last time I was to set foot in the country.

The process of passport control and check-in was straightforward, and we entered a waiting room with the bag security conveyor belts in the middle, manned by staff all sitting around. They told me to sit down, they'd let us know when they were ready. The last of the three Premier League games was on, so for an hour I was able to watch that. Not much was going on, people just relaxing, or mothers trying to placate their babies. All the shops were shut apart from a small cafe.

With ten minutes of the match to go, it was announced that we could go through security but knowing that it would take a while (and it seemed like we were the only flight) I just watched the end of the game. At full time I took my place in the queue and passed through without issue. Security had not been as strict as at some of the more western countries. I was glad; I never feel in danger in airports. Taking my shoes off always seems really over the top and I dream of the days it will be relaxed.

I had 1000 rupees still to spend so I cleaned myself out at the souvenir shop/cafe which was open.

I have never missed a take-off because I was asleep before, but I did out of Kathmandu. The 3.30am take-off and the relaxed atmosphere meant I sat in my seat and put my music on. It is a shame I missed it, as I think I'd have liked to see Thamel and the Monkey Temple from above, but I awoke as we were past the centre and heading for the hills. Last time I'd flown out of Kathmandu, the take-off made the front page of the *Kathmandu Post* – now I didn't even notice it myself.

There was a spare seat behind me, so I had no qualms about putting my seat fully back and prepared to get some sleep. The man next to me was fully masked, and seemed genuinely scared on the two occasions I spoke to him unmasked, so I just kept quiet for the four hours we were in the air.

At Doha, we had to go through security despite it being a transfer, something that never happened on the outward flight. It was half an hour to the gate being announced so I looked for some food and a drink. There was a Harrods concession and a Hamleys toy shop; it really was an expensive place. I wasn't especially hungry, just bored, so I kept my money in my pocket, waited for the gate to be called and walked the half a mile to where the plane would be.

They started calling people to check in straightaway despite there being about an hour and a half to the flight, yet on the other side of the gate, where there was

Hamleys at Doha airport.

another waiting area, there were no facilities, not even toilets. It was really odd. As soon as we were allowed on the plane, there were queues for the loo.

I sat next to an Aussie lady called Anne. Well, not quite next to her, I had the window and she had the aisle, and there was no one between us. She was happy to chat, and so we did. Not for all seven hours of the flight, but I reckon for four of them. She was an expat Brit returning to Liverpool to attend to several family things. She was good company and it was my most enjoyable flight of the four I had made. A good way to end.

At the airport it took ages to get my bags, but Jane was patient, and when we saw each other, the proverbial sunshine moment occurred. It was so good to see her.

I was back in England, and I was pleased to be back.

On the way home we stopped for a sandwich, and by luck, Jim made his first video call from Thailand. He was as surprised to see me as I was by the phone call. Then it was back via Burton and a visit to my parents. Then finally back to Nottingham where Matt is now living with us before he goes travelling. From seeing no one in person for a while, I caught up with nearly the whole family.

10 OCTOBER 2022   DAY 20: THE FLIGHT HOME

I was home, and after the bath I had been thinking of for a few days, it was back in my own bed after three weeks away, my adventure was complete.

Post-trip news

I went on the scales the following morning, and despite drinking every night for a week, accompanied by burgers, steaks, pizzas and egg sandwiches I was below 104kg. I'd lost a further two kilograms. I wonder what it would have been straight after the walk.

I had also raised £1,200 for Teenage Cancer Trust. There was a flurry of activity on EBC day. Thanks to everyone who sponsored me.

Since coming home, I have watched *Aftershock: Everest and the Nepal Earthquake*, the three-part Netflix documentary about the 2015 earthquake in Nepal which killed thousands. A less underserving country and people I can think of. RIP to all those who died, and thoughts are with those still trying to come to terms with mourning their losses and trying to rebuild. the country.

ACKNOWLEDGEMENTS

My first thanks go to Nepal Outfitters, especially Raj, for organising the trip. I took a chance by booking direct, rather than going through a UK operator, but there was no need to worry. The communication was excellent throughout the process, the trip was well planned and the accommodation was great in Kathmandu and on the trek. I would thoroughly recommend them.

https://www.outfitternepal.com/

My second thanks are to Anton and Indra, my companions on the trip. I hope that you enjoyed being with an Englishmen as much as I enjoyed being with a

Anton, Indra, Sontos and I in Lukla after our final meal together.

ACKNOWLEDGEMENTS

German and Nepali. Only you had the exact same experience as me, and that is something that we will share forever. The offer to come and visit me in England will always stand. Don't be strangers.

Although Anton and Indra were my direct walking companions, there were many others on the trek who added to my experience. Those who followed the walk to Base Camp on the same day as me will recognise the feelings about the weather and the views as we all followed the same path. Special mention to Mark and Keith, my two Scottish friends who were on the same plane from Lukla and became a big part of the experience. I also want to single out Alex, Ben and Robbie, three students from Oxford University. The same age as my kids, you were fun, interesting and determined. In no particular order, but all adding greatly to my experience were Selina and Jonathan, Michael, Don and Jerry, Line and Liva, Cindy and Brecht, Pritima, Bernard, Robert and Anna and Daniel and Eilish. Photos of most of you are in the book somewhere, so thanks to those who sent me their 'best' ones.

The people of Nepal are some of the most incredible I have met. Helpful, friendly, organised and welcoming, you do your country proud. If anyone is reading this and is in any doubt about whether you should go, it is not just the scenery that makes the trip worthwhile.

This brings me on to the unsung heroes of any trek, the porters. The backbone of the tourism industry, whether it is carrying the kit of the tourists or the things needed to keep the industry going, you zoomed past us regularly. I hope that we contribute positively both to your livelihood and your opinion of foreigners. We need you more than you can imagine.

Outside of Nepal, I want to thank all those who accompanied me on my training walks. Helen and Ed, Boggie, Denise and Rich, Lee and Andrew (twice), Matt, Lois and Nick, Pete and Ali, and not forgetting Dan (twice) and Jane (three times). You gave me the motivation to go, and the company to really enjoy myself.

I also want to mention the British countryside here too, especially the Peak District. Some of the greatest diversity of panorama you will see. We are so lucky to live in such a fabulous country for walking. The pictures from my training walks will show you what a beautiful and varied place it really is.

Also, thanks to Gareth, my editor. You showed me all my written tics and changed all my abbreviations so that they made sense.

I have known Matt and Michelle for many years now – my designer and production manager respectively. They brought this book to publication with all the skill and judgement that I have come to expect. Rarely seeing each other now as you live in different parts of the country, I know that I can depend on you despite this distance and I hope you never forget how important you are to JMD Media Ltd as a company and to me personally.

Last, and most importantly I want to thank my family. My mum and dad who are always supportive and encourage me in everything I do. My children Jim, Matt and Dan – you have all grown into fun, curious, interesting, adventurous, polite and caring adults and you make me so proud every day. Finally my wife Jane, the love of my life and more supportive than she really knows. We make a great team.

Cheers Nepal.